DEFENDING
the FAITH

DEFENDING
the FAITH

*Upholding Biblical Christianity
and the Genesis Record*

Dr. Henry Morris

Master
Books

First printing: August 1999
Second printing: February 2003

ISBN: 0-89051-324-4
Library of Congress: 99-66473

Printed in the United States of America

Please visit our website for other great titles:
www.masterbooks.net

For information regarding author interviews, please contact the publicity department at (870) 438-5288.

Acknowledgments

I would like to thank my long-time friend and colleague, Dr. Emmett Williams, for reviewing the manuscript for this book, and then especially for writing the Foreword. Many years ago, Emmett and I were together on the Virginia Tech engineering faculty and in the College Baptist Church of Blacksburg (now Harvest Baptist). We later served together for several years on the board of the Creation Research Society, and he is currently president of the society. For those unfamiliar with it, the Creation Research Society is a membership association of several hundred scientists with post-graduate degrees in science who are also committed Christians, believing in literal biblical creationism. The society has been publishing a quarterly journal of research and review papers on scientific biblical creationism for over 35 years, playing a key role in the modern revival of creationism.

I also thank Dr. John Morris, president of the Institute for Creation Research (and my son!) for a thorough review of the manuscript. Both he and Dr. Williams made many helpful suggestions, which I have tried to incorporate.

Thanks, also, to Ruth Richards, who typed the manuscript, and Jim Fletcher and his associates at Master Books who edited and published it. Many sections were modified from previous articles published by ICR as well as CRS and various hitherto unpublished manuscripts.

Contents

Foreword

hen most people retire, they like to travel, but since Dr. Henry Morris had already spent so many years traveling and lecturing on Bible-science topics, he and Mrs. Morris are now content to stay at home. Many retirees devote considerable time to such pleasures as fishing, yet Henry Morris, who spent much of his youth in El Paso, never became enamored with water sports. He prefers to "fish for men" through his biblical apologetic writings. Upon retirement, he shed most of the administrative duties that had encumbered him in the many places he had labored since the early 1950s (most recently as president of the Institute for Creation Research) and now spends a major portion of his time in earnestly defending the Christian faith with his writings. And we who are creationists in the true sense of the word are fortunate to be able to read his excellent books.

Dr. Morris, with his firm stand on biblical truth and its application to so many scientific subjects, is an encouragement to all of us. This book, *Defending Our Faith*, is the latest in a long series of books and articles exhorting Christians to stand fast on biblical creationism. As always, the author points out the glaring weaknesses in humanistic musings on origins which ignore the Creator. Since some Christians feel that they must twist biblical truth to accommodate atheistic scientism, Henry Morris carefully illustrates the absurdity of such compromise. Presenting the superiority of the biblical viewpoint, which honors the Creator, he examines many scientific disciplines from the vantage of a young earth-worldwide flood approach.

The issue of time (young earth vs. ancient earth), the period of creation activity, thermodynamics and the application of the first and second laws to so-called evolutionary development, cosmology versus "In the beginning God created the heavens and earth," and historical geology in light of the Noachian Deluge are covered in sufficient detail to show the superiority of the creationist worldview.

We must heed the author's advice and admonition and earnestly contend for the faith ourselves. May the Lord continue to bless Dr. Morris and his efforts and may readers be edified as they read this book. For the Creator, the Lord Jesus Christ, is honored as He should be.

Emmett L. Williams
President, Creation Research Society

Introduction

n his very last epistle, the apostle Paul passionately exhorted his young son in the faith, Timothy, over and over again that he should "keep the faith." He said this in different ways, but in all of these exhortations he was showing deep concern that the true faith set forth in the Holy Scriptures be firmly defended and maintained in all its original clarity and purity.

Note some of these exhortations:

Hold fast the form of sound words, which thou hast heard of me, in faith and love which is in Christ Jesus (2 Tim. 1:13).

The things that thou hast heard of me among many witnesses, the same commit thou to faithful men, who shall be able to teach others also (2 Tim. 2:2).

Continue thou in the things which thou hast learned and hast been assured of, knowing of whom thou hast learned them (2 Tim. 3:14).

I charge thee therefore before God and the Lord Jesus Christ, who shall judge the quick and the dead at His appearing and His kingdom; Preach the word (2 Tim. 4:1–2).

And note especially the concluding words of his first letter to Timothy:

O Timothy, keep that which is committed to thy trust,

avoiding profane and vain babblings, and oppositions of science falsely so called (1 Tim. 6:20).

It has always been essential for Bible-believing Christians to "earnestly contend for the faith," that faith which had been once-for-all "delivered unto the saints" (Jude 3), because that faith is always under attack by the evil one. In fact, these satanic efforts were prophesied to become so intense in the last days, that Jesus sadly had to say: "When the Son of man cometh, shall He find [that] faith on the earth?" (Luke 18:8).

This is why that prince of preachers, Charles Haddon Spurgeon, was moved to exclaim: "We must defend the faith" (see page 19). It is why Martin Luther said: "Where the battle rages, there the loyalty of the soldier is proved!" (on page 20).

Despite what some observers claim is a religious revival taking place today, marked by much emotional expression in diverse forms, the world in general seems to be rapidly descending into a morass of wickedness and apostasy.

As far as attacks on Biblical Christianity are concerned, they seem to focus primarily on the inerrancy of Scripture, the full deity of Jesus Christ, and the foundational truth of God's supernatural creation of all things in the beginning. Satan and the world system which He controls (note 1 John 5:19; 2 Cor. 4:3–4; etc.) can put up with a great deal of religious fervor and moralistic reforms, but he must destroy faith in these basic truths at all costs if he ever hopes to prevail in his long war against God.

That is why I felt constrained many years ago to devote my own limited resources of time and ability primarily to defending and proclaiming this precious faith entrusted to us by our great God and Savior Jesus Christ. There have been — and are — many others, of course, who have felt the same constraint, and I would hope that God would raise up many more defenders of the faith in these last climactic days of this age.

Why Defend the Faith?

One of my favorite (yet most convicting) Scripture verses is 1 Peter 3:15: "But sanctify the Lord God in your hearts: and be ready always to give an answer to every man that asketh you a reason of the hope that is in you with meekness and fear."

This is not a suggestion to believers, but a commandment. The Greek language in the original indicates the following amplified paraphrase is an appropriate exposition of its thrust. "But firmly establish the Lord God [that is, the Lord Jesus Christ] on the throne of your life, and always be ready to give a systematic, scientific, legal defense of your Christian faith to anyone who raises questions about the logical and sound basis of that faith, while always doing so in a gentle, respectful, reasonable manner."

This is not an easy commandment to obey, but it is vitally important that all serious Christians try. To be able to "give an answer" (the Greek word is *apologia*, from which is derived our word "apologetics"; it is a legal term, used in the sense of a courtroom "defense"), the believer must spend quality time in diligent study of the Word and the evidences — both internal and external — of its divine origin and authority. The "answer" required is the Greek *logos*, from which we derive our word "logic" and all the various "ologies" (theology, geology, biology, etc.). In combination with the Greek preposition *apo*, it even becomes our other word, *apologia*.

Very early in my own life, as a young engineering instructor at a humanistically oriented university, I became convinced of the urgent need in these last days of both defending and proclaiming, as well as expounding, our biblical Christian faith. Most of my own books have been developed around this need, and this particular book is in a way a sort of capsulized summary and updating of many of these earlier works.

Actually, *Defending the Faith* is also structured around a number of articles published by me during the past five years. Many of them are taken from our ICR periodical *Acts & Facts*, and some from other Christian publications. These have been modified as needed for continuity, completeness, and suitability for use in a single book focusing on the one major theme of defending our faith. I hope and pray it will be helpful to any who are led to read it.

Most of all, of course, I trust it will honor the Lord Jesus and His wonderful Word in these last days before His return.

Chapter I

We Must Defend the Faith

Christ, the Bible, and Creation

f we are going to defend our Christian faith effectively, we must first of all understand exactly what it is. As "Christians," we must follow Christ. He is our "example," the "author and finisher of our faith" (1 Pet. 2:21; Heb. 12:2). All evangelical Christians, regardless of church denomination, believe in Jesus Christ as the unique Son of God, and have accepted Him as their Savior and Lord. They seek to obey His great commission to all His followers: "Go ye therefore, and teach all nations, baptizing them in the name of the Father, and of the Son, and of the Holy Ghost: Teaching them to observe all things whatsoever I have commanded you: and, lo, I am with you alway, even unto the end of the world, Amen" (Matt. 28:19–20).

Therefore, we ought to teach His "all things" the same way He did. He is our authority for He created and upholds all things (Col. 1:16: Heb. 1:3).

Among many other truths which He taught, there are two basic doctrines on which all the others depend. One is the absolute verbal inerrancy of Scripture; the other is the special creation of all things by God in the beginning.

The problem is that many Christians, who *believe* that they believe these truths, disagree on what they mean. Therefore, on the assumption that all who really believe on the Lord Jesus Christ will accept His authority as to what He understood to be their meaning, let us look first at what He taught about the Bible and then at what He taught about creation.

In the days when He was on earth, He had access only to the Old Testament, of course, but the Gospel records make it clear that He accepted these Scriptures as coming without error from God. He quoted from them often and referred to them even more often, always indicating unequivocally that He accepted their records as true and authoritative.

For example, in answering a question about the vital issue of marriage and divorce, He simply quoted from the Genesis account of the first husband and wife, saying: "Have you not read, that he which made them at the beginning made them male and female, and said, For this cause shall a man leave father and mother, And shall cleave to his wife: and they twain shall be one flesh? Wherefore they are no more twain, but one flesh. What therefore God hath joined together, let not man put asunder" (Matt. 19:4–6).

Here the Lord was quoting from Genesis 1:27 and Genesis 2:24, the two complementary accounts of the creation of the first man and woman, accepting both accounts as true and compatible, and as establishing the divine pattern for all future marriages.

When resisting the three temptations by Satan in the wilderness, He defeated the old deceiver merely by quoting an appropriate verse of Scripture, each from the Book of Deuteronomy (Matt. 4:4, 7, 10, citing Deut. 8:3; 6:16; 10:20; respectively). "It is written," He said, and that settled it, even against the greatest enemy of all!

Christ undoubtedly accepted the verbal inspiration of the Bible — the words, not just the thoughts. On one occasion, the Jews were about to stone Him because, they said, "Thou makest thyself God." He then quoted Psalm 82:6 in His defense against them. "Is it not written in your law, I said, Ye are gods? If he called them gods, unto whom the word of God came, and the scripture cannot be broken; Say ye of him whom the Father hath sanctified, and sent into the world, Thou blasphemest, because I said, I am the Son of God?" (John 10:33–36).

Our purpose here does not require an exposition of these verses, except to note that Christ's argument depends entirely on the use of one word "gods" in Psalm 82:6. Christ believed in verbal inspiration!

Even more striking is His statement in Matthew 5:18. "For verily I say unto you, Till heaven and earth pass, one jot or one tittle shall in no wise pass from the law, till all be fulfilled." The "jot" was the smallest letter of the Hebrew alphabet, and the "tittle" was a small mark used to distinguish between two similarly shaped letters. There could hardly be anywhere a stronger statement of *literal* inspiration of the Old Testament writings. It was made by the Lord Jesus Christ himself, and surely all true Christians should hold the same high view of biblical authority that He did.

As far as the New Testament is concerned, He assured us that His own words would be accurately preserved. "Heaven and earth shall pass away," He said, "but my words shall not pass away" (Mark 13:31). Their preservation, as well as the writings of all the New Testament, would be accomplished by His apostles, through the Holy Spirit. "When he, the Spirit of truth, is come, he will guide you into all truth . . . and he will shew you things to come" (John 16:13). "He shall teach you all things, and bring all things to your remembrance, whatsoever I have said unto you" (John 14:26).

Then, at the very end of the New Testament, Jesus speaks again, this time from heaven. "For I testify unto every man that heareth the words of the prophecy of this book. If any man shall add unto these things, God shall add unto him the plagues that are written in this book: And if any man shall take away from the words of the book of this prophecy, God shall take away his part out of the book of life, and out of the holy city, and from the things which are written in this book" (Rev. 22:18–19).

Note again the emphasis on "the words of the book," not just the spiritual concepts. Lest anyone question whether these warnings were actually from Christ, the very next verse settles it: "He which testifieth these things saith, Surely I come quickly. Amen. Even so, come, Lord Jesus" (Rev. 22:20).

There is no doubt, therefore, in view of such statements as we have cited, that the Lord Jesus Christ believed and taught the absolute verbal inerrancy of all the Bible. Therefore, we who believe Him and seek to follow Him must do the same. All of His apostles, as well as His prophets of the Old Testament, did so, and so should we.

There are many other reasons, of course, for believing in the inspiration, infallibility, and authority of the Bible. Its writers (Moses, Isaiah, Paul, etc.) all claimed to be writing with such authority. The Bible contains hundreds of fulfilled prophecies and scores of remarkable scientific insights, with no demonstrable errors. Its historical records square with all the known facts of archaeology and secular history. Its unique and powerful message of salvation and God's plans for His creation was written by over 40 different writers over a period of at least 1,500 years, yet all parts are consistent with all others and with innumerable internal evidences of divine inspiration. There is no other book like this in the whole wide world!

But the greatest evidence of all is that Christ (the second Person of the holy Trinity) accepted and taught its inerrant authority in all things: He taught the historicity of the great events recorded in Genesis, for example, especially including the account of the creation, as we have already noted (see Matt. 19:3–8). He referred to the historical fact of Abel's murder, speaking of "all the righteous blood shed upon the earth, from the blood of righteous Abel unto the blood of Zacharias" (Matt. 23:35).

He also accepted the historical reality of the worldwide flood in the days of Noah: "As it was in the days of Noe, so shall it be also in the days of the Son of man. They did eat, they drank, they married wives, they were given in marriage, until the day that Noe entered into the ark, and the flood came, and destroyed them all" (Luke 17:26–27). The notion that this event may have affected only those living in a certain region is negated by His comparing it to His second coming. "The flood came, and took them all away; so shall also the coming of the Son of man be" (Matt. 24:39). One would think that, if Christ believed in the global flood, our modern progressive creationists would do well to rethink their advocacy of a "local flood."

The Lord also taught the historicity of the catastrophic destruction of Sodom and Gomorrah in the days of Abraham (Luke 17:29), the miraculous provision of manna to the children of Israel in the wilderness (John 6:32, 49), the burning bush revelation to Moses (Luke 20:37), the incident of the brazen serpent in the wilderness (John 3:14), the unique wisdom of Solomon (Matt. 12:42), the amazing experience of Jonah in the belly of the whale (Matt. 12:40), the remarkable prophecies of Daniel (Matt. 24:15), and all the other "hard to believe" records of the Old Testament Scriptures.

He even taught the fact of a recent creation! "From the beginning of the creation God made them male and female," He said (Mark 10:6). That is, according to Christ (who was there!), God made Adam and Eve right at the beginning of His great creation — not after a 4.6 billion year process of slow development, as the modern scientific establishment (who were not there!) would have us believe.

The same truth of recent creation was also implied by Him in Luke 11:50, when He referred to "the blood of all the prophets, which was shed from the foundation of the world." That is, God's prophets have been suffering bloody persecution since the very foundation of the world, in the time of Abel, not just starting 4.6 billion years since the imaginary evolution of the earth out of a primordial cloud of dust and rocks.

When Christ spoke of a coming period of "affliction, such as was not from the beginning of the creation which God created" (Mark 13:19), He was implying that there had been many lesser afflictions on God's people in the world ever since the beginning of the created world.

We suggest that those Christians who question the truth of any portion of the Bible or who try to "wrest the Scriptures" (2 Pet. 3:16) to make them accommodate some current scientific claim or some "private interpretation" (2 Pet. 1:20) ask themselves if they are prepared to explain to the Lord their reasons for doing so. Remember that "every one of us shall give account of himself to God" (Rom. 14:12). Would it not be better in that day to have believed and taught what Christ believed and taught? With respect to the great historical records of early history, we need to remember His rebuke of the religious leaders of the time when He was on earth. "If ye believe not his [Moses] writings," He said, "how shall ye believe my words?" (John 5:47).

He said that "the scripture cannot be broken" (John 10:35). Evolutionists may try to break it; New Agers and occultists may try to break it; secularists and hedonists may try to break it; all manner of skeptics and doubters and even compromising Christians may try to break it. But the Scripture cannot be broken!

Defending Biblical Creationism

In the next-to-last book of the Bible, the apostle Jude exhorts us to "earnestly contend for the faith which was once delivered to the saints" (Jude 3). His warning refers primarily to professing Christians who would dilute the faith instead of defending it.

I recently ran across the following exhortation from that great "prince of preachers," Charles Haddon Spurgeon, and I would like to share it with you. I don't know where it first appeared over a hundred years ago, but it is so relevant to the modern situation that it could have been written yesterday. Here it is:

> We must defend the Faith; for what would have become of us if our fathers had not maintained it? . . . Must

we not play the man as they did? If we do not, are we not censuring our Fathers? It is very pretty, is it not, to read of Luther and his brave deeds? Of course, everybody admires Luther! Yes, yes, but you do not want anyone else to do the same today. . . . We admire a man who is firm in the Faith, say four hundred years ago . . . but such a man today is a nuisance, and must be put down. Call him a narrow-minded bigot, or give him a worse name if you can think of one. Yet imagine that in those ages past, Luther, Zwingli, Calvin, and their compeers had said, "The world is out of order; but if we try to set it right we shall only make a great row, and get ourselves into disgrace. Let us go to our chambers, put on our nightcaps and sleep over the bad times, and perhaps when we wake up, things would have grown better." Such conduct upon their part would have entailed upon us a heritage of error. These men loved the Faith and the name of Jesus too well to see them trampled on. Note that we owe them, and let us pay to our sons the debt we owe to our fathers.

To the same effect is that stirring statement from Martin Luther, which I have kept in the fly leaf of my Bible for about 40 years.

If I profess with the loudest voice and clearest expression every portion of the truth of God except precisely that little point which the world and the devil are at that moment attacking, I am not confessing Christ, however boldly I may be professing Christ. Where the battle rages, there the loyalty of the soldier is proved, and to be steady on all the battlefield besides, is mere flight and disgrace, if he flinches at that point.

The world and the devil are focusing their attack today on the great truth of biblical creation more than on any other doctrine. If we refuse to defend this component of God's "everlasting gospel" (Rev. 14:6,7), it matters little what we do about the rest. Unbelievers attack all the Bible, of course, especially the miracles and prophecies, but they always direct their most passionate attacks against the truth of recent creation and its corollary doctrine, the global cataclysm of the flood. If they can destroy these two doctrines, the rest will fall eventually. That is why the apostle Peter stresses these two great facts of history as the real antidote to the naturalistic world view, the notion that "all things continue as they were from the beginning of the creation" (see 2 Pet. 3:3–6). He calls it "willful ignorance" to reject or ignore the two great biblical truths of special supernatural creation and the global cataclysm of the great flood.

The sad aspect of this conflict is that so many "evangelicals" are trying to force the evolutionary ages of geology into the Genesis account of creation. Instead of defending our biblical Christian faith, they are trying to accommodate it to the unbelieving world view of evolutionary naturalism. They will affirm their belief in the resurrection of Christ and His imminent return, and these are indeed vital doctrines, but they are not defending the true Christian faith when they dilute the historical authenticity of the foundational chapters of the Bible.

Some will even refute Darwinism and do an excellent job of it. But then they still try to accommodate the evolutionary ages of the naturalists, which in turn requires rejecting the worldwide cataclysm of the flood. They seem indifferent to the fact that this means accepting a billion years of a suffering, dying biosphere before Adam's fall brought sin and death into the world.

It is even sadder when they feel that this compromising approach will convince the scientific establishment to accept Christ and the gospel. They may use various terms to soften the concept — such terms as "intelligent design," "process creation," "theistic evolution," and the like — but it will not make a dent in the world view of the naturalists. They will continue smugly in their unbelief, regardless of the accommodations some Christians make to their system.

For example, an official policy statement of the National Association of Biology Teachers on teaching evolution says:

> Explanations employing non-naturalistic or supernatural events, whether or not explicit reference is made to a supernatural being, are outside the realm of science and not part of a valid science curriculum.[1]

One of evolution's most articulate and influential spokesmen, Dr. Stephen Jay Gould of Harvard, rejects one of the best-written books of the "intelligent design" school, in scathing words such as the following:

Johnson's current incarnation of this false strategy, *Darwin on Trial,* hardly deserves to be called a book at all. . . . The book, in short, is full of errors, badly argued, based on false criteria and abysmally written. . . . Johnson is not a "scientific creationist" of Duane Gish's ilk — the "young earth" biblical literalists who have caused so much political trouble of late, but whom we beat in the Supreme Court in 1987. He accepts the earth's great age and allows that God may have chosen to work via natural selection and other evolutionary principles. . . . The book is scarcely more than an acrid little puff."[2]

Now Gould's review is grossly unfair, and Phil Johnson wrote an excellent reply to it (which *Scientific American* refused to print), but the point is that it did not change Gould's opinion at all.

The fact is that no dilution of the creation/flood record of God's inspired Word, no matter how well-motivated and persuasively written, is going to budge the evolutionary establishment in science or education one iota. They hold their position for religious reasons, not scientific, and scientific arguments for "intelligent design" are rejected just as vigorously as arguments for recent creation or a global flood.

The American Scientific Affiliation has been advocating a compromise between evolution and creation for about 50 years. Their widely distributed book, *Teaching Science in a Climate of Controversy*, was a collection of well-planned essays designed to encourage such a middle-of-the-road system for classroom teaching. The result was a series of bitter attacks by the evolutionists. The *Science Teacher* magazine, for example, published a series of essays by leading scientists repudiating it, entitled "Scientists Decry a Slick New Packaging of Creationism" (May 1987, p. 36–43). One of the authors, Dr. Lynn Margulis, called it "treacherous," a polemic designed "to coax us to believe in the ASA's particular creation myth."

The excellent book *Of Pandas and People* was written to present biology in terms of "intelligent design," without any reference to God, the Bible, or creation, hoping that it could be adopted as a high school biology textbook. Again, nothing doing! It was merely a sneaky way of getting creationism into the schools, said its opponents, and they won. The Creation Research Society textbook *Biology: A Search for Order in Complexity*, published in 1970 with a similar goal, had already met the same fate.

I don't believe any sort of compromise on this issue will ever get a fair hearing, let alone be adopted for public use, so why repeat the same old mistakes? Do we really believe the Bible to be the inspired word of God? Do we believe that God speaks clearly? Do we really think that current scientific majority opinion is always right?

Another very popular advocate of compromise says that teaching recent creation and worldwide flood views will keep people from coming to Christ. "Because of the implausibility of such a position," says Dr. Hugh Ross, "many reject the Bible out of hand without seriously investigating its message or even reading for themselves the relevant passages."[3]

Dr. Ross does not document this statement, and he is wrong. Many scientists *do* accept the biblical record at face value, and there are now thousands of scientists who have become young-earth creationists, not to mention multitudes of non-scientists.

What the compromise approach does, however, is not to bring the lost to Christ but causes many who are already Christians to doubt their faith as they go down the slippery path of compromise.

We do want urgently to win people to Christ, and many have come, through the biblical message of the great gospel of creation and redemption. But it is even more important to be true to God's clear revelation.

> In six days the Lord made heaven and earth, the sea, and all that in them is, and rested the seventh day (Exod. 20:11).

> By the word of the Lord were the heavens made . . . For he spake, and it was done; he commanded, and it stood fast (Ps. 33:6–9).

> But from the beginning of the creation God made them male and female (Mark 10:6).

> By man came death (1 Cor. 15:21).

> Whereby the world that then was, being overflowed with water, perished (2 Pet. 3:6).

> How long halt ye between two opinions? If the Lord be God, follow him (1 Kings 18:21).

Yes, we must defend the faith; for what would have become of us if our fathers had not maintained it? Where the battle rages, there the loyalty of the soldier is proved.

The World Plus the Word

The 19th Psalm is one of the most magnificent writings in the Bible and indeed in all literature. As in all the psalms, the structure is poetic as it extols the majesty of creation in its first six verses, followed by the far greater glory of the Scriptures in the final eight. It displays remarkable scientific insight as well as profound spiritual truth.

Testimony of the World of God

"The heavens declare the glory of God; and the firmament sheweth his handywork" (Ps. 19:1). The "firmament" (Hebrew *raqia*, meaning "expanse") was indicated as the space between the primeval "waters above the firmament" and those below (Gen. 1:7), so it seems to have essentially the same meaning as our modern scientific concept of "space."

Then, verse 2 tells us that the marvels displayed by God in "space" are also being shown through "time." "Day unto day uttereth speech, and night unto night sheweth knowledge." These remarkable verses are speaking of the space-time universe in which are shown forth all the multitudinous workings of God and all the beautiful and intricate designs in His creations.

In fact, they are all "declaring the glory of God." We know from the New Testament that, in the deepest sense, this can only mean the Lord Jesus Christ, who is the very "brightness of his glory" (Heb. 1:3), for we ultimately have "the light of the knowledge of the glory of God in the face of Jesus Christ" (2 Cor. 4:6). In one way or another, the gospel is being "preached to every creature [in every creation] which is under heaven" (Col. 1:23).

That is, for those who have eyes to see and ears to hear, "the invisible things of Him from the creation of the world are clearly seen, being understood by the things that are made," so that those who will not see and hear the witness of God in creation are "without excuse" (Rom. 1:20). The heavens declare the glory of God, but sadly, "all have sinned and come short of the glory of God" (Rom. 3:23).

This testimony of the created world has "no speech nor language" (note that "where" in verse 3 is not in the original Hebrew of this verse). Nevertheless, "their line is gone out through all the earth, and their words to the end of the world" (v. 4). This verse is quoted in the great missionary passage of Romans 10 as saying "their sound went into all the earth" (Rom. 10:18) and as proving that all men have had access to the evidence of God's power and love. Jesus Christ is "the true Light, which lighteth every man that cometh into the world" (John 1:9).

The problem is that "men loved darkness rather than light, because their deeds were evil," so would not come to the light (John 3:19–20). The "line" of Psalm 19:4 is a reference to the measuring line of the surveyor, indicating that God's measurement of human response to His revealed glory in creation somehow conditions any further revelation He might give to men and women.

In the structures and processes of "nature," there is abundant witness to His "eternal power and Godhead," leaving men and women "without excuse" when they have "changed the glory of the uncorruptible God into an image made like to corruptible man, and to birds and four-footed beasts, and creeping things" (Rom. 1:20, 23), attempting to replace the God of creation with an atheistic or pantheistic evolutionary pseudo-creation. God's measuring line thus finds them far "short of the glory of God."

The most magnificent of God's structures is the sun, which provides the energy for maintaining practically all earth's natural processes. "In them [that is, in space and time] hath he set a tabernacle for the sun, Which is as a bridegroom coming out of his chamber, and rejoiceth as a strong man to run a race" (Ps. 19:4–5).

At first, the metaphors of bridegroom and runner seem strange figures to apply to the glorious light of the sun, which — physically speaking — is nothing less than the "light of the world," sustaining its very life. But that actually makes it a beautiful type of the world's Creator, the Lord Jesus Christ. He indeed is the heavenly bridegroom, coming forth to choose and claim His bride, the Church, and the heavenly runner, encouraging us who are in His Church to "run with patience the race that is set before us, Looking unto Jesus the author and finisher of our faith; who for the joy that was set before him endured the cross" (Heb. 12:1–2).

"His going forth is from the end of the heaven, and his circuit unto the ends of it: and there is nothing hid from the heat thereof" (Ps. 19:6). This verse is often derided by skeptics as teaching that the sun goes around the earth, instead of the earth rotating on its axis.

But the writer was more scientific than his critics. There is no fixed point of zero motion in the universe, so far as astronomers know. The sun, indeed, is moving in a gigantic orbit in the Milky Way galaxy, and the galaxy itself is moving among the other galaxies. So the circuit of the sun is, indeed, from one end of the heavens to the other.

However, the Psalmist was really using the scientifically correct terminology of "relative motion." No one knows scientifically where a fixed point of zero motion may be, so all motion must be referenced to some assumed fixed point. For practically all measurements by surveyors, navigators, and astronomers, the most useful (therefore, the most scientific) zero point is the earth's surface at the location of the observer. That is exactly what the Psalmist has assumed.

And note the significance of the statement that "there is nothing hid from the heat thereof." This refers mainly to the sun's effect on the earth, and scientists now know that the heat energy transmitted to the earth by solar radiation empowers all activity on earth, either directly (e.g., winds, rains) or indirectly (plant life through photosynthesis, and, therefore, also animal and human life). Through "fossil fuels" derived from buried organisms, it even drives our machinery. It is significant that the science which deals with all these energy transfers is called thermodynamics (meaning "heat power") and its two basic laws are the best-proved and most universally applicable laws of science.

These two laws testify plainly to the existence and power of God. The second law (the law of decreasing available energy, as the universe heads downward toward an eventual "heat death," with the sun and stars all burned out) tells us that there must have been a primeval creation, or else the universe would already be "dead"! The first law (law of energy conservation) tells us that no energy is now being created, so the universe could not have created itself. The only scientific conclusion is that "In the beginning God created the heaven and the earth" (Gen. 1:1).

When this verse speaks of the sun's "going forth," however, it is not referring only to its transit across the sky, but to the "outgoing" of its radiant heat energy. It is the same Hebrew word as in Deuteronomy 8:3 which reminds us that man cannot live by bread alone, but "by every word that proceedeth out of the mouth of the Lord." It is also used in the remarkable prophecy of the coming birth of Christ in Bethlehem, where we are told that His "goings forth have been from of old, from everlasting" (Mic. 5:2).

Here, also, the sun is a beautiful type of Christ, picturing both the Living Word and the written Word of God. He is the eternally begotten Son of God, everlastingly proceeding from the Father and declaring Him (John 1:18), while the Holy Scriptures "for ever settled in heaven" (Ps. 119:89), can continually sustain our spiritual lives, just as the sun does our physical lives.

As marvelous as God's witness in the creation may be, however, it can never bring lost men to salvation. The sun may sustain their lives, but it can never save their souls.

Testimony of the Word of God

But God's Word can! "The law of the Lord is perfect, converting the soul" (Ps. 19:7). We are saved by grace through faith, but "faith cometh by hearing, and hearing by the word of God" (Rom. 10:17). Therefore, the Apostle exhorts us to "receive with meekness the engrafted word, which is able to save your souls" (James 1:21). We can only know the One who is the Living Word through His revelation in the written Word, "the holy scriptures, which are able to make thee wise unto salvation through faith which is in Christ Jesus" (2 Tim. 3:15).

That is why we, like the Psalmist, must read, believe, and love the Holy Scriptures. The psalmist David only had a relatively small portion of the Scriptures available in his day, yet he could say: "More to be desired are they than gold . . . sweeter also than honey . . . in keeping of them there is great reward" (Ps. 19:10–11).

Note David's further convictions. "The testimony of the Lord is sure. . . . The statutes of the Lord are right . . . the commandment of the Lord is pure. . . . the judgments of the Lord are true and righteous altogether" (Ps. 19:7–9). And Paul echoes with similar conviction: "All Scripture is given by inspiration of God, and is profitable for doctrine, for reproof, for correction, for instruction in righteousness" (2 Tim. 3:16). Combining the witness of David and Paul, we are assured that "The law of the Lord is perfect (Ps. 19:7). . . . that the man of God may be perfect" (2 Tim. 3:17).

The psalm ends with a prayer, asking God for cleansing through the Word. "Cleanse thou me from secret faults" (or sins of ignorance, v. 12). "Keep back thy servant also from presumptuous sins" (or willful acts of disobedience, v. 13). Otherwise, long-continued deliberate rejection of God's Word may become "the great transgression" (v. 13) from which there is no deliverance.

Then he prays, and so should we: "Let the words of my mouth and the meditation of my heart, be acceptable in thy sight, O Lord, my strength, and my redeemer" (v. 14).

Defending the Gospel

Although many Christians would argue that the Gospel simply needs to be preached rather than defended, the apostle Paul would not agree with them. He wrote to the church at Philippi, "I am set for the defence of the gospel" (Phil. 1:17). Furthermore, he had insisted that "In the defence and confirmation of the gospel, ye all are partakers of my grace" (Phil. 1:7).

In these verses, the word "defense" is *apologia* in the Greek, meaning a systematic legal defense in a court case in which the defendant is under attack. It is the word from which we get our English word "apologetics." Paul thus was set to give an apologetic (not "apologizing"!) for the Gospel, which was under attack by the Greek skeptics and Jewish legalists. The word "confirmation" is self-explanatory. Paul was determined both to defend the Gospel against its enemies and also to establish its validity for its friends. We must follow his example as "partakers" (that is, "participants"), like the Philippians, with Paul.

The Gospel centers on the death, burial, and resurrection of Christ (1 Cor. 15:1–4), dying for our sins and being raised for our justification. But that is not all there is to the Gospel. It covers the entire scope of the person and work of the Lord Jesus Christ. It has no foundation apart from His work as Creator and no future hope except for His promised return as King. That means, first of all, if we would defend and establish the Gospel, we must defend and establish the truth of creation, as revealed in God's Word.

The most important of all the good fruits of creationism is Christianity itself. Many evangelicals seem unaware that all the key doctrines of the Christian faith are founded on the truth of creation. The Gospel of Christ, however, begins with creation. In Revelation 14:6–7 we read this testimony of the apostle John: "And I saw another angel fly in the midst of heaven, having the everlasting gospel to preach unto them that dwell on the earth, and to every nation, and kindred, and tongue, and people, Saying with a loud voice, Fear God, and give glory to him; for the hour of his judgment is come: and worship him that made heaven, and earth, and the sea, and the fountains of waters." Please note: This is the *everlasting* Gospel. Its rejection is connected by the angel with the coming judgment, but its message centers on the Creator! The very foundation of the Gospel that saves from coming judgment is the creation and its Creator.

The Gospel is connected with creation because Jesus Christ himself is the Creator. Only the Creator of all men could ever die for sins and then defeat death to become the redeeming Savior of all who believe on His name. One of the greatest passages on the person and work of Christ is Colossians 1:16–20. It begins with this great affirmation: "For by him [Christ] were all things created, that are in heaven, and that are in earth, visible and invisible, whether they be thrones, or dominions, or principalities, or powers: all things were created by him, and for him: And he is before all things and by him all things consist" (v. 16–17). Only because He was the Creator of all things could He then make "peace through the blood of his cross, by him to reconcile all things unto himself" (v. 20). The reason we need Him to be our Savior is that we have sinned against Him as our Creator, and we must know and believe this in order to know and believe on Him.

Another passage which teaches how important the biblical doctrine of creation is to a saving, living faith is found in Hebrews. Chapter 11 of this book is well known as the great passage on faith. This exposition, however, really begins with the last two verses of chapter 10. In verse 38 we are told that "the just [or justified] shall live by faith." In the next verse the author argues that true Christians are "them that believe [i.e., that have faith] to the saving of the soul" (v. 39). But what is this faith by which we are saved and by which we must live? Its first object according to chapter 11, verse 3, is this: "Through faith we understand that the worlds were framed by the Word of God, so that things which are seen were not made of things which do appear."

This passage, incidentally, precludes theistic evolution (i.e., the doctrine that God oversaw the evolutionary process). God the Creator did not use pre-existing materials to form the "things which are seen" by the slow process of evolution. He spoke the worlds into existence merely by His Word. As Scripture declares elsewhere: "By the word of the Lord were the heavens made; and all the host of them by the breath [literally, 'spirit'] of his mouth. . . . For he spake, and it was done" (Ps. 33:6–9).

We ought not judge anyone's heart, but professing Christian evolutionists should at least ask themselves, "How can we really have a living, saving faith in Christ when we deny His clearly revealed work in creating all things out of nothing by His powerful Word?"

The doctrine of the special creation of all things by the omnipotent, omniscient Creator is the foundation of a true doctrine of Christ, the true Gospel and true saving faith. Upon this foundation must be erected the doctrines of the redemptive work of Christ and of the coming judgment and the reconciliation of all things to God. A sound structure can be built only on a firm foundation. A tree producing good fruits must grow from strong roots.

True evangelism, then, must also begin with an exposition of creation. John's Gospel is most instructive in this regard. In his concluding testimony, John notes that his Gospel has the specific purpose of winning people to Christ. "These are written, that ye might believe that Jesus is the Christ, the Son of God; and that believing ye might have life through his name" (John 20:31). But note carefully, then, the incomparable words with which he begins: "In the beginning was the Word, and the Word was with God, and the Word was God. The same was in the beginning with God. All things were made by him; and without him was not any thing made that was made. . . . He was in the world, and the world was made by him, and the world knew him not. . . . And the Word was made flesh, and dwelt among us, (and we beheld his glory, the glory as of the only begotten of the Father) full of grace and truth" (John 1:1–14).

At this point, the question naturally arises, "Given that true evangelism begins with the doctrine of creation, does this mean that we must always proclaim the biblical account of origins before we present the Gospel message?" The answer is, "No. We must do this only when the circumstances warrant it."

The strategy of the disciples is instructive. When they preached to their Jewish brethren in the synagogues, they did not need to begin with an emphasis on creation, for the Jews already knew and believed the Old Testament, acknowledging God as Creator and the truth of creation. The disciples could immediately go beyond this. They "reasoned with them [the Jews] out of the Scriptures, opening and alleging, that Christ must needs have suffered, and risen again from the dead; and that this Jesus . . . is Christ" (Acts 17:2–3).

On the other hand, when the disciples preached to pagans, who neither knew the Scriptures nor believed in a Creator God, they began by laying a foundation of creationism. For example, at Athens, Paul proclaimed the "God that made the world and all things therein"

(Acts 17:24). He drew out the implications from this and then went on to the great testimony of Christ's resurrection. Similarly, Paul urged the pagans at Lystra to "turn from these vanities unto the living God, which made heaven, and earth, and the sea, and all things that are therein" (Acts 14:15).

We should follow these examples today, as we try to win people to Christ. To those who already know the Scriptures, believing in God and creation, we can use the Scriptures and the Resurrection to proclaim Christ's salvation. When we witness to pagans (whether on the mission field or on the American college campus), we need to first convince them that there is a Creator to whom they are responsible. From there, we can go on to preach Christ, the Scriptures, and the great gift of salvation.

Defending the King James Bible

Now the clearest and most emphatic expositions of the inerrancy of Scripture, the truth of special creation, and the fullness of the Gospel are found in the time-tested King James authorized translation of the Bible. Although many Christians have started using one of the modern English translations, abandoning the King James Version, it may be well to review a few of the reasons why many still prefer the latter.

One reason is that all the 50 or more translators who developed the King James Bible were godly men who believed implicitly in the inerrancy and full authority of Scripture and in the literal historicity of Genesis, with its record of six-day creation and the worldwide flood. This has not been true of many who have worked on the modern versions.

Furthermore, the King James translators (54 men altogether) were great scholars, at least as proficient in the biblical languages as any who have come after them. They were familiar with the great body of manuscript evidence, as well as all the previous translations. They worked diligently on the project (assigned to them by King James) for over seven years (completed in 1611), with the result that the "Authorized" version eventually displaced all those that had gone before and has withstood the test of wide usage in all English-speaking countries ever since.

There have been over 120 English translations of the complete Bible published *since* the King James, as well as over 200 New Testaments. Even if one really feels that he ought to switch to a modern translation, how can he decide which, if any, is really the inspired word of God? I personally have perused in some depth at least 20 of them, and am personally convinced that the old King James is still the best.

For a long time, the "official" version used in each Bible-believing church was the King James, with the others used occasionally for reference study by teachers and pastors. Now, however, confusion reigns. Congregational reading is no longer possible in most churches, and Scripture memorization, which has been an incalculable blessing in my own Christian life, is almost a lost art these days.

And what about our belief in verbal inspiration? If it's only the "thought" that counts, then the words are flexible, and we can adjust them to make them convey any thought we prefer. Exact thoughts require precise words.

Even many King James Bibles have footnotes referring to what are said to be "better manuscripts" which indicate that certain changes should be made in the King James text. But what are these manuscripts and are they really better? It is significant that almost all of the new versions of the New Testament are based on what is known as the Westcott-Hort Greek text, whereas the King James is based largely on what is known as the Textus Receptus. As far as the Hebrew text of the Old Testament is concerned, the King James is based on the Masoretic text, while the modern versions rely heavily on Kittel's revised Masoretic text.

The Masoretic text was compiled from the ancient manuscripts of the Old Testament by the Masoretes, Hebrew scholars dedicated to guarding and standardizing the traditional Hebrew text as "handed down" (the basic meaning of Masoretic) from the earlier Hebrew scribes, who had in turn meticulously copied the ancient Hebrew manuscripts, scrupulously guarding against error. As far as the Hebrew text developed by Rudolf Kittel is concerned, it is worth noting that Kittel was a German rationalistic higher critic, rejecting biblical inerrancy and firmly devoted to evolutionism.

The men most responsible for alterations in the New Testament text were B.F. Westcott and F.J.A. Hort, whose Greek New Testament was largely updated by Eberhard Nestle and Kurt Aland. All of these men were evolutionists. Furthermore, Westcott and Hort both denied biblical inerrancy. Nestle and Aland, like Kittel, were German theological liberals.

Westcott and Hort were also the most influential members of the English revision committee which produced the English Revised Version of the Bible. The corresponding American revision committee which developed the American Standard Version of 1901 was headed by another liberal evolutionist, Philip Schaff. Most new versions since that time have adopted the same presuppositions as those of the 19th century revisers.

Furthermore, the Westcott-Hort text was mainly based on two early Greek manuscripts, the Sinaiticus and Vaticanus texts, which were rediscovered and rescued from long (and well-deserved) obscurity in the 19th century. Since these are both said to be older than the 5,000 manuscripts that support the Textus Receptus, they were called "better." This was in spite of the fact that they frequently disagreed with each other as well as with the Textus Receptus and also contained many obvious and flagrant mistakes.

The fact that these two manuscripts may have been older does not prove they are better. More likely it indicates that they were set aside because of their numerous errors. Thus, they would naturally last longer than the good manuscripts which were being used regularly, and had to be recopied when they began to wear out.

So one of the serious problems with most modern English translations is that they rely heavily on Hebrew and Greek manuscripts of the Bible developed by liberals, rationalists, and evolutionists, none of whom believed in the verbal inspiration of the Bible. Is this how God would preserve His word? Would He not more likely have used devout scholars who believed in the absolute inerrancy and authority of the Bible?

Furthermore, the beautiful prose of the King James is a treasure which should not be lost. It has been acclaimed widely as the greatest example of English literature ever written. Apart from a few archaic words which can be easily clarified in footnotes, it is as easy to understand today as it was 400 years ago. This is why the common people today still use and love it. The King James uses mostly one and two-syllable words, and formal studies have always shown its readability index to be tenth grade or lower.

It is also noteworthy that the King James was produced during the period when the English language and literature had reached their zenith of power and expressiveness. This was the age of Shakespeare, for example. Modern English is merely a decadent remnant of its former beauty and clarity. It is no wonder that a Bible translation produced at that special time in history has endured for almost 400 years, meeting the needs and guiding the culture of over ten generations of English-speaking peoples. Why should this generation suddenly want to change it?

We have abandoned today many fine points of grammar commonly used in 1600. For example, we forget that "thee," "thou," and "thine" were used to express the second person singular, with "you," "ye," and "yours" reserved for second person plural. Today we use "you" indiscriminately for both singular and plural, thereby missing the precise meaning of many texts of Scripture.

Furthermore, the translators were not only biblical scholars but accomplished writers, and one of their goals had been to produce a Bible that would "sing" with beauty and power, as well as retaining literal faithfulness to the original texts, which had themselves been written with majestic musical beauty.

With all these factors in mind, do we not most honor the Lord and His revealed word by having it read and used in that form of our language which was in use when the English language was at its best, instead of in our modern jargon? All modern versions are inferior to the King James in this important regard.

Other versions are better than no version, of course, and their users can certainly profit from them. However, I believe after studying, teaching, and loving the Bible for over 55 years, that Christians — especially creationists! — need to hang on to their old King James Bibles as long as they live. God has uniquely blessed its use in the great revivals, in the worldwide missionary movement, and in the personal lives of believers, more so than He has with all the rest of the versions put together, and "by their fruits ye shall know them" (Matt. 7:20).

It is the most beautiful, the most powerful, and (I strongly believe) the most reliable of any that we have or ever will have, until Christ returns.

Endnotes
1   Statement on Teaching Evolution, adopted March 15, 1995 (National Association of Biology Teachers).
2   Stephen Jay Gould, *Scientific American,* July 1992, p. 118–121.
3   Hugh Ross, *The Fingerprint of God* (Orange, CA: Promise Publishing Co., 1991), p. 144.

Chapter II

The Christ of the Bible

n a very real sense, Christianity *is* Christ, so that defending the Christian faith must focus especially on the person and work of Christ. If He was merely a great teacher, as the liberals allege, or merely a great prophet, as Jews and Muslims teach, or just one of many manifestations of the cosmic consciousness, as New Age gurus might argue, then our Christian faith is a delusion. The Bible teaches — and Jesus claimed — that He is the only begotten Son of God, nothing less than the one God of creation incarnate in human flesh.

This is an amazing concept, and it is hardly surprising that most people reject or ignore it. But if it is true, as genuine Christians have always believed, then it is supremely important, for it means that in Him alone is eternal salvation.

In this chapter, therefore, we shall survey some of the reasons and evidences for believing that Jesus Christ is God — evidences that seem quite compelling to us Christians.

Before Time Began

When the writings of all the world's religions are compared, it is found that only the biblical revelation speaks of a special creation of all things in the beginning — a creation out of nothing. All other religions and philosophies of men, both ancient and modern, have espoused evolutionary systems, starting with eternally existing matter.

The Bible, unique among the sacred writings of mankind, begins with an eternal, omnipotent, personal God. He brought all things into being, not out of primeval chaos or eternal matter, but out of nothing except His own infinite power and wisdom. Special creation is a concept found only in the Bible. To the ancient Israelites, accustomed as they were to thinking in terms of the evolutionary cosmologies of the Egyptians and the Canaanites, this was a radically new idea. The writer of Genesis, therefore, had to be quite clear and emphatic in his account of creation in order to keep his contemporaries from reading their evolutionary preconceptions into it.

This is why the first chapter of Genesis teaches so plainly and definitely that all things, "the heavens and the earth . . . and all the host of them" (Gen. 2:1), were spoken into existence and brought into their finished perfection directly by God alone. God was not in any way dependent upon pre-existing matter or upon natural processes in their accomplishment. There was nothing at all before the creation period — only God.

Our minds cannot fully grasp the idea of an eternal God existing independently of the universe which He created. But for that matter, neither can we comprehend the idea of eternal chaotic matter or of an infinite chain of secondary causes extending back to eternity. Our minds are finite and are bound by the framework of the space-mass-time universe in which we function. They cannot successfully comprehend infinity and eternity or any kind of existence outside of space and time.

But what we cannot comprehend, we can believe. Millions of people through the ages have found both mental and spiritual rest through simple faith in an eternal Creator, revealed and incarnate in Jesus Christ. This, unlike the "evolution-out-of-nothing" idea, is a concept that involves a cause adequate to produce the effect!

The special creation of our space-mass-time universe is declared in the introductory statement of the Word of God: "In the beginning [time] God created the heaven [space] and the earth [mass]" (Gen. 1:1). The tri-universe, thus spoken into existence, reflects the triune nature of its Creator. The triune God — Father, Son, and Holy Spirit — is thus the source of all meaning and reality.

Skeptics sometimes attempt to ridicule the biblical chronology by saying, "But if the creation took place only 6,000 years ago, what was God doing before that?" One can surely see, however, that this is the same question as "What was God doing prior to the hypothetical creation of the universe five billion years ago?" Infinity minus 6,000 is exactly the same as infinity minus 5 billion.

In either case, there is only one way in which we could possibly learn anything about events prior to the creation. We can only know what God has been pleased to reveal in His Word. And there are a few such glimpses given us in the Holy Scriptures.

We are given an insight into the heart of God when we hear Christ pray to the Father, "Thou lovedst me before the foundation of the world" (John 17:24). The three persons of the godhead shared a mutual love and fellowship in their eternal counsels.

In these counsels we are told that somehow the triune God made plans for the history of the universe: "Known unto God are all his works from the beginning of the world" (Acts 15:18). Ephesians 1:11 tells of God's plans for the inhabitants of the earth prior to their creation: "Being predestinated according to the purpose of him who worketh all things after the counsel of his own will."

We also learn that a certain body of people would be created who, before they even existed, were "chosen . . . in him before the foundation of the world" (Eph. 1:4). But God, knowing that man would choose to rebel against His will and would thereby deserve nothing but punishment and separation from Him, undertook also to work out a marvelous plan of salvation. It was agreed that God's eternal Son would become a man and would endure the punishment and separation from God which men deserved. He was "foreordained before the foundation of the world" (1 Pet. 1:20) to be "the Lamb slain from the foundation of the world" (Rev. 13:8).

On the basis of this great sacrifice, God could then promise eternal life "before the world began" (Titus 1:2) to all who would come to God's Son believing that promise. The marvelous redemption thus planned by the triune God was "the hidden wisdom, which God ordained before the world unto our glory" (1 Cor. 2:7).

Finally, having planned and provided all details, God could then proceed to the actual work of creating the universe and its inhabitants, thence to the work of redemption, and finally to the effectual calling and salvation of believers through the preaching of the gospel.

It is God, and He alone, "who hath saved us, and called us with an holy calling, not according to our works, but according to his own purpose and grace, which was given us in Christ Jesus before the world began" (2 Tim. 1:9).

God's Only Begotten Son

One of our favorite Christmas Scripture verses is 1 John 4:9. "In this was manifested the love of God toward us, because that God sent his only begotten Son into the world, that we might live through him." The marvelous incarnation in human flesh of the only begotten Son of God is not the end of the story, of course. The next verse explains that we have life through Him because God "sent his Son to be the propitiation for our sins" (1 John 4:10). Our Heavenly Father gives us eternal life instead of the eternal hell that we deserve because His only begotten Son died in our place for our sins. "For he hath made him to be sin for us, who knew no sin; that we might be made the righteousness of God in him" (2 Cor. 5:21).

Consider, though, the significance of this revelation that Jesus Christ is the Father's "only begotten" Son. This unique phrase is used with reference to the Lord Jesus just four other times, and all five verses contain vitally important truths concerning Christ. These verses are as follows:

(1) "And the Word was made flesh, and dwelt among us, (and we beheld his glory, the glory as of the only begotten of the Father,) full of grace and truth" (John 1:14).

This is the key verse of the Incarnation, assuring us that the man Jesus, who dwelt among us for a time, was also the eternal Word who was "in the beginning with God" and that He "was God" and that "all things were made by him" (John 1:1–3). He was God the Creator manifest in the flesh.

(2) "No man hath seen God at any time; the only begotten Son, which is in the bosom of the Father, he hath declared him" (John 1:18).

The Father is omnipresent, and therefore invisible to mortal eyes, but as Jesus said: "He that hath seen me hath seen the Father" (John 14:9). Men have seen and heard the Father in the person of His only begotten Son. Whenever God has been seen by men, it has been through the Son who has revealed Him.

(3) "For God so loved the world, that he gave his only begotten Son, that whosoever believeth in him should

not perish, but have everlasting life" (John 3:16).

This verse, of course, is the most magnificent of all gospel verses; many would call it the greatest verse in the Bible. It assures us that if we simply put our trust in our great Creator, who has become man in order to die for our sins and then to defeat death and become our Savior, our sins will be forgiven, and we shall live forever with Him.

(4) "He that believeth on him is not condemned: but he that believeth not is condemned already, because he hath not believed in the name of the only begotten Son of God" (John 3:18).

Other than the name of the Lord Jesus Christ, "There is none other name under heaven given among men, whereby we must be saved" (Acts 4:12). In view of all that our Creator/Savior has done for us, this verse gives clear warning that those who refuse or neglect to believe on the person and work of God's only begotten Son, will die in their sins, condemned forever by the Father whose Son they have spurned.

(5) "God sent his only begotten Son into the world, that we might live through him" (1 John 4:9).

This great Christmas verse was discussed above and is a wonderful summary verse on salvation that Christians now often write on their Christmas cards.

But why was it important for the Holy Spirit, who inspired these five great verses, to stress that the Lord Jesus was the incarnate only begotten Son of God. Many modern English translations of the New Testament apparently do not consider it important, for they render the phrase merely as "only son." It is so rendered in the Living Bible, the Revised Standard Version, the God's Word translation, the 20th Century New Testament, the New Living Translation, the Moffatt, Goodspeed, and Williams translations, and many others. The New International Version renders it "one and only son." There are still a few, however — the best-known being the New American Standard and the New King James — that render it correctly (as in the King James Version) as "only begotten Son."

The Greek word for "only begotten" is *monogenes*, the very form of which clearly denotes "only generated." As monotheism connotes only one God and monosyllable means a word of only one syllable, so *monogenes* means only one genesis or only one generated — or, more simply, only begotten. It does *not* mean "one," or even "one and only." It is worth noting that, although Christ is called the Son, or Son of God, frequently in the New Testament, He is *never* (in the Greek original) called the "only" Son of God.

The fact is, that to call Him the only Son of God would make the Bible contradict itself, for He is not the only Son of God, and certainly not the "one and only" Son of God. Angels are several times called the sons of God (e.g., Job 38:7) since they had no fathers, being directly created by God. Likewise, Adam was called the son of God (Luke 3:38), because he was directly created. The same applies even to fallen angels (Gen. 6:2), and even to Satan (Job 1:6), because they also were created beings. The term is also used in a spiritual sense, of course, for those who have become "new creations" in Christ Jesus by faith (2 Cor. 5:17; Eph. 2:10; etc.). In this sense, we also are "sons of God" (e.g., 1 John 3:2) by special creation — not physically but spiritually.

But it is never applied in this sense to Christ, for He is not a *created* Son of God (as the Jehovah's Witnesses and other cultists teach), but a *begotten* Son of God — in fact, the *only begotten* Son of God. He never had a beginning, for He was there in the beginning (John 1:1). In His prayer to the Father in the upper room, He spoke of "the glory which I had with thee before the world was" (John 17:5).

In that wonderful Old Testament Christmas prophecy about His coming human birth in Bethlehem (Mic. 5:2), we are told that His "goings forth have been from of old, from everlasting." His human body was, indeed, "brought forth" from "she which travaileth" (Mic. 5:3). But long before that, He had been everlastingly going forth from "the bosom of the Father." As noted in John 1:18, He was still "in the bosom of the Father," even while He was on earth manifesting the Father.

This is beyond our full comprehension, of course, for it is all part of the mystery of the triune godhead. Christ is "the image of the invisible God" (Col. 1:15), for as He said: "I and my Father are one" (John 10:30).

He is not just the *only begotten* Son of the Father, but He is also the *eternally begotten* Son of the Father. He is eternally "in his bosom," yet always "going forth" to "declare" the Father — once as the creating Word, occasionally in pre-incarnate theophanies, also through the Holy Spirit conveying God's written Word (which had been eternally "settled in heaven" (Ps. 119:89) down to man through divinely chosen prophets, then ultimately appearing as the incarnate Word to live forever as the God/man.

The doctrine of "eternal generation" was what the older theologians called this great truth. He did not *become* the only Son by His virgin birth. He *was* the only begotten Son from eternity, "set up from everlasting" (Prov. 8:23).

But that is not all. He was not just the only begotten Son in the beginning, He soon also became the "first begotten of the dead" in time (Rev. 1:5). He was "declared to be the Son of God with power . . . by the resurrection from the dead" (Rom. 1:4). When Paul at Antioch preached on the Resurrection, he declared that God "hath raised up Jesus again; as it is also written in the second psalm, Thou art my Son, this day have I begotten thee" (Acts 13:33).

He is the only begotten Son eternally and now the first begotten Son by resurrection, "the first-fruits of them that slept" (1 Cor. 15:20). What a wonderful Savior is Jesus Christ, our Lord!

The Lord Jesus is not only the unique Son of God by eternal generation and by resurrection, but also by divine inheritance. God has "spoken unto us by his Son, whom he hath appointed heir of all things" (Heb. 1:2).

His unique human birth, miraculously conceived with a divinely created body in a virgin's womb, had also marked Him as the incarnate Son of God. To Mary, the angel had said: "Fear not . . . that holy thing which shall be born of thee shall be called the Son of God" (Luke 1:30–35).

His unique righteousness, in both character and action, still further marks Him as Son of God, for He alone possessed the divine nature from the beginning. He said on one occasion: "The Son can do nothing of himself, but what he seeth the Father do: for what things soever he doeth, these also doeth the Son likewise" (John 5:19).

He was even identified as God's Son by heavenly proclamation. "There came a voice from heaven, saying, Thou art my beloved Son, in whom I am well pleased" (Mark 1:11).

The Lord Jesus Christ is thus Son of God by miraculous conception and virgin birth, by heavenly proclamation, by His uniquely perfect human nature, by divine inheritance, and by triumphant resurrection.

But, most of all and first of all, He is Son of God by eternal generation — the second person of the Holy Trinity, the only begotten Son of God!

There is another great Christmas verse. "For unto us a child is born," known and beloved by every born-again Christian. That child was the infant Jesus, born of the virgin, as prophesied hundreds of years in advance (Isa. 7:14), in the little town of Bethlehem, as also prophesied (Mic. 5:2). At the same time, "Unto us a son is given." That Son was the only begotten, eternally begotten Son of God. "And the government shall be upon his shoulder," for He holds the whole wide world in His hand! "And his name shall be called Wonderful, Counsellor, The mighty God, The everlasting Father, The Prince of Peace" (Isa. 9:6).

As one with the everlasting Father in the triune godhead, He is also the mighty God. He is our Creator, our Redeemer, our resurrected Savior, our King of kings, and Lord of lords. "Wherefore he is able to save them to the uttermost that come unto God by him" (Heb. 7:25).

Christ, Creation, and the Koran

As we have seen, the Bible teaches that Jesus, while fully human (except for sin), was at the same time the one eternal Son of God, the only begotten of the Father. Of the three persons in the godhead (Father, Son, Holy Spirit), He was the Creator and sustains all things (John 1:1–3; Col. 1:16–17; etc.).

People of all religions recognize the greatness of His character and teachings, but they stumble over this great truth. Even the other two great monotheistic religions, Islam and Judaism, refuse to believe that He is God. Both Jews and Muslims acknowledge Him as one of their prophets, but that is as far as they will go. Muslims even believe in His virgin birth and second coming, but not His deity.

Orthodox Jews and orthodox Muslims believe — at least superficially — in the Old Testament, especially the books of Moses. Thus, they, like Bible-believing Christians (and unlike people of the pantheistic religions such as Buddhism, Hinduism, etc.), accept the Genesis record of special creation as the true account of primeval history. This fact at least gives Christians an effective basis of agreement with them upon which we can build as we seek to defend and proclaim our Christian faith to them.

It is not only men and women of these other religions who need to understand and believe the great truths concerning the person and work of Jesus Christ. The same is true of multitudes of nominal Christians who don't fully believe or appreciate them, not to mention all those who profess atheism, humanism, or no faith at all. First of all, we can look at the Muslim faith, as based on Mohammed's teachings in the Koran.

This is the faith of multitudes around the world, and it is growing rapidly. There are, indeed, a number of key points of agreement between Bible-believing Christians and Qur'an (or Koran)-believing Muslims.

As far as creation is concerned, for example, the Koran explicitly teaches the special creation of all things in six days by one God. For example, note the following excerpts from the writings of Mohammed in the Koran:

> We created the heavens and the earth and all that
> is between them in six days, and no weariness touched
> us (50:37, p.93).[1]

The "we" and "us" in this verse are not referring to other gods, of course, but probably constitute majestic plurals. The Koran is very specific in denying the existence of other gods.

> The gods whom they call on beside God, create
> nothing, but are themselves created. . . . Your God is
> the one God (16:20–23, p. 201).

Noah, his ark, and the deluge also are mentioned at several places in the Koran. For example:

> Before them the people of Noah treated the truth
> as a lie. . . . So we opened the gates of Heaven with
> water, which fell in torrents, and we caused the earth to
> break forth with springs, and their waters met by settled
> decree. And we bare him on a vessel made with planks
> and nails (54:9–13, p. 77).

Instead of Mount Ararat, the Koran says that the ark finally grounded on a mountain with a different name.

And the water abated, and the decree was fulfilled, and the Ark rested on Al-Djoudi (11:46, p. 219).

However, this is not necessarily a contradiction, since many Muslim scholars say that Al Djoudi was a generic name for any high mountain.

It may be surprising to many Christians that Mohammed accepted the books of Moses (including Genesis) and also the Psalms and the Gospels as coming from God. However, Mohammed believed that these had become distorted in various ways, so that these mistakes had to be corrected by him in the Koran. Christians, of course, maintain that the Bible is right in all such conflicts, and that any distortions are only in the Koran.

In any case, the Koran does teach that Jesus was a great prophet and even that He was born of a virgin.

Remember when the angel said, "O Mary! Verily God announceth to thee the Word from Him. His name shall be Messiah Jesus the son of Mary . . . She said, How, O my Lord! Shall I have a son when man hath not touched me?" He said, "Thus: God will create what He will; when He decreeth a thing, He only saith, Be, and it is" (3:40–42, p. 390).

Note that Jesus is thus called both "the Word" and "Messiah Jesus" in this passage.

However, although He is thus called "the Word" (as He is in the Bible — John 1:1, 3, 14), the Koran repeatedly denies that He is the Son of God. For example:

The Messiah, Jesus, son of Mary, is only an apostle of God, and His Word which he conveyed into Mary, and a Spirit proceeding from himself. Believe therefore in God and his apostles, and say not, "Three:" (there is a Trinity) — Forbear — it will be better for you. God is only one God! Far be it from His glory that He should have a son! (4:169, p. 428).

Thus, the Koran teaches emphatically that there is only one God, denying not only the polytheism of the pagans but also God's triunity.

The Bible, of course, reveals that Christ is the eternal and only begotten Son of God, the second person of the godhead. Furthermore, only God himself can be man's Savior from sin. The Creator must become man in order to redeem men from sin and death. In spite of the similarities between the Koran and the Bible as far as creation is concerned, there is a great gulf between the two when it comes to salvation.

Muslims can rejoice with Christians over the birth of Christ, for they also believe He was virgin-born and sent from God. They believe He was a great teacher (even speaking from His cradle!) and performed mighty miracles. But they still miss the glorious truth that He became Emmanuel ("God with us" — Matt. 1:23) when He was born. Consequently, Mohammed and his followers also are unable to appreciate the marvelous significance of His atoning death and victorious resurrection. Here is what the Koran says about that:

> Yet they slew him not, and they crucified him not, but they had only his likeness. . . . they did not really slay him, but God took him up to himself" (4:156, p. 427).

Christ did ascend back to heaven, of course, but only after He had died on the cross for all our sins and then defeated sin and Satan and death itself by His bodily resurrection.

It is sad that Mohammed and his Muslim followers have not understood this wonderful truth, for it leaves them without a Savior and without any assurance of salvation. The Koran does speak of an eternal paradise for the righteous and an eternal hell for the unrighteous (including, but not limited to, all who are not Muslims).

> A picture of the Paradise which God promised to them that fear Him. The rivers flow beneath its bowers: its food and its shades are perpetual. This is the reward of those who fear God; but the reward of the unbelievers is the Fire (13:35, p. 337).

> Whoso desireth any other religion than Islam, that religion shall never be accepted from him, and in the next world he shall be among the lost (3:79, p. 394).

But not even true believers in Islam are exempt from judgment:

> The weighing on that day, with justice! And they whose balances shall be heavy, these are they who shall

be happy. And they whose balances shall be light, these
are they who have lost their souls, for that to our signs
they were unjust (7:7–8, p. 294).

Not even devout Muslims (with the possible exception of those
who are considered martyrs for their faith) can have any assurance of
salvation before the Day of Judgment.

To the Christian, this seems very sad. Many Muslim people are
devoutly religious in their faith, trying to live righteous lives according to the instructions in the Koran. Yet they — like all men and
women everywhere — are sinners by nature and practice, for "all
have sinned and come short of the glory of God" (Rom. 3:23), and
therefore all need a Savior, since "the wages of sin is death" (Rom.
6:23).

The Lord Jesus Christ *is* the *only one* who can be such a Savior.
Even the Koran acknowledges that He was just and righteous him-
self (3:41, p. 390). On the cross, therefore, "Christ also hath once
suffered for sins, the just for the unjust, that he might bring us to
God" (1 Pet. 3:18). Then He "was raised again for our justification"
(Rom. 4:25).

But when Mohammed denied the substitutionary death and resurrection of the Lord Jesus on the cross, he cut himself and his followers off from the only one who could take away their sins and
make them truly righteous before God.

Jesus said: "No man cometh unto the Father, but by me" (John
14:6), and He vindicated His otherwise incredible claim by rising
from the dead. Whether Mohammed believed it or not, the fact is that
Jesus did defeat death by His own bodily resurrection and then
"showed himself alive after his passion by many infallible proofs,
being seen of them forty days, and speaking of the things pertaining
to the kingdom of God" (Acts 1:3).

Mohammed never claimed to be sinless, as Jesus both claimed
and demonstrated himself to be. Mohammed died in Medina and
was buried, but the tomb of Jesus is empty, for He rose from the dead
and, 40 days later, ascended to the right hand of His Father in heaven
(Mark 16:19).

As we remember again the great incarnation of God, when "the
Word was made flesh, and dwelt among us" (John 1:14), we should
remember the millions of Muslims in prayer. They also believe, as
we do, that God sent Him into the world by miraculous conception

and virgin birth, but they still need salvation through receiving Him as personal Savior. "For God sent not his Son into the world to condemn the world; but that the world through him might be saved" (John 3:17).

Genesis and the Resurrection

The bodily resurrection of Jesus after His death on the cross is the greatest event in history after the creation itself and is the crowning proof that He was the only begotten Son of God, as He had claimed. Only God himself can defeat death. Abraham is dead, Moses is dead, Mohammed is dead, but Jesus Christ is alive after being dead and entombed three days. He has ascended back to heaven in His resurrection body and will never die again. The resurrection of Christ can be said to be the most certain fact of history, and we shall survey some of the proofs shortly.

First, however, it is well to note that it had been foreshadowed in many Old Testament types and prophecies, as well as specifically predicted by Jesus himself many times. Nevertheless, when it happened, it came as a surprise even to His own disciples. Such a thing seemed impossible. They could believe in the survival of a soul after death (even the pagan religions teach that) and maybe in a future resurrection of all the dead at the final judgment (Jews and Muslims believe that), but to return from physical death by one's own power was an event never seen before or since, and the disciples could not believe it would really happen. If they had really known and believed the Old Testament, however, not to mention the clear promises of Christ himself, they should have been expecting it.

One of the primary goals of Christians should be to call as many people as we can "back to Genesis," as the foundational book in which to find answers to the problems of life and death. We're on solid ground when we do this, because that is exactly what the Lord Jesus Christ did after His resurrection.

"What manner of communications are these that ye have one to another, as ye walk, and are sad?" (Luke 24:17) was the question Christ asked two of His followers as He joined them walking home one evening. Not recognizing Him, Cleopas then told Him sadly how their master, Jesus, had been crucified and buried; but now His body was missing from the tomb, and they and the others didn't know what to do.

Then, after Jesus mildly rebuked them for not knowing and believing their Bible, we are told that "beginning at Moses and all the prophets, he expounded unto them in all the Scriptures the things concerning himself" (Luke 24:27). Although they did not yet recognize the resurrected Christ, their hearts "burned within them" (see verse 32) while "He opened the Scriptures to them," and they heard a more wonderful biblical exposition than anyone had ever heard before.

And note that he went back to Genesis to begin! In the Old Testament there are numerous explicit references to the future Messiah who would redeem the lost world, but there are none in Genesis — none, that is, that speak directly of His substitutionary death and bodily resurrection. Yet Genesis is where Jesus began as He expounded to them all the Scriptures concerning himself.

Therefore, He must have shown them instead some of the beautiful types and shadows of these great events, as revealed through the lives of the ancient patriarchs. Perhaps we also can discern some of these types as we study the Book of Genesis.

Adam and His Bride

For example, note the beautiful manner in which Adam and Eve were created. Adam's body was carefully and lovingly molded by God himself out "of the dust of the ground" (Gen. 2:7), without father or mother. Then "The Lord God caused a deep sleep to fall upon Adam." This was not merely an anaesthetized sleep to deaden pain, for there was as yet no pain in God's "very good" world. To all appearances, however, it was a sleep at least simulating death and, while Adam was in that "deep sleep," God opened Adam's side and "took one of his ribs."

However, the word translated "rib" (Hebrew, *tsela*) seems to mean something more than just a rib bone. It occurs more than 40 times in the Old Testament and is only translated "rib" here. It is most frequently translated "side." Evidently God opened one of Adam's sides and took some of his flesh as well as his bone. From these He made Eve, and presented her to Adam as his bride. Adam then exclaimed: "This is now bone of my bones, and flesh of my flesh" (see Gen. 2:21–23).

Now when Adam's side was opened, no doubt blood flowed out as well. Thus Adam "died" and shed his blood so that, when he arose from his deep sleep, he would have a wife to love and cherish all the days of his new life. The symbolic teaching of this great event at the beginning of history is explained by the apostle Paul in Ephesians 5:25, 27, and 30. "Husbands, love your wives, even as Christ also loved the church, and gave himself for it . . . That he might present it to himself a glorious church. . . . For we are members of his body, of his flesh, and of his bones." Christ's side was opened, and His blood was shed, that we who love Him might become His spiritual Bride.

"And so it is written, The first man Adam was made a living soul; the last Adam was made a quickening [that is, 'life-giving'] spirit. . . . The first man is of the earth, earthy: the second man is the Lord from heaven" (1 Cor. 15:45–47).

Noah and the Ark

Another wonderful type in Genesis is the account of Noah and the ark of safety which he prepared to save those who otherwise would have died in the flood (see Gen. 6:5–8:19). Noah here is a type of the Heavenly Father (in fact, he was the human father of all people on the earth today), and the ark is a type of God's provision for deliverance from His own just wrath on sin.

Noah "prepared an ark to the saving of his house; by the which he condemned the world" (Heb. 11:7). The very waters of the flood which drowned all the ungodly antediluvian population bore up the ark, "wherein few, that is, eight souls were saved by water. The like figure whereunto even baptism doth also now save us . . . by the resurrection of Jesus Christ" (1 Pet. 3:21).

In fact, the glorious Resurrection took place on the anniversary of the very day when the ark finally rested on the mountains of Ararat after the flood had fully performed its mission — that is, "in the seventh month, on the seventeenth day of the month" (Gen. 8:4). The seventh month of the ancient civil calendar had been designated by God as the first month of Israel's religious calendar, and the Passover sacrifice was to be slain on the 14th day of that month (Exod. 12:2, 6). "Christ our passover (was) sacrificed for us" (1 Cor. 5:7) and, three days after He had shared the Passover supper with His disciples, He rose from the dead "on the seventeenth day of the seventh month."

Because Noah prepared the ark which endured the beatings of the flood on its own structure, thereby protecting those within its walls, the refugees were delivered from the old world and emerged to a new life. Similarly, "If any man be in Christ, he is a new creature: old things are passed away; behold, all things are become new" (2 Cor. 5:17). Like those in the ark, we "have fled for refuge to lay hold upon the hope set before us" (Heb. 6:18).

Abraham and His Son

Perhaps the most beautiful type in Genesis is the record of Abraham and Isaac. "By faith Abraham, when he was tried, offered up Isaac; and he that had received the promises offered up his only begotten Son . . . Accounting that God was able to raise him up, even from the dead; from whence also he received him in a figure" (Heb. 11:17–19).

The account itself is found in Genesis 22:1–19. It is a remarkable testimony to Abraham's strong faith (note Rom. 4:20) that, in a time when no one had ever come back to life after dying, Abraham believed that God would raise His own beloved Son from the dead.

This was especially shown when he told the two young men who had accompanied him and Isaac to wait for them, assuring them that "I and the lad will go yonder and worship, and come again to you" (Gen. 22:5). He fully intended to obey God in sacrificing his son, but had such strong faith in God's promises (e.g., Gen. 15:5–6) that he believed God would then restore him to life.

That he did indeed rise from the dead "in a figure" assures us that the experience was intended by God to serve as a type of the sacrifice and resurrection of His own beloved and only begotten Son.

Abraham thus is a type of the Heavenly Father willing to sacrifice His own Son, and Isaac is a type of the beloved Son willing to be sacrificed to do the will of His Father. Isaac was not a little lad at this time, but a strong young man, easily capable of escaping if he wished, but the Scripture says twice that "they went both of them together" (Gen. 22:6, 8) to the place of sacrifice. "Herein is love, not that we loved God, but that he loved us, and sent his Son to be the propitiation for our sins" (1 John 4:10).

Other Types in Genesis

Perhaps these were among the wonderful teachings from Genesis shared by the Lord Jesus with the two disciples as they walked along together on that evening after His resurrection. There probably were many others, too. There is the great protevangelic promise of Genesis 3:15, for example, assuring us of the ultimate defeat of the evil one who now has "the power of death, that is, the devil" (Heb. 2:14).

The blood of Abel, shed by his brother Cain, also foreshadows Christ, whose blood was, in effect, also shed by his brethren (note Matt. 27:25). Abel's blood "crieth unto me from the ground," God said (Gen. 4:10), but we listen now "to Jesus the mediator of the new covenant, and to the blood of sprinkling, that speaketh better things than that of Abel" (Heb. 12:24).

Then there is the lovely story of Isaac and Rebekah, along with Abraham's servant, sent into a distant country to find a bride for his master's son (Gen. 24). In the typology implied, Isaac pictures the Son after He has returned from the place of sacrifice to stay with His Father, the servant represents the Holy Spirit sent into the world to find and prepare a Bride (that is, the Church) and Rebekah, of course, represents the Bride.

We cannot know for sure whether these were among the passages expounded by the Lord Jesus, but they certainly could have been. There well may have been others in Genesis also, as well as throughout the Old Testament, as Jesus opened to them "in all the Scriptures the things concerning himself" (Luke 24:27). Like the experience of the two disciples on the road to their home in Emmaus, so today our own hearts also "burn within us," as we learn to seek and find the Lord Jesus Christ, not only as our great Creator but also as our sin-bearing Savior and ever-living Lord in Genesis and all the Scriptures.

Prophecies of the Resurrection

Now that we have noted some of the beautiful types of the resurrection in Genesis, we can look next at some of the more explicit prophecies in other books of the Old Testament.

Just as creation is the most certain truth of real science, so the bodily resurrection of Jesus Christ is the most certain fact of genuine history. And as creation by God required His substitutionary death and bodily resurrection to give purpose and meaning to history, so Christ's resurrection required the power of the Creator to make it happen.

As we shall see later, the historical fact of Christ's resurrection is confirmed by "many infallible proofs" (Acts 1:3), including His many appearances to the disciples after His death, the amazing changes in the disciples after they were convinced He had risen, the unanswerable evidence of His empty tomb, and the entire subsequent history of the Christian church.

Before His resurrection took place, however, there was no historical record to give such assurance, and the only hope of resurrection during the thousands of years before Christ came had to be gleaned from the prophecies in God's inspired Word. There were indeed many such prophecies, but only those who loved the Word and had a real concern for God's purpose in creation could discern them. From our perspective today, we can see them more clearly since they have already been fulfilled, providing strong evidence of the divine inspiration of the Bible. We today, therefore, have less excuse for ignoring God's Word than they did and so must be judged more severely if we do so.

For example, consider the remarkable prophetic picture of the substitutionary death of the coming Savior in Isaiah 53. After describing His sufferings, the record says that "He was cut off out of the land of the living. . . . And he made his grave with the wicked, and with the rich in his death" (Isa. 53:8–9). But then it promises that "when thou shalt make his soul an offering for sin . . . he shall prolong his days, and the pleasure of the Lord shall prosper in his hand" (Isa. 53:10). This prophecy can only be understood in terms of the Resurrection.

Similarly, in the graphic portrayal of Christ's unspeakable sufferings by crucifixion in Psalm 22, the Scripture prophesies that He will cry in His heart that "I am poured out like water, and all my bones are out of joint: my heart is like wax; it is melted in the midst of my bowels. . . . thou hast brought me into the dust of death" (Ps. 22:14–15). But that is not the end, for He later testifies that: "My praise shall be of thee in the great congregation . . . your heart shall live for ever. All the ends of the world shall remember and turn unto the Lord: and the kindreds of the nations shall worship before thee" (Ps. 22:25–27). Again, this clearly requires interpretation in terms of His resurrection after death.

His victorious resurrection is even intimated in the very first prophesy of the Bible, the "protevangelium" of Genesis 3:15. There God told Adam and Eve that although the old serpent, Satan, would bruise the heel of the coming seed of the woman, the divine seed would ultimately be victorious and would destroy the wicked one.

A prophecy that was used by the apostles when they first began proclaiming Christ's resurrection is found in Psalm 16 (note Acts 2:25–28; 13:35–37). The first eight verses of this fascinating psalm are best understood as coming from the lips of Christ as He prayed in the Garden of Gethsemane just before His arrest and crucifixion. But then He prays: "My flesh also shall rest in hope. For thou wilt not leave my soul in hell; neither wilt thou suffer thine Holy One to see corruption. Thou wilt show me the path of life: in thy presence is fulness of joy; at thy right hand there are pleasures for evermore" (Ps. 16:9–11). These verses speak poetically first of His burial, then His descent in the spirit into Hades, followed by His return into His body, resting in the tomb before decay could begin, then His resurrection and ascension into heaven to be seated at the Father's right hand. This verse, incidentally, contains the first of 21 references in the Bible to His present position at the right hand of God the Father.

Then there is the prophecy of Psalm 40:1–3. "I waited patiently for the Lord; and he inclined unto me, and heard my cry. He brought me up also out of an horrible pit, out of the miry clay, and set my feet upon a rock, and established my goings. And he hath put a new song in my mouth, even praise unto our God: many shall see it, and fear, and shall trust in the Lord."

Psalm 110:1 gives special insight concerning His ascension after the resurrection. "The LORD said unto my Lord, Sit thou at my right hand, until I make thine enemies thy footstool." Literally, this reads: "Jehovah said unto Adonai," using two names of God as the Father is apparently speaking to the Son. This particular verse is applied to Christ no less than five times in the New Testament.

A similar conversation is recorded in Psalm 2:7: "The LORD hath said unto me, Thou art my Son; this day have I begotten thee." This verse is quoted in Acts 13:33 as fulfilled in Christ's resurrection.

In what is perhaps the oldest book in the Bible, the patriarch Job asks the universal question: "If a man die, shall he live again?" (Job 14:14). A little later, however, his strong faith in a future resurrection returns, and he exclaims: "For I know that my redeemer liveth, and that he shall stand at the latter day upon the earth: And . . . in my flesh shall I see God" (Job 19:25–26).

There is a cryptic reference to the resurrection of both the nation of Israel and also her Messiah in Hosea 6:2: "After two days will he revive us: in the third day he will raise us up." Also note Zechariah

12:10: "They shall look upon me whom they have pierced, and they shall mourn for him, as one mourneth for his only son."

There are also a number of types in the Old Testament that speak of Christ's death and resurrection and were so applied by New Testament writers. We have already noted the story of Abraham and Isaac, as referred to in Hebrews 11:17–19. "By faith Abraham, when he was tried, offered up Isaac . . . his only begotten son. . . . Accounting that God was able to raise him . . . from the dead; from whence also he received him in a figure." In this passage, the writer is comparing Abraham's sacrifice of Isaac to the Heavenly Father offering his Son, with Isaac's return comparable in type to Christ's resurrection.

With reference to Jonah, the Lord Jesus himself made the analogy: "For as Jonas was three days and three nights in the whale's belly; so shall the Son of man be three days and three nights in the heart of the earth" (Matt. 12:40).

There are others, both types and specific prophecies, but the ones discussed above seem the most directly applicable. Even these are often given other interpretations. It is obviously easier to interpret most prophecies after their fulfillment than before. Even the disciples of Christ seem to have been caught unawares by His resurrection, in spite of their obvious knowledge of the Scriptures.

Yet they *could* have and *should* have known what was coming. This fact is evident from the rebuke Christ gave to the two disciples as they walked together on the road to Emmaus. "O fools, and slow of heart to believe all that the prophets have spoken: Ought not Christ to have suffered these things, and to enter into his glory? And beginning at Moses and all the prophets, he expounded unto them in all the Scriptures the things concerning himself" (Luke 24:25–27).

Even if they were uncertain about the meaning of the Scriptures, however, they had many direct prophecies from Christ himself. Just after Peter made his great confession of the deity of Christ (Matt. 16:16), we read that "from that time forth began Jesus to show unto his disciples, how that he must . . . be killed, and be raised again the third day" (Matt. 16:21; see also John 2:19; Matt. 17:22,23; 20:17–19; 26:32; John 10:17–18; etc.).

But whatever reasons they may have been able to give for their own blindness, we today have no excuse at all if we reject Him and His victorious physical resurrection after His death for our sins. We have all the information they had and far more, since we have the complete Bible, vindicated and verified by almost 2,000 years of Christian history, and by all the internal and external evidences of its divine inspiration and authority.

In fact, the substitutionary death, burial, and resurrection of Christ are so important that they constitute the very heart of the saving gospel of the Lord Jesus Christ (1 Cor. 15:1–4). True creation is the sure foundation of the gospel (Rev. 14:6–7), and the Second Coming of Christ to establish His eternal kingdom is the blessed hope of the gospel (Matt. 4:23). But the death and resurrection of Christ constitute the very heart of the gospel and its power to bring salvation to all who believe it.

Although creation is the foundation, it is not the entire structure, and it is sad that many who believe in creation are still unsaved, because they "obey not the gospel of our Lord Jesus Christ" (2 Thess. 1:8).

If any reader is in this dangerous position, we would earnestly urge him or her to receive Christ, who "was dead" but is now "alive for evermore" (Rev. 1:18), by faith, as personal Lord and Savior.

> If thou shalt confess with thy mouth the Lord Jesus, and shalt believe in thine heart that God hath raised him from the dead, thou shalt be saved (Rom. 10:9).

> If we believe that Jesus died and rose again . . . so shall we ever be with the Lord (1 Thess. 4:14–17).

> Neither is there salvation in any other: for there is none other name under heaven given among men, whereby we must be saved (Acts 4:12).

> Believe on the Lord Jesus Christ, and thou shalt be saved (Acts 16:31).

Amazing Prophecies by Christ

Creationists often hear this criticism from other evangelicals: "You creationists are causing controversy and division among Christians; you should just be preaching Christ and the gospel, not creation!"

But that would be impossible. The "everlasting gospel" includes the worship of "Him that made heaven, and earth, and the sea, and the fountains of waters" (Rev. 14:7). That One who made all things is Jesus Christ, "For by him were all things created, that are in heaven, and that are in earth" (Col. 1:16).

Since this "everlasting gospel" is to be proclaimed by an angel from heaven (Rev. 14:6), it cannot have been any different from the gospel of Christ as preached by Paul (note Gal. 1:8).

These and similar Scriptures ought to be enough to convince Bible-believing Christians that the Lord Jesus Christ is the God of creation, and that He must be worshipped as Creator as well as Savior.

The problem is, however, that many Bible-believing Christians have allowed themselves to be influenced by Bible-rejecting skeptics, who not only deny the fact of creation, but also the gospel and the deity of Christ. These unbelievers deride such beliefs, saying that they depend entirely on the teachings of a long-outmoded, error-filled Book that has little relevance to our modern scientific age.

These teachings *are* found in the Bible, of course, but the Bible *is* the inspired Word of God, whether people believe it or not. However, there are certain overwhelming proofs of the truth of the Bible, and of the deity of Christ that do not depend on whether the Bible was inspired by God or not, or even whether its records are historically accurate.

For example, consider the words attributed to Jesus (whether or not the reporting of them was correct) in Matthew 24:35. "Heaven and earth shall pass away," He is said to have said, "But my words shall not pass away."

What an arrogant, foolish statement that seems to be, reputedly spoken by an outwardly uneducated, unpublished, itinerant preacher, with a small band of ignorant followers in an insignificant captive state in the Middle East! Why, the man must have been mad to make such a claim! Or so it would seem, *unless it were somehow true.*

As a matter of fact, for almost 2,000 years, His words have not passed away! This claim constitutes an amazing prophecy, fulfilled in worldwide outreach, with the words of Christ probably read and believed by more people than any other words ever spoken. He may never have written a book, but His Bible is the world's all-time best seller, and more books have been written about Him and His teachings than those of any other man in history.

And consider also His claim in John 8:12, "I am the light of the world: he that followeth me shall not walk in darkness, but shall have the light of life." How could an uncultured carpenter from a despised village in a small province ever presume to assert that *he* was the very light that would enlighten the entire world? Absurd!

Yet there have been millions down through the centuries who have testified that He was, indeed, the light of *their* world! Furthermore, He has been the inspiration for the world's greatest music, its finest art, and multitudes of hospitals, schools, and charitable institutions of all kinds. The world today would, indeed, be in gross darkness had it not been for the multitudes of concerned and caring men and women who have followed Him.

Still another remarkable fulfilled prophecy is found in Matthew 16:18. "Upon this rock I will build my church; and the gates of hell shall not prevail against it." Unbelievers may be able to find various problems with His church (that is, with all those believers who stand upon the rock of Peter's great confession, in Matthew 16:16, that Jesus is the Christ, the Son of the living God), but they cannot ignore the fact that the church *exists*! That small body of 12 unpromising disciples has somehow become a great host of millions in every age, in spite of intense opposition and persecution continually seeking to destroy it. How could such things be, unless Christ really is the Son of God?

That is not all. In John 12:32, Jesus is quoted as saying, "And I, if I be lifted up from the earth, will draw all men unto me." The writer then comments that, in saying this, He was "signifying what death he should die." It may not have taken a great deal of prophetic insight to predict that He would die by being lifted up on a cross, for that was a common method of executing those convicted either as common criminals or as enemies of their Roman rulers in those days.

But how could Jesus be so presumptuous as to prophesy that His crucifixion would "draw all men" to *Him*! Such an ignominious and excruciating death would seem to repel men, not draw them. How would people ever happen even to hear about it?

But they *have* heard about it, all over the world. Though not all individuals have believed on Him, multitudes *have* believed, and the rest have at least had to make a decision about Him. If "all" is understood to mean "all kinds," it is literally true that men and women of all nations and all walks of life have been irresistibly drawn to His cross and to Him as the One who died there for their sins. As the hymn writer sang: "That old rugged cross, so despised by the world, has a wondrous attraction for me." The cross also has come to adorn thousands of pulpits and church steeples, as well as ladies' pendants and many other places.

Christ made many other such claims (or at least those who wrote the records say He did) which seem either utterly false or impossibly presumptuous or completely mad, but which have turned out to be remarkably fulfilled prophecies for 2,000 years. They provide an impregnable testimony to His deity, for only God knows the end from the beginning.

We shall consider just one more of these claims. To His small band of disciples, He predicted: "Ye shall be witnesses unto me both in Jerusalem, and in all Judaea, and in Samaria, and unto the uttermost part of the earth" (Acts 1:8). "This gospel of the kingdom shall be preached in all the world for a witness unto all nations; and then shall the end come" (Matt. 24:14).

That was quite an order for such a motley and seemingly insignificant group. The task was clearly impossible, even if they were willing to try. But then, the account says they watched Him ascend up to heaven, and a few days later they received power when the Holy Ghost came on them, and somehow the absurdly impossible prophecy is really being fulfilled.

The gospel has penetrated the remotest parts of the world, and at least some converts "of all nations, and kindreds, and people and tongues" (Rev. 7:9) will one day stand before the Lord Jesus Christ praising Him for His great salvation. This very book is a part of the fulfillment of that prophecy, as it also seeks to witness for Him.

These amazing claims of Christ all have become marvelously fulfilled prophecies, even though they might have seemed insanely arrogant and impossible when they were first spoken. Further, as noted before, they do not even depend on the inerrancy or historicity of the accounts in the Bible where they are recorded. They are true and fulfilled prophecies regardless of the authenticity of the records.

As a matter of fact, these and other such claims also themselves become yet another evidence, not only of the deity of Christ, but also of the veracity of the Scriptures, because it is the Scriptures that tell us that this was what Jesus taught.

"Search the Scriptures . . ." He said, "they are they which testify of me" (John 5:39). "Till heaven and earth pass, one jot or one tittle shall in no wise pass from the law, till all be fulfilled" (Matt.

5:18). "And the Scripture cannot be broken" (John 10:35).

If Jesus is the only begotten Son of God, as He claimed, then He is a member of the eternal triune godhead, one with the Father and the Holy Spirit. In the days of His humanity, He could pray in full confidence to the Father who had sent Him. "Now, O Father, glorify thou me . . . with the glory which I had with thee before the world was" (John 17:5).

He was there before the world was, and the Scripture says that "all things were made by him" (John 1:3). He is, as the ancient creeds have said, "very God of very God." He is our Creator and it is He who had to pronounce the great curse on His whole creation when man brought sin and death into the world (Rom. 5:12; 8:20–22).

But then, in the fullness of time, He came forth from the Father to bear the great curse himself, because of "His great love wherewith he loved us" (Eph. 2:4). He suffered and died in payment for both the universal "sin of the world" (John 1:29) and also for the individual "sins of the whole world" (1 John 2:2). The great Creator has become our forgiving Savior!

The final and compelling proof of His deity, of course, is His bodily resurrection, demonstrated by "many infallible proofs" (Acts 1:3). Christ has defeated sin and death once for all and made effective forever, for every person who receives it, His great gift of salvation through repentance and faith in Him.

Proofs of the Resurrection

Just what are these "many infallible proofs" to which Luke refers in Acts 1:3? As a matter of fact, many entire volumes have been written by qualified scholars — historians, lawyers, scientists, theologians — setting forth the evidence for Christ's resurrection and refuting the quibbling objections that have been raised against it.

In this small book, however, it should suffice to mention just three key evidences that Christ really died, was buried, and three days later rose from the dead. This is the very heart of His saving gospel. Note carefully the following verses:

> Moreover, brethren, I declare unto you the gospel which I preached unto you, which also ye have received, and wherein ye stand; By which also ye are saved, if ye keep in memory what I preached unto you, unless ye have believed in vain.

> For I delivered unto you first of all that which I also received, how that Christ died for our sins according to the Scriptures; And that he was buried, and that he rose again the third day according to the Scriptures (1 Cor. 15:1–4).

Then, the apostle Paul proceeds to give the first of the proofs — that of His many appearances to His followers. They *saw* Him alive on various occasions. Paul even points out that on one such occasion, "He was seen of above five hundred brethren at once; of whom the greater part remain unto this present" (1 Cor. 15:6).

That is, when Paul was writing the Corinthian letter, about 20 years after the Resurrection, almost 500 people were still living who could testify truthfully that they had seen Jesus alive after His crucifixion, and who could easily have testified *against* this statement by Paul if it were untrue. As Luke says: "He shewed himself alive after his passion by many infallible proofs, being seen of them forty days, and speaking of the things pertaining to the kingdom of God" (Acts 1:3).

They not only saw Him, but they heard Him *speak*! Some of them even shared a meal with Him (John 21:13–15; Luke 24:29–31). He showed them the wounds in His hands and side, and even invited them to touch Him (John 20:27).

They were not seeing a ghost, as some might have thought, nor were they dreaming or having hallucinations, as others have charged. Sometimes He was in a room with them, another time He walked with two of them on a road, once he was out in the open with them. Visions and hallucinations of the same thing do not happen to so many different people on so many varied occasions. A ghost does not have flesh and bones and eat bread with those watching Him. No, the appearances were real, and He was a real person in a real physical body (though it was now immortal and glorified after His resurrection).

A second infallible proof became established soon after His appearances to the disciples, especially after He had ascended to Heaven and sent the Holy Spirit to empower them. They began preaching Christ and the resurrection so powerfully and convincingly, that multitudes were converted to the faith. This led to a great wave of persecution against them, as the political and religious leaders tried unsuccessfully to stamp out this growing Christian movement.

They could easily have stopped it, of course, simply by showing the people that Jesus' body was still in the tomb.

This they could not do. It was neither in Joseph's tomb nor in any other tomb. It had ascended to heaven, and they could not reach it there!

Thus, the evidence of the empty tomb, which convinced the apostle John first of all (John 20:3–8) has never been refuted, and it can be explained only by the Resurrection.

Some have concocted the notion that this was somehow all a monstrous plot. Perhaps, they suggest, Jesus did not really die and somehow managed to get out of the tomb before the Romans sealed it. Then all the stories of seeing and talking with Him were fabricated, with hundreds in on the plot. Jesus himself was too weak from the terrible ordeal on the cross to do anything himself, so the disciples hid Him away somewhere while they spread the story of a resurrection. Then, still later, Matthew, Mark, Luke, and John all wrote down their fabricated tales, or else someone else using their names did this, and the Christian church was born.

What nonsense! In fact, the third infallible proof of the Resurrection is the sudden change in the behavior of the disciples, from hiding in fear of their lives (only John dared be at His crucifixion) to boldly proclaiming the Resurrection! They gladly suffered all manner of persecution and torture, finally even martyrdom, as a result of their fearless preaching. Would these multitudes of people — not only the disciples, but also their many converts — do all this for something they knew to be a hoax? Although some may have renounced their professed faith in fear of death, not one ever confessed or implied it was all a lie.

These are other evidences that could be added. As mentioned above, many large volumes have been written in defense of the bodily resurrection of Christ. These three, however, ought be enough to convince any honest seeker of truth — the many appearances to His followers, the empty tomb, and the amazing change in the disciples who gladly suffered imprisonment, torture, and death because of preaching His resurrection and His deity.

As the apostle Paul wrote (and he also was one who suffered much for Christ's sake):

> And if Christ be not raised, your faith is vain; ye are
> yet in your sins. Then they which are fallen asleep in Christ
> are perished. If in this life only we have hope in Christ,

we are of all men most miserable. But now is Christ risen from the dead, and become the firstfruits of them that slept (1 Cor. 15:17–20).

Therefore, my beloved brethren, be ye steadfast, unmovable, always abounding in the work of the Lord, forasmuch as ye know that your labor is not in vain in the Lord (1 Cor. 15:58).

We *know* our service for Christ is not in vain, for we *know* He died for our sins, was buried, and rose again!

Endnotes

1 The references as given in this section refer, in order, to the sura (or chapter) in the Koran, then the verse, and lastly the page number in the 1909 Everyman's Library edition. The chapters and verses, however, refer to the Arabic edition, which have been arranged differently in the English translation as issued in the edition published by the Everyman's Library (J.M. Dent & Son, Ltd., London, 1909).

Chapter III

Back to Genesis

Beginning at the Beginning

he most harmful, vicious, and influential attacks against our Christian faith have been the supposedly scientific arguments against the biblical records of ancient history, especially those of special creation and the worldwide flood. Therefore the next five chapters will focus on the defense of biblical and scientific creationism. The evolution model of origins and the uniformitarian model of earth history can be shown to be utterly false, both biblically and scientifically. The Genesis record is true and can withstand all these attacks.

The greatest Bible teacher of all time was the Lord Jesus Christ and, when He wanted to teach His friends about himself and His great plan for the world, He began by teaching them the Book of Genesis, the first of the books of Moses.

Right after His resurrection, He met two of His followers walking home to Emmaus and confused about the apparent ending of His ministry when He died on the cross. First, He gently rebuked them for their lack of faith. Then, "Beginning at Moses and all the prophets, he expounded unto them in all the Scriptures the things concerning himself" (Luke 24:27).

This greatest of all Bible teachers thus began this most wonderful of all Bible lessons by starting at the Book of Genesis. In our imaginations, we can walk along beside them there, for He has told us to "follow his steps" (1 Pet. 2:21). Genesis is the foundation book

~ *63* ~

of the Bible, and thus arguably the most important book. We certainly need to understand it first of all, and believe it, if we are ever to really understand and truly believe the rest of God's revelation.

My own first book, written over 50 years ago, stressed the wonderful truth of creation and the harmful fallacy of evolution. This is a timeless message, needed more and more as time goes on.

In that first book, I said, for example, "Evolution is not so much a science as it is a philosophy or an attitude of mind — and since no one was present to watch the supposed great evolutionary changes of the past, it is manifestly impossible to prove scientifically that they actually did take place."[1]

Then, with respect to the Genesis record of creation, I stressed that "the account in Genesis can by no stretch of the imagination be made to agree with the supposed development of life as presented to us by evolutionary geologists."[2] I pointed out then, just as we still do today, that "the Bible says that death entered the world as a result of the sin of the first man and woman." By the evolutionary-age scenario, however, "the bones of dead millions of God's creatures were in the ground long before man was even on the scene."[3]

I was not the first writer to point out these truths, by any means, for they have long been self-evident to anyone who really believed the Bible to be God's infallible and clearly understandable Word. Many others before me also have noted the grave dangers to family life, church integrity, and national survival if the evolutionary system should ever truly prevail in the hearts and minds of most people. In that first book of mine (written so long ago), after noting that communism, fascism, immoralism, and most other evil systems and practices were based on the assumption of evolution, I concluded that, "by the very fact of goodness and beauty in the world, it is hard to believe that such a theory could really be true."[4]

In those days, however, the Scopes trial of 1925 was still of fairly recent memory. The *Humanist Manifesto* had been published in 1933 by John Dewey, Julian Huxley, and other leading evolutionists, and true confidence in the Genesis record had almost vanished from the world of science and education. Evolutionism seemed triumphant, and even biblical fundamentalists had retreated to the "gap theory" or some other such compromise by which Bible teachers naively hoped to avoid dealing with the long ages of evolutionary geology and all the poisonous effects on Christianity and human life which that concept was generating. This hope was futile, of course, for a world view based on random variation, natural selection, and survival of the fittest was bound to pander to the sinful self-centered nature of fallen mankind. It had already produced two world wars and soon captivated the "baby boom" generation as well. In fact, the worldwide triumphant celebrations of the Darwinian Centennial in 1959 widely (but prematurely) proclaimed the death of God and the end of Bible-centered Christianity.

Many writers[5] have attributed the beginnings of the modern revival of scientific biblical creationism to the catalytic effects of the book, *The Genesis Flood*,[6] published in 1961. If this is true, I believe the reason for the book's effectiveness was its frank acceptance of the Genesis record (even in the title of the book!) as absolutely and literally true, showing that Genesis also provided a better basis for understanding the scientific data concerning primeval history than any evolutionary model could ever do.

Our later books and other publications have shown that the literal Genesis record of supernatural creation is the foundation of the true gospel, the true doctrine of Christ, true evangelism, genuine saving faith, and of all the key aspects of biblical Christianity. True science, true education, the true institution of marriage and family — and even our original American government — also were based on Genesis creationism.

Indeed, all truth, in every area of life, finds its beginning in the Genesis record of creation and the other events of primeval history. That is why God placed it first in the Bible.

Our homes, our churches, our nation, and our world all need to get back to Genesis and begin there. The word "genesis" means "beginning," and we need to begin at the beginning!

But that is not all, of course. Genesis is the foundation, but the foundation is not the complete structure. The Lord Jesus Christ is our Creator, but He has also become our Redeemer and will one day be acknowledged by all the world as King of kings, and Lord of lords. That must be our ultimate goal — to win the world and all its systems back to God, in Christ. All this is implied in God's great "dominion mandate," as given first to Adam (Genesis 1:26–28), then renewed and enlarged to Noah (Gen. 9:1–7). This first divine commission to mankind has never been withdrawn and, in fact, has now been supplemented and extended by Christ's "Great Commission" to His followers (Matt. 28:18–20; Acts 1:8). We must diligently try not only to win the lost to Christ but also to bring the world itself back to God. We must try not only to win individual scientists and educators to Christ but also to win *science* itself, and *education* itself, to Christ. The same is true for every sphere of human life, for all this is implied in God's primeval command to "have dominion" over all the earth and all its creatures. Even many churches need to be brought back to the true God of creation and to His inspired and authoritative word (beginning at Genesis!) as their basic rule of faith and practice.

No single organization could accomplish such a task, of course, and it will never be really completed until Christ himself returns to "make all things new" (Rev. 21:5). However, we should all at least be intelligently and fervently working toward this end, with this great challenge as our goal, doing what we can.

As we study Genesis and its marvelous accounts of creation, the Fall and Curse, the global flood, the confusion of tongues, and the other events of the earliest ages of history, we must realize we are reading true history — not some myth or allegory. The accounts were written originally by the ancient patriarchs who were there as eyewitnesses, then handed down from father to son until they reached Moses, who compiled and edited them into our present wonderful Book of Genesis.[7]

Six Real Days of Creation

There are many Christians who say they believe the Bible, but still seem unable to believe its very first chapter. The biblical record says that God created the universe and everything in it in six days, then rested on the seventh day.

This fact is stated explicitly, not only in the first chapter of the Bible, but also in the fourth of God's Ten Commandments.

> Remember the Sabbath Day to keep it holy. Six days shalt thou labor and do all thy work: But the seventh day is the Sabbath of the Lord thy God: in it thou shalt not do any work . . . For in six days the Lord made heaven and earth, the sea, and all that in them is, and rested the seventh day (Exod. 20:8–11).

It could not be said any more plainly. The six days of man's work week (still being observed thousands of years later, all over the world) were the same kind of days as in God's work week. Furthermore, in all the written Word of God, this section alone was not only inspired by God, but also inscribed by God.

> For in six days the Lord made heaven and earth, and on the seventh day he rested and was refreshed. And he gave unto Moses, when he had made an end of communing with him upon Mount Sinai, two tables of testimony, written with the finger of God (Exod. 31:17–18).

In spite of this clear testimony from the Creator himself, the modern world view is that the universe has been evolving for about 15 billion years, and that the earth and its inhabitants have been evolving almost 5 billion years, and this creates a problem.

Christians must decide, therefore, whether they should interpret the scientific data in terms of God's revelation or try to interpret the Genesis record of creation to fit the evolutionary ages. Most Christian intellectuals take the latter approach and then attack those whom they call "young-earth creationists." An example of this is found in the writings of Bradley and Olsen:

> The Hebrew word *yom* and its plural form *yamim* are used over 1,900 times in the Old Testament. . . . Outside of the Genesis 1 case in question, the two hundred plus occurrences of *yom* preceded by ordinals all refer to a normal twenty-four hour day. Furthermore, the seven hundred plus appearances of *yamim* always refer to a regular day. Thus, it is argued that the Exodus 20:11 reference to the six *yamim* of creation must also refer to six regular days.[8]

Bradley and Olsen think that such exegesis doesn't apply to the creation week. Here is their reasoning.

> These arguments have a common fallacy, however. There is no other place in the Old Testament where the intent is to describe events that involve multiple and/or sequential indefinite periods of time.

There is, of course, no hint in either Genesis 1 or Exodus 20:8–11 that the writer's intent was to "describe events that involve . . .

indefinite periods of time." The accounts are written as simple statements of fact, using straightforward language that everywhere else
in the Bible denotes literal days. Another writer, Dr. Pun, agrees.

> It is apparent that the most straightforward under-
> standing of the Genesis record . . . is that God created
> heaven and earth in six solar days, that man was created
> on the sixth day, that death and chaos entered the world
> after the Fall of Adam and Eve.[9]

But Dr. Pun seems to doubt that God understood what He was
saying, since He said it ". . . without regard to all the hermeneutical
considerations suggested by science." That is, he thinks that "science" should govern our biblical hermeneutics. Dr. Pun goes on to
say:

> The recent Creationist position . . . has denied and
> belittled the vast amount of scientific evidence amassed
> to support the theory of natural selection and the antiquity
> of the earth.

All three of these men are leading evangelical scientists (Pun at
Wheaton College, Bradley at Texas A & M, Olsen from Colorado
School of Mines) and all claim to believe in biblical inerrancy and
the historicity of Genesis. Their "day-age theory," however, seems
quite illogical. If Genesis doesn't mean what it says, then why accept
its historicity at all?

Liberal theologians *don't* accept it, as a matter of fact. One leading Hebrew scholar is James Barr, professor of Hebrew Bible at
Vanderbilt University and former regius professor of Hebrew at Oxford University in England. Although he does not believe in the historicity of Genesis 1, Dr. Barr does agree that the writer's *intent* was
to narrate the actual history of primeval creation. Others also agree
with him.

> Probably, so far as I know, there is no professor of
> Hebrew or Old Testament at any world-class university
> who does not believe that the writer(s) of Genesis 1–11
> intended to convey to their readers the ideas that (a) cre-
> ation took place in a series of six days which were the
> same as the days of 24 hours we now experience. . . . Or,
> to put it negatively, the apologetic arguments which sup-

pose the "days" of creation to be long eras of time, the figures of years not to be chronological, and the flood to be a merely local Mesopotamian flood, are not taken seriously by any such professors, as far as I know.[10]

While men such as Bradley, Olsen, and Pun may have worthy motives in trying to retain creationism in the face of the supposed evidence for macroevolution and an ancient earth, it seems obvious that Barr's position is more realistic. If God did not mean what He said in the very first chapter of His Book, then why should we take the rest of it seriously?

It seems to me that we should take Scripture as the literal Word of God, intended to be understood by its readers in every generation and every nation — especially *this* chapter, which is the foundation of all the rest. If God had meant to convey the idea of long ages, He could easily have used a number of other Hebrew words and phrases to convey that idea. All the ancients were already familiar with the concept of long ages of evolutionary change in their various nature religions.

The idea of a six-literal-day creation, however, was a radical departure from what the early Hebrews could have heard from their pagan neighbors; so God was very specific in using plain words to preclude any such misunderstanding. For example, He defined the word "day" the very first time He used it. "God called the light Day, and the darkness he called Night. And the evening and the morning were the first day" (Gen. 1:5). The word "day" in Genesis does *not* mean a geological period!

Furthermore, the order of events in Genesis flagrantly contradicts the order assigned by evolutionary astronomers and geologists in well over a dozen ways.[11]

Although there are many, many references to creation throughout the Bible, there is no hint anywhere of long ages before man's creation. The fact that men and women and various human activities were present from the very foundation of the world is indicated in the New Testament by Peter (Acts 3:21), by Paul (Rom. 1:20), by John (1 John 3:8), by the father of John the Baptist (Luke 1:69–70), and especially by the Creator, the Lord Jesus Christ himself (Luke 11:50; Mark 10:6; 13:19).

Perhaps most important of all is the fact that acceptance of the geological ages (with their billions of fossil remains in the sedimentary rocks) makes God out to be the Creator of evil and suffering, directly allowing a billion years of cruel struggle for existence before He created Adam and Eve. Even a humanist sees this.

> Nature makes everything in vain. After all, what is evolution? A mindless process built on evil; that's what it is. . . . So natural selection seems smart to those who see only the surviving products, but as a design process it is idiotic. And the raw brutality of the process is offensive.[12]

It seems clear that those who truly believe the Bible ought to repudiate this hoary day/age theory once and for all. However, this means repudiating the evolutionary age system, and to many Christian intellectuals, this costs too much. So most of them go on promoting this system of great ages (despite the lack of any genuine scientific proof of any ages before the beginning of recorded history). For example, the president of a leading evangelical college has noted:

> For at least six decades, Wheaton's faculty . . . have held that the "days" of Genesis are most likely to have been extended periods of time. Further, they have also noted that the Bible does not comment on the exact origin of species as described today.[13]

Most main-line denominations, many Christian colleges and seminaries today, as well as most Christian student organizations, and even a few Christian apologetics and creation-oriented organizations would agree with that position. We could become more popular here at ICR, and we would have bigger meetings, more book sales, and more open doors, if we would go and do likewise.

But, this we cannot do and still remain faithful to the Word of God. We hope you understand. We believe God does.

The Gaps in the Gap Theory

Another popular device for trying to accommodate the evolutionary ages of the geologists and astronomers in the creation record of the Bible has been the "gap theory" — also called the "ruin-and-reconstruction" theory.

According to this concept, Genesis 1:1 describes the initial creation of the universe. Following this, the standard events of cosmic evolution took place, which eventually produced our solar system about five billion years ago. Then, on the earth, the various geologic ages followed, as identified by their respective assemblages of fossils (trilobites, dinosaurs, etc.).

But then occurred a devastating global cataclysm, destroying all life on earth and leaving a vast fossil graveyard everywhere. This situation is then said to be what is described in Genesis 1:2. "And the earth was without form and void; and darkness was upon the face of the deep." The cataclysm is thought to have occurred as a result of the rebellion of Satan and his angels against their Creator in heaven, with God then casting them out of heaven to the earth.

Those who advocate the gap theory agree that the six days of the creation week were literal days, but they interpret them only as days of re-creation, with God creating again many of the kinds of animals and plants destroyed in the cataclysm.

The gap theory was developed mainly for the purpose of accommodating the great ages demanded by evolutionary geologists. This idea was first popularized by a Scottish theologian, Thomas Chalmers, early in the 19th century. In this country, the famous *Scofield Reference Bible* made it an almost universally accepted teaching among fundamentalists.

The *Scofield Bible* notes on Genesis 1 include the following:

> The first act refers to the dateless past, and gives scope for all the geologic ages. . . . The face of the earth bears everywhere the marks of such a catastrophe. There are not wanting intimations which connect it with a previous testing and fall of angels. . . . Relegate fossils to the primitive creation, and no conflict of science with the Genesis cosmogony remains.[14]

However, serious conflicts *do* remain. In fact, there are few, if any, professionally trained geologists and astronomers (to my knowledge there are none) who accept the gap theory. The promoters of this theory have mostly been Bible teachers who hoped they could place these great ages in a gap between the first two verses of Genesis, and thus not have to deal with them at all.

With the modern revival of scientific biblical creationism, many of these teachers have abandoned the gap theory in favor of strict creationism. Most advocates of the gap idea were men of strong biblical faith, and when they were shown its biblical fallacies, plus its scientific inadequacies, they were quite willing to reject the evolutionary ages scheme altogether.

Many of us had naively assumed that the gap theory was moribund, and so had concentrated most of our critiques on the other compromise theories (day-age theory, framework theory, etc.). But it now appears that the gap theory is still being advocated by a number of evangelical theologians.

For example, the *Nelson Study Bible*, (1997), in its footnotes on Genesis 1:1 and 1:2, says:

> Here it means that God renewed what was in a chaotic state. God changed chaos into cosmos, disorder into order, emptiness into fullness. . . . The two words, without form and void, express one concept — chaos. The earth had been reduced to this state — it was not the way God had first created it.[15]

The editors and contributors to this volume — 43 in all — include many well-known evangelical leaders. Yet they feel they must allow for the geological ages, and so they opt for what amounts to the old gap theory again, with its pre-Adamic cataclysm. The notes in this study Bible do allow a worldwide flood, but there are no relevant comments on the effects of sin and the curse on the animal kingdom, and no mention of the billions of fossils now preserved in the earth's sedimentary rock beds.

The reason geologists will not accept the gap theory is that it contradicts their assumption that the past is continuous with the present. There is no room in their naturalistic approach to science for a global cataclysm that would destroy all life and then require a new creation of plants, animals, and people such as the gap theory proposes.

Any cataclysm that would leave the earth "without form and void" (or "a shapeless chaotic mass" as *The Living Bible* expresses it), with "darkness on the face of the deep" everywhere, would require a worldwide nuclear or volcanic explosion that would effectively disintegrate the whole crust of the earth. All pre-cataclysm mountains would be blown into the sea and billions of tons of rocks and dust blown into the atmosphere, leaving the earth covered with "the deep" everywhere and "darkness" covering the deep everywhere.

Such a cataclysm would disintegrate any previously deposited sedimentary deposits with their fossils and thus obliterate all evidence of any previous "geological ages." Thus, the gap theory, which is supposed to accommodate the geological ages, requires a cataclysm which would destroy all evidence for the geological ages.

The gap theory is also unsound theologically. The God of creation is an omnipotent and omniscient God, and is also a God of grace, mercy, and love. The very concept of the geological ages, on the other hand, implies a wasteful and cruel "god," and therefore probably no god at all.

The supposed geologic ages are identified in terms of the fossils found in the earth's sedimentary rocks, and there are multiplied billions of them there. But fossils speak of death — even violent death. The preservation of dead animals requires rapid burial if they are to last very long. There are many regions, for example, where there are millions of fossil fish preserved in the rocks. There are dinosaur fossil beds on every continent, as well as great beds of fossil marine invertebrates practically everywhere. These may indeed speak of cataclysmic death and burial, but not a cataclysm operating slowly over billions of years, as the geological ages imply. If the gap theory were valid, it would mean that God had instituted an ages-long system of suffering and death over the world, before there were ever any men and women to place in dominion over that world, and then suddenly destroy it in a violent cataclysm. Why would an omnipotent, merciful God do such a wasteful and cruel thing as *that*?

They cannot blame Satan, either. According to the gap theory, Satan's fall took place at the end of the geological ages, followed by the great pre-Adamic cataclysm on the earth. Thus, the geological ages, with their eons of cruelty and waste, took place even before Satan's sin. God himself would be solely responsible for the whole debacle, if it really happened.

If the Bible actually teaches the gap theory, however, then there might be some reason to try to accommodate it in our theology. But the Bible does *not* teach it! If there really *had been* billions of years of animals suffering and dying before Genesis 1:2, why would God say nothing about it? The best they can offer in support of such a notion are some out-of-context quotes from Isaiah and Jeremiah, along with an *ad hoc* translation of Genesis 1:1,2.

And why would God send such a devastating cataclysm at all?

Satan's fall did not occur until *after* the creation week of Genesis 1, for at that time God had pronounced the whole creation "very good" (Gen. 1:31). At present, however, "the whole creation groaneth and travaileth in pain together" (Rom. 8:22) because of the great curse pronounced by God on man's dominion (Gen. 3:17–19), as a result of sin.

This groaning creation has indeed experienced one global cataclysm — one not inferred from vague hints in out-of-context quotes, but rather one described in great detail in Genesis 6–9 and referred to often and unambiguously in later passages — namely, the worldwide flood in the days of Noah. Most of the vast fossil graveyards in the earth's crust can best be explained as one of the results of the flood.

This awesome spectacle of destruction and death was not part of God's "very good" creation. There was no death in the world until sin was in the world (Rom. 5:12; 1 Cor. 15:21; etc.). In fact, death itself is "the wages of sin" (Rom. 6:23). Our future deliverance from sin and death has been purchased by the substitutionary death of Jesus Christ, who is "the propitiation for our sins and . . . also for the sins of the whole world" (1 John 2:2).

But if "death reigned," not "from Adam to Moses" as the Bible says (Rom. 5:14), but had already reigned for billions of years before Adam, then death is not the wages of sin but instead was part of God's creative purpose. How then could the death of Christ put away sin? The gap theory thus undermines the very gospel of our salvation, as well as the holy character of God.

The fact is that no such gap exists between the first two verses of Genesis at all. The second verse merely describes the initial aspect of the creation as "without form and void" — that is, with neither structure nor inhabitants. The rest of the chapter tells how God produced a marvelous structure for His created universe, with multitudes of plant and animal inhabitants for the earth, all to be under the dominion of its human inhabitants created in the image of God. It was only then that God pronounced the creation "finished" (Gen. 2:1).

It is time for those who believe the Bible and in the goodness and wisdom of God to abandon the gap theory once and for all (as well as the day-age theory, which is even worse) and simply believe what God has said. The gap theory has no scientific merit, requires a very forced biblical exegesis, and leads to a God-dishonoring theology. It does not work, either biblically or scientifically.

Sin and the Groaning Creation

One of the hardest things to understand is how anyone who claims to believe in a God of love can also believe in the geological ages, with their supposed record of billions of years of suffering and death before sin came into the world. This seems clearly to make God a God of waste and cruelty rather than a God of wisdom and power and love.

Atheistic evolutionists seem to understand this easily enough, so why can't Christians? Richard Dawkins, arguably Europe's leading Darwinian evolutionist, comments as follows:

> The total amount of suffering per year in the natural world is beyond all decent contemplation. During the minute that it takes me to compose this sentence, thousands of animals are being eaten alive, many others are running for their lives, whimpering with fear, others are being slowly devoured from within by rasping parasites, thousands of all kinds are dying of starvation, thirst and disease. . . . The universe that we observe has precisely the properties we should expect if there is, at bottom, no design, no purpose, no evil and no good, nothing but pitiless indifference.[16]

Why would any Christian charge God with creating that kind of world?

The fact is, He did *not* create that kind of world. At the conclusion of God's six days of creating and making all things, He placed it all under man's dominion and then pronounced it all to be "very good" (Gen. 1:26, 28, 31).

There was, therefore, nothing bad in that created world, no hunger, no struggle for existence, no suffering, and certainly no death of animal or human life anywhere in God's perfect creation (plant "life," created as food for men and animals, does not "die" in the biblical sense). There was no carnivorous activity at that time, for God had said: "And to every beast of the earth, and to every fowl of the air, and to every thing that creepeth upon the earth, wherein there is life, I have given every green herb for meat, and it was so" (Gen. 1:30).

One can understand how people could find these words of God hard to believe, but how can they *say* they believe them, and then believe also in billions of years of animals living and dying in the manner described above by Dawkins, before man brought sin into the world and God's Curse on his dominion?

As Dawkins said, the universe seems to have "no purpose . . . nothing but pitiless indifference." It is enslaved under what the Bible calls "the bondage of corruption" (Rom. 8:21). In fact, we see "that the whole creation groaneth and travaileth in pain together until now" (Rom. 8:22). It is certainly not the "very good" creation that it was when God first finished creating and making it.

As a matter of fact, the world as seen by Dawkins is exactly what Bible-believing Christians would expect to see in "this present evil world" (Gal. 1:4), a world seemingly without God. When the first man and woman rebelled against God's word in favor of the word of the evil one, God *did* withdraw His presence from them. "Cursed is the ground for thy sake," He told Adam (Gen. 3:17) and then banished Adam and Eve and their descendants from His holy presence. Animals, too, were victims of the Curse (Gen. 3:14), and so were the plants (Gen. 3:18), for all were part of man's dominion.

That was when death was introduced into the world. "By man came death" (1 Cor. 15:21). "Unto dust shalt thou return," God told Adam (Gen. 3:19), and ever since that time, "in Adam all die" (1 Cor. 15:22). "By one man's disobedience many were made sinners" (Rom. 5:19). Therefore, "death passed upon all men, for that all have sinned" (Rom. 5:12).

The animals, not having moral natures, were not guilty of sin, of course, but they also shared in the Curse, for they were — like Adam — made of the dust of the ground that God had cursed. Like Adam's body, their bodies also must return to the ground. Henceforth, "Death reigned . . . even over them that had not sinned after the similitude of Adam's transgression" (Rom. 5:14). Thus, there is death in the world only because there is sin in the world. It is *this* great truth that causes evolutionists to stumble over God and His word. By stretching the six days of creation into great ages, many evolutionists can put up with the Genesis "story" of creation, but they simply cannot tolerate the record of man's Fall and God's curse as the cause of suffering and death in the world. The "distinguished professor of philosophy" at Colorado State University points out this problem quite explicitly.

The real problem is with the Fall, when a once-para-disiacal nature becomes recalcitrant as a punishment for human sin. . . . This does not fit into the biological para-digm at all. Suffering in a harsh world did not enter chro-nologically after sin and on account of it. There was struggle for long epochs before human arrival.[17]

A prominent anti-Christian philosopher, Michael Ruse, sees the problem better than most Christians.

Either humankind is in a state of original sin or it is not. If it is, then there was reason for Jesus to die on the cross. If it is not, Calvary has as much relevance as a gladiator's death in the Coliseum.[16]

In other words, by diluting or ignoring the effects of the Fall, one inevitably — though perhaps unintentionally — is undermining the very gospel itself.

Another humanist further stresses this aspect, even gloating over what such accommodations are accomplishing.

And the creationists have also shown irrefutably that those liberal and neo-orthodox Christians who regard the creation stories as myths or allegories are undermining the rest of Scripture, for if there was no Adam, there was no fall; and if there was no fall, there was no hell; and if there was no hell, there was no need of Jesus as Second Adam and Incarnate Savior, crucified and risen. As a re-sult, the whole biblical system of salvation collapses.[19]

Evolutionists seem to comprehend this. Why can't Christians?

It does no good to suggest, as some have done, that maybe God's judgment of death on Adam applied only to spiritual death. The Curse was pronounced on "the ground," and Adam's body was eventually to return to "the dust." That means *physical* death! Furthermore, if God's judgment only involved spiritual death, then why did man's future redemption from death require the brutal *physical* death of Jesus Christ on the cross? Actually the Curse involved both. When Adam sinned and the Curse was pronounced, he *immediately* died spiritually and also *began* to die physically.

These biblical constraints do require believers to make what to many seems a very difficult choice. If the Fall and the Curse really happened as the Bible says, then the whole creation was brought under the bondage of corruption at that time.

In turn, this must mean that the great fossil graveyard in the earth's crust all over the world cannot be a record of the progressive creation of life over many long ages, but must actually be a record of the worldwide destruction of life in one age, when "the world that then was, being overflowed [cataclysmically overwhelmed] with water, perished" (2 Pet. 3:6), at the time of the great flood.

Furthermore, all of this took place only a few thousand years ago, not many millions of years ago, regardless of the spurious evidences of vast ages of time that have been proposed by those scientists committed to naturalism and uniformitarianism. The Lord Jesus (who was *there* at the beginning!) made this plain when He said, quoting Genesis 1:27: "From the beginning of the creation, God made them male and female" (Mark 10:6). Not billions of years *after* the beginning, but there right at the beginning, God made Adam and Eve.

God would never be guilty of creating the kind of world now seen by such men as Dawkins and the other leaders of evolutionary thought. A world of pain, cruelty, suffering, and death is the result of man's sin, not of God's love.

God's love was manifested not only in creating a perfect world to begin with, but then — even more — of paying the terrible price to redeem it once man had almost ruined it. How sad is the testimony of John 1:10. "He was in the world, and the world was made by him, and the world knew him not." Yet how glorious is the truth that "God sent not his Son into the world to condemn the world; but that the world through him might be saved" (John 3:17).

Yes, "the wages of sin is death, but the gift of God is eternal life, through Jesus Christ our Lord" (Rom. 6:23). For all who receive that priceless gift by faith, "to them gave he power to become the sons of God, even to them that believe on his name" (John 1:12). And in that new world to come, "there shall be no more curse" and "there shall be no more death" (Rev. 22:3; 21:4).

The Tree of Life

The wonderful tree of life, discussed in the two "book ends" of the Bible, Genesis and Revelation, is one of the most fascinating (yet enigmatic) subjects in all the inspired word of God. It is first mentioned in Genesis 2:9:

And out of the ground made the Lord God to grow every tree that is pleasant to the sight, and good for food; the tree of life also in the midst of the garden, and the tree of knowledge of good and evil.

The fruit of this tree was "good for food" and Adam was told that he could "freely eat" of it (Gen. 2:16).

However, he was *not required* to eat its fruit to stay alive! He was created by God to live without dying, with only one restriction — that is, he was *not* to eat of "the tree of knowledge of good and evil," for that would cause him to die (Gen. 2:17).

Later that same day, Eve was created, after Adam had first given names to each basic kind of animal — that is, specifically, only the "beast of the field" and the "fowl of the air" (Gen. 2:19), those that would be most likely to be in close proximity and possible fellowship with humans. He could easily have accomplished this in a few hours. Then Eve was created and was given the same instruction about eating as Adam had received, for she referred to these instructions when the serpent tempted her some time later.

Despite God's clear warning, she and Adam both then rebelled against God's word and ate of the tree of knowledge of good and evil, and thus "sin entered into the world" (Rom. 5:12). As a result, death also came into the world when God — true to His word — told them that "unto dust shalt thou return" (Gen. 3:19).

Furthermore, God's curse was pronounced on the very "ground" itself, out of which the bodies of both animals and men had been formed (Gen. 3:17; 1:24; 2:7), so that "the whole creation groaneth and travaileth in pain together until now" (Rom. 8:22). Thus, "by man came death," and "in Adam all die" (1 Cor. 15:21–22).

Then God cast Adam (with Eve) out of His beautiful garden, "lest he . . . take also of the tree of life, and eat, and live for ever" (Gen. 3:22).

This seems to create a problem, possibly even an apparent contradiction in God's words. God cannot contradict himself, of course, so this is our problem, not His. Many so-called "progressive" creationists, as well as theistic evolutionists, argue that Adam and Eve must already have been eating regularly of the tree of life in order to stay alive, even before they sinned. Otherwise they would have died physically even if they had never sinned, or so the argument goes. Then they argue that the death pronouncement by God on their sin was a "spiritual" death, not physical.

This idea, of course, contradicts the clear statement of God that they would die physically, as well as spiritually, with their bodies returning to the dust. Furthermore, it makes a travesty of Christ's death on the cross for our sins! Why would Christ have to die *physically* — and such a horrible physical death at that! — in order to atone for man's "spiritual" death?

But our accommodationist brethren are anxious to preserve the "old-earth" dogma of the evolutionists at all costs and so are willing to adjust Genesis and the gospel in whatever ways they need to do so in order to avoid conflict with modern scientism. They insist that we must accept the evolutionary ages of geology, with their billions of fossils and their billion-year spectacle of suffering and death before sin entered the world, in order to be acceptable to the intellectual community.

Nevertheless, the Genesis record — supported as literal history throughout all the rest of Scripture — is explicitly clear in teaching that physical suffering and death were introduced into the world only when Adam sinned. Thus, even if Adam and Eve had continued to eat the delicious fruit of the tree of life after they had sinned, they would eventually have died anyway because God had said so! However, this health-promoting fruit might have enabled them to live an inordinately long time before dying. Even as it was, Adam lived 930 years (Gen. 5:5).

The solution to our problem may well be that the Hebrew word *olam* (translated "for ever" in Gen. 3:22) could legitimately be translated "a very long time." For example, in Isaiah 42:14 God says: "I have long time [*olam*] holden my peace." It is obvious that "for ever" is not warranted in this context, for God will not hold His peace forever! Similarly, note Deuteronomy 33:15: ". . . precious things of the lasting [*olam*] hills." The hills may last a long time, but not forever. The Hebrew *olam* is translated "old time" in Joshua 24:2, and is applied to the "*ancient* landmark" in Proverbs 22:28 and the "*ancient* people" in Isaiah 44:7.

There are a number of other such examples. The word *olam* certainly does not have to mean "forever" unless the context so indicates. Therefore, it would be legitimate to read Genesis 3:22 as follows: ". . . lest he . . . take also of the tree of life and eat and live an excessively long time." There is thus no necessary indication in this verse that death was in the world before Adam brought sin into the world.

How long the Garden of Eden survived in the primeval world after the expulsion of Adam and Eve has not been revealed. If not destroyed earlier, it was certainly carried away by the devastating waters of the great flood, when "the world that then was, being overflowed with water, perished" (2 Pet. 3:6).

But the marvelous tree of life will be planted once again "in the midst of the paradise of God" in the new earth which God will create some day and "they that do his commandments" will then "have right to the tree of life" (Rev. 2:7; 22:14).

And note its remarkable character! "On either side of the river, was there the tree of life, which bare twelve manner of fruits, and yielded her fruit every month: and the leaves of the tree were for the healing of the nations" (Rev. 22:2).

Not just one tree of life as in the original Garden of Eden, but many such trees will be planted there with their beautiful and nutritious fruits, freely available to all who "do his commandments" — that is, to everyone in the Holy City. The fruit will be different every month,[18] but always "pleasant to the sight, and good for food." Furthermore, its leaves will also be of great value, since they are for "the healing of the nations." This cannot mean that without these healing leaves the people in these "nations of them which are saved" (Rev. 21:24) would otherwise become sick and die because God has assured us that in the Holy City, "there shall be no more death, neither sorrow, nor crying, neither shall there be any more pain: for the former things are passed away" (Rev. 21:4). The leaves will not be needed to heal sickness any more than the fruit of that original tree of life in Eden was needed to prevent death.

It is significant that the Greek word translated "healing" in this verse (*therapeia*) is translated "household" in Matthew 24:45 and Luke 12:42, referring to the staff of servants employed in keeping the affairs of a great house running efficiently. It is the source of our English word "therapy." Thus, the leaves of the tree will be for the "therapy," or the effective services, of the nations in the new earth. As the fruits of the tree will surely contain many nutrients for happy vigorous service by Christ's servants in the ages to come (Rev. 22:3), so its leaves may contain a complex of chemical substances useful in the occupations and general economy of those ages.

It is pointless to speculate as to the exact nature of the tree of life, for God has not told us, and there is no tree like it in the present world. The same is true with reference to the tree of knowledge of good and evil. God is well able to create any kind of tree He wishes, and we do well to leave it at that!

Because of the marvelous nature of the tree of life, however, the writer(s) of Proverbs used it (under divine inspiration of course) as a symbol of four wonderful truths.

First, the true wisdom "is a tree of life to them that lay hold upon her" (Prov. 3:18). That true wisdom can be none other than Christ (1 Cor. 1:30, Col. 2:3).

Second, "the fruit of the righteous is a tree of life" (Prov. 11:30). Indeed, "the fruit of the Spirit is in all goodness and righteousness and truth" (Eph. 5:9). A life such as that will be like a tree of life to all who encounter it.

Third, "when the desire cometh, it is a tree of life" (Prov. 13:12). That is, fulfilled hope, like true wisdom and righteousness, is so vitalizing as to be a source of renewed vigorous life.

Fourth, "a wholesome tongue is a tree of life" (Prov. 15:4). Therefore, "let your speech be alway with grace, seasoned with salt, that ye may know how ye ought to answer every man" (Col. 4:6).

We can eagerly, yet patiently and fruitfully, look forward to enjoying the delicious, nourishing fruit of the tree of life in the Holy City some day. In the meantime, we can pray that God will help us to be like little, life-giving trees ourselves through growing in true wisdom, living righteously, offering hope to the lost in our midst, and using our God-given abilities of communication graciously and meaningfully to all those we meet.

The Great Global Flood

The biblical flood in the days of Noah has become a great divide between two watersheds of belief. On the one hand there are those who say it is either a purely mythological event or else possibly a local or regional flood. This group includes practically all evolutionists, but it also includes the "old-earth creationists."

These all accept the so-called geological ages as the approved record of earth history, recognizing that a global hydraulic cataclysm would have destroyed any evidence for such geological ages. The geological ages concept and a worldwide devastating flood logically cannot coexist.

On the other hand, "young-earth creationists" accept the biblical record of the flood as a literal record of a tremendous cataclysm involving not only a worldwide flood, but also great tectonic upheavals and volcanic outpourings that completely changed the crust of the earth and its topography in the days of Noah.

Those of us who hold this view are commonly ridiculed as unscientific and worse, so it would be more comfortable and financially rewarding if we would just go along with the evolutionary establishment, downgrade the flood, and accept the geological ages.

But this we cannot do for a number of, what seem to us, compelling reasons. In fact, I have made a list of 100 reasons for believing in a global flood. For those who are interested, the list is included in two of my books, *The Genesis Record* and *The Defender's Study Bible.*[21]

A few of the many biblical reasons for believing in the global flood are briefly summarized below. For those who believe in the Bible as the inerrant word of God, these should be sufficient.

1. Jesus Christ believed the Old Testament record of the worldwide flood. Speaking of the antediluvian population, He said: "The flood came, and took them all away" (Matt. 24:39). Evolutionary anthropologists are all convinced that people had spread over the entire earth by the time assigned to Noah in biblical chronology, so an anthropologically universal flood would clearly have required a geographically worldwide flood.

2. The apostle Peter believed in a worldwide hydraulic cataclysm. "Whereby the world [Greek, *kosmos*] that then was, being overflowed [Greek, *katakluzo*] with water, perished" (2 Pet. 3:6). The "world" was defined in the previous verse as "the heavens . . . and the earth." Peter also said that "God . . . spared not the old world, but saved Noah . . . bringing in the flood [Greek, *kataklusmos*] upon the world of the ungodly" (2 Pet. 2:5). Note also that these words *katakluzo* and *kataklusmos* (from which we derive our English word "cataclysm") are applied exclusively in the New Testament to the great flood of Noah's day.

3. The Old Testament record of the flood, which both Christ and Peter accepted as real history, clearly teaches a global flood. Therefore, it seems to us that *Christians*, professing to believe in Christ and follow Him, can do no less. For example, the record emphasizes that "all the high hills, that were under the whole

heaven . . . and the mountains were covered" (Gen. 7:19–20) with the waters of the flood. This must have included Mount Ararat on which Noah's ark landed, and which is now 17,000 feet high. This was no *local* flood!

4. Since "all flesh died that moved upon the earth . . . all that was in the dry land" (Gen. 7:21–22), Noah and his sons had to build a huge ark to preserve animal life for the post-diluvian world — an ark that can easily be shown to have had more than ample capacity to carry at least two of every *known species* of land animal (marine animals were not involved, of course). Such an ark was absurdly unnecessary for anything but a global flood.

5. God promised that never "shall there any more be a flood to destroy the earth" (Gen. 9:11), and He has kept His word for over four thousand years, if the flood indeed was global. Those Christians who say it was a local flood, however, are in effect accusing God of lying, for there are many devastating local floods every year.

Scientific Reasons

The earth's surface and sedimentary crust also bear strong witness to the historicity of a worldwide flood, and the early geologists (Steno, Woodward, etc.) taught this. Most modern geologists have argued, on the other hand, that the earth's crust was formed slowly over billions of years. Yes, but consider the following significant facts.

1. All the mountains of the world have been under water at some time or times in the past, as indicated by sedimentary rocks and marine fossils near their summits. Even most volcanic mountains with their pillow lavas seem largely to have been formed when under water.

2. Most of the earth's crust consists of sedimentary rocks (sandstones, shales, limestones, etc.). These were originally formed in almost all cases under water, usually by deposition after transportation by water from various sources.

3. The assigned "ages" of the sedimentary beds (which comprise the bulk of the "geologic column") have been deduced from their assemblages of fossils. Fossils, however, normally require very rapid burial and compaction to be preserved at all. Thus every sedimentary formation appears to have been formed rapidly —

even catastrophically — and more and more present-day geologists are returning to this point of view.

4. Since there is known to be a global continuity of sedimentary formations in the geologic column (that is, there is no *worldwide* "unconformity," or time gap, between successive "ages"), and since each unit was formed rapidly, the entire geologic column seems to be the product of continuous rapid deposition of sediments, comprising in effect the geological record of a time when "the world that then was, being overflowed with water, perished."

5. It is also significant that the types of rocks, the vast extent of specific sedimentary rock formations, the minerals and metals, coal and oil found in rocks, the various types of structures (i.e., faults, folds, thrusts, etc.), sedimentary rocks grossly deformed while still soft from recent deposition, and numerous other features seem to occur indiscriminately throughout the various "ages" supposedly represented in the column. To all outward appearances, therefore, they were all formed in essentially the same brief time period.

6. The fossil sequences in the sedimentary rocks do not constitute a legitimate exception to this rule, for there is a flagrant circular reasoning process involved in using them to identify their supposed geologic age. That is, the fossils have been dated by the rocks where they are found, which in turn had been dated by their imbedded fossils with the sequences based on their relative assumed stages of evolution, which had ultimately been based on the ancient philosophy of the "great chain of being." Instead of representing the evolution of life over many ages, the fossils really speak of the destruction of life (remember that fossils are dead things, catastrophically buried for preservation) in one age, with their actual local "sequences" having been determined by the ecological communities in which they were living at the time of burial.

7. The fact that there are traditions of the great flood found in hundreds of tribes in all parts of the world (all similar in one way or another to that in the Genesis record) is firm evidence that those tribes all originated from the one family preserved through the cataclysm.

This brief discussion is a mere introduction to the large array of scientific and biblical evidences that could be cited for the great flood

of the Bible, global in extent and cataclysmic in character and results. The book, *The Genesis Flood*[22] (co-authored by Dr. John
Whitcomb and myself back in 1961), supplemented by many subsequent books and especially by many writers and articles in the *Creation Research Society Quarterly* scattered over its 35 years of publication, as well as various other creationist journals, provides an
abundance of further evidence and documentation of the global extent and cataclysmic nature of the flood.

One can understand why atheistic and pantheistic evolutionists
have to interpret earth history in terms of great ages and evolution,
rather than creation and the flood. They really have no other choice,
once they have decided to reject the God of creation and His record
in the Bible. However, it is very difficult to understand why men and
women who do believe in God and His word do this. The Bible is
explicitly clear on the global deluge, and sound scientific evidence
supports it.

But this position does mean that the geological ages could never
have happened, and too many establishment-oriented Christians are
not yet willing to take such a stand. And that's rather sad in these last
critical days.

In the meantime, further discussion of biblical geology is given
in chapter 7 of this book.

The Naive Literalist

At a Christian Bookseller's Association convention in Denver,
a leading Christian publisher asked a Master Books representative,
"How can you people possibly believe in a literal six-day creation of
all things?" The implication, of course, was that it is simply naive to
believe Genesis literally, in view of the overwhelming "scientific"
evidence that the cosmos and the earth itself are billions of years old.

The answer to his question is simple enough. We believe that
"In six days the Lord made heaven and earth" because the One who
made heaven and earth said He did it in six days!

Furthermore, He even wrote down this revelation himself on a
tablet of stone (Exod. 20:11; 31:17–18). Perhaps it is naive to believe that God is able to tell the truth and say what He means, but I
guess that's a weakness of us literalists!

I'm more or less accustomed to this patronizing attitude by now.
Fifty years ago, Bernard Ramm, in his famous book *The Christian
View of Science and Scripture*, called me a "naive literalist" in his

evaluation of my first creationist book, *That You Might Believe* (which had been published in 1946).

Actually, I had been a theistic evolutionist during my college days, and only gradually "evolved" into a naive literalist. When I began to study the Bible seriously after getting out of college, I soon found that it was impossible to harmonize the Bible with evolution, and so became a "progressive creationist," trying to correlate the ages of geology with the days of creation in Genesis. This was the position advocated in most of the evangelical colleges and seminaries at the time (and still is, for that matter). This idea didn't satisfy very long, however, as it seemed so inconsistent with Genesis. The order of events in Genesis was contradictory at many points with that inferred by the geologists and, furthermore, it was crystal clear that the writer of Genesis (in reality, God himself) meant the "days" to be understood as literal days. In fact, He defined the word "day" (Hebrew, *yom*) as a literal day the very first time He used it (Gen. 1:5). The universal practice of keeping time in seven-day weeks can only be understood as a memorial to the creation week, as clearly explained in Exodus 20:8–11. We work six days and rest one day, because that's what God did. There is no other rational explanation for the seven-day week.

Consequently, I switched to the "gap theory," which was being taught in most "fundamentalist" colleges and seminaries. This theory takes the days of creation literally, but still hangs on to the geological ages by inserting them in a postulated time gap between Genesis 1:1 and Genesis 1:2.

But there soon appeared overwhelming problems with the gap theory, too. It purported to retain the geological ages by a device which no geologist would ever accept. That is, it required a global cataclysm terminating the geological ages (in order to leave the earth "without form and void," as in Gen. 1:2) which would have destroyed all the geological evidence identifying the geological ages! Since the whole system of evolutionary geological ages is based on the premise of a uniformitarian continuity of these "ages" with the present age, there is no room there for such a worldwide cataclysm. The gap theory defeats itself geologically.

Even more serious were its theological and biblical problems. The main difficulty which persuaded me that the gap theory could not be valid was the inferred existence of eons of suffering and death in the world before man brought sin into the world (as per Rom. 5:12; 1 Cor. 15:21; etc.). Even though advocates of this theory attribute the cataclysm to Satan's sin in heaven, the geological ages supposedly occurred long before that. Thus, God himself becomes responsible for bringing suffering and death into the world, not as a judgment on sin, but simply because it pleased Him to do it. This makes God out to be a sadistic monster — not the gracious, omniscient, omnipotent, loving God of the Bible.

This problem of death before sin also affects the day/age theory, of course, as well as any other compromise that attempts to harmonize the geological age system with the God of the Bible. Thus it became clear that I would have to give up one or the other — either take Genesis literally or reject it altogether.

So I became a naive literalist! This was over 50 years ago, and I have been a literalist ever since. It would have been much easier to go along with the popular view, but this would have dishonored the Lord and His Word. God has blessed this decision, and I have never regretted it. At that time, however, it seemed that almost no one else in the whole Christian world, especially the academic Christian community, was willing to take a stand on the scientific validity of a literal six-day creation of the universe and the subsequent earth-destroying flood. At least I could never find any, and no one had published books or articles to that effect.

Now, however, there are thousands of scientists and hundreds of thousands of others who are uninhibited literal creationists. Many of these have been brought to Christ and to assurance of salvation by this non-compromising approach to the gospel. It has not proved true, as many have claimed, that people reject Christ as Savior if they think they must also believe in literal creationism. It really works the other way: most non-Christians clearly understand the inconsistency of professing to believe on Christ while rejecting the foundational chapters of His Word. When they learn that they really can trust Genesis as literally true and scientifically defensible, it becomes easier for them to make an unequivocal decision to receive the Lord Jesus Christ as Creator, Redeemer, and Lord. Many have done just that. Furthermore, many reticent Christians become boldly witnessing Christians when they also make this discovery.

On the other hand, Christians who compromise on this foundational revelation are laying a shaky foundation for their own lives.

One does not come to Christ for salvation on his own personal terms. If he comes at all, he must come as a lost soul, dead in sins, deserving nothing but eternal separation from the One who created him and then died for his sins. It is arrogant for a hell-bound sinner to impose conditions upon God's offer of salvation, presuming to tell God which parts of His Word he will believe and obey before he does God the favor of accepting His offer of salvation. If reluctance to accept the Genesis revelation is the stumbling block keeping a person from accepting Christ, then there is grave doubt that he would ever truly believe on Him anyway. Jesus said: "If ye believe not his [Moses'] writings, how shall ye believe my words?" (John 5:47).

Except for peer pressure, it would actually be easier to believe in a young earth than in a billion-year-old earth. Our own life spans are normally less than a hundred years, our nation is barely two hundred years old, and all known recorded history occupies less than about five thousand years. The oldest known living thing (the bristlecone pine) is also less than five thousand years old. If it were not for the Bible, which reveals that the world is six thousand or so years old, we would have no objective historical reason to think it was older than about five thousand years in age at the outside!

The human brain cannot even comprehend millions or billions of years — the very idea is alien to anything we have ever experienced. So where did the idea originate? It did not come from modern science, for all the ancient pantheistic religions (Egypt, Sumeria, India, etc.) assumed the universe to be infinitely old, going through endless cycles of evolution and renewal.

Modern scientists, of course, seek to justify the idea of an ancient cosmos by simply assuming that processes have always functioned essentially as they do now, and that these processes have evolved the cosmos into its present diverse and complex forms. This is their premise of "uniformitarianism," or naturalism. This assumption eliminates God and special creation simply by definition. It also denies any subsequent supernatural interruption of those natural processes, such as in the biblical judgment of the worldwide cataclysmic flood.

Without these assumptions, there is nothing in the real world that even *looks* older than, say, six thousand years! As the apostle Peter prophesied: "In the last days scoffers" will willfully ignore the fact "that by the word of God the heavens were of old" and also the fact that "the world that then was, being overflowed with water, perished" (2 Pet. 3:3–6). And now, the earth's surface *looks* like it was restructured by an incredible worldwide water cataclysm. As the apostle Paul explained, those who deny the revealed truth of special creation of all things in the beginning have "changed the truth of God into a lie, and worshipped and served the creature more than the Creator" (Rom. 1:25).

For those who are willing to believe that God has told the truth in His Word, and who have eyes to see, there is actually overwhelming evidence in the real physical and biological worlds of both special creation and the great flood — evidences which completely obliterate the supposed evidences of an old earth, based as they are entirely on the false premise of evolution and uniformitarianism.

Call it naive literalism if you will. I call it simply taking God at His Word, and then seeking to explain all real scientific data in that context. We may not yet have answers to every problem, but at least our tentative answers are better than their false answers, because our answers are derived from implicit confidence in God's plainly revealed Word.

In that day when we all give account to God, it will be easier to explain why we had *too much* confidence in His Word (if that is possible) than why we placed more confidence in the fallible philosophies of men.

We literalists may not be so "naive" after all. I think a better word is "realistic."

Endnotes
1 Henry M. Morris, *That You Might Believe* (Chicago, IL: Good Books, Inc., 1946), p. 26–27.
2 Ibid., p. 27.
3 Ibid., p. 28.
4 Ibid., p. 31.
5 See, for example, the recent thoroughly documented volume by Dr. Ronald Numbers, Professor of History of Science and Medicine at the University of Wisconsin, entitled *The Creationists* (New York: Adolph Knopf Co., 1992), especially p. 184–213, 338.
6 John C. Whitcomb and Henry M. Morris, *The Genesis Flood* (Phillipsburg, NJ: P & R Publishing, 1961).
7 The writer's commentary on Genesis gives a summary of the evidence for this understanding of the original writing of the book. See *The Genesis Record* (Grand Rapids, MI: Baker Book House, 1976), p. 22–30.

8   Earl D. Radmacher and Robert D. Preuss, editors, *Hermeneutics, Inerrancy and the Bible*, "The Trustworthiness of Scripture in Areas Relating to Natural Science," by Walter L. Bradley and Roger Olsen (Grand Rapids, MI: Zondervan Publishing House, 1984), p. 299.

9   Pattle P.T. Pun, "A Theory of Progressive Creationism," *Journal of the American Scientific Affiliation,* vol. 39, March 1987, p. 14.

10 James Barr, letter to David Watson, 1984.

11 The contradictions have been pointed out in many books. See, for example, the brief tabulation in *The Young Earth* by John D. Morris (Green Forest, AR: Master Books, 1994), p. 33.

12 Arthur Falk, "Reflections on Huxley's Evolution and Ethics," *The Humanist*, vol. 55, November/December 1955, p. 23–24.

13 Richard Chase, "Teaching Science," *Wheaton Alumni*, April/May 1990, p. 4.

14 C.I. Scofield, editor, The Scofield Reference Bible (New York: Oxford University Press, 1909, 1945), p. 3–4.

15 Earl D. Radmacher, editor, The Nelson Study Bible (Nashville, TN: Thomas Nelson Publishers, 1997), p. 4.

16 Richard Dawkins, "God's Utility Function," *Scientific American*, vol. 273, November 1995, p. 85.

17 Homes Rolston III, "Does Nature Need to be Redeemed?" *Zygon*, vol. 29, June 1994, p. 205–206.

18 Michael Ruse, "A Few Last Words — Until the Next Time," *Zygon*, vol. 29, March 1994, p. 78.

19 A.G. Mattill Jr. "Three Cheers for the Creationists," *Free Inquiry*, vol. 2, Spring 1982, p. 17.

20 Note the incidental reference to "months." Time had a beginning when God created it (Gen. 1:1), but it will have no end. The words "time no longer" in Revelation 10:6 are in the sense of "delay no longer."

21 Henry M. Morris, *The Genesis Record* (Grand Rapids, MI: Baker Book House, 1976),
    Henry M. Morris, *The Defender's Study Bible* (Grand Rapids, MI: World Publishing, Inc., 1995).

22 John C. Whitcomb and Henry M. Morris, *The Genesis Flood* (Phillipsburg, NJ: P & R Publishing, 1961).

Chapter IV

The Rhetoric of Evolution

n chapter 3 it was stressed that none of the various devices that have been proposed by Christian evangelicals to accommodate evolution and the geological ages in the Christian faith will work. The biblical record is adamant. God's Word teaches the creation of all things in six literal days, followed later by the global cataclysm of the great flood, and nothing else. All attempts to compromise this system with the Bible fail.

Evolution Is Not Science

But actually, there is no need to compromise anyhow. Evolution and the geologic ages cannot be defended by real science, only by rhetoric, and that rhetoric often becomes bombast or ridicule or belligerence, rather than reason.

It is obvious that, despite loud protests, evolution does not fit the traditional definition of science at all. That is, no one has ever observed evolution happening, and the essence of the scientific method is experimentation and observation. In all human history, there has never been a documented case of real "vertical" evolution. All observed changes are "horizontal" within limits (these may be called microevolution, but they are really just variations or recombinations). Mutations may be "vertical" on rare occasions, but if so, they are "downward," not "upward." Most observed mutations are neutral or reversible; otherwise they are harmful, representing "mistakes" or "deteriorations."

Furthermore, the laws of thermodynamics, which are discussed in chapter 5, seem to say true upward evolution is not even possible. And still furthermore, the record of the past, as preserved in the fossils in the great beds of sedimentary rock, seems equally emphatic in saying that true evolution never happened in any past geologic age, either. Although many extinctions are documented in the fossils ("downward" evolution?), there are no "transitional" series of fossils documenting "upward" evolution from one kind to some higher kind of organism.

So, if there is no observational evidence of past, present, or possible evolution, then evolution cannot even be discussed *scientifically*. It can be discussed naturalistically, of course, with all kinds of "just-so stories" and supposed similarities, but naturalism is a philosophy, not a science. Unless one can prove there is no God, or else that He cannot create anything even if He exists, then creation is at least a logical possibility. And there is one thing for sure — atheism can never be proved! As a matter of fact, the Bible calls it foolishness. "The fool hath said in his heart, There is no God" (Ps. 14:1).

Thus, evolutionists have to resort to rhetoric, not science, in defending evolution and opposing creation. In this chapter, we shall look at some of their arguments, with this in mind.

We acknowledge, of course, that creation cannot be demonstrated scientifically either. But that's the point! Creation was an event of the past, and so cannot be observed happening now. That's the essence of the creation model. Evolution, on the other hand, supposedly operating by the natural processes which are occurring now, *should* be happening now and all through past history. Thus, the utter absence of real evidence for evolution is not just an argument against evolution, it is a positive argument for creation in the past. What we see in the real world is exactly what would be predicted on the basis of a completed past creation.

What Evolutionists Say

Evolutionary scientists sometimes say the most fascinating things. When confronting creationists, they always present a unified front, insisting that total evolution is a certain fact of science, proved beyond reasonable doubt. Creation, on the other hand, they say, is nothing but religion. Sometimes they even get ugly about it. One of England's top evolutionary biologists, Richard Dawkins, recently made the following pronouncement:

I think a case can be made that *faith* is one of the world's great evils, comparable to the smallpox virus but harder to eradicate.[1]

Dawkins was speaking of religious faith, in general, especially any faith that opposes his neo-Darwinism, which he equates to proven science.

However, while they can be of one mind about creationism, they also squabble vigorously among themselves when they assume we creationist Christians are not listening. A humanist, Rob Wipond, writes:

Scientists can be tired, ornery, and incredibly irrational when they wake up in the morning. Some do lie, some do falsify data. . . . They can be greedy; they may well have weak powers of logic, while no one else has the time or money to debunk their arguments.

Wipond then proceeds to argue that belief in evolution is itself based on blind faith, stating that so-called "*rational thinking* may just be a highly sophisticated and powerful method of self-delusion." He goes on to say:

But then, it merely exposes how much the belief in evolutionary theory is ultimately based upon a similar kind of blind faith. It shows there is no definitive, final proof for evolution, either. There are just a lot of suggestive facts that make some of us formulate an argument, every bit as tautological as the quote-the-Bible-to-prove-creationism-is-right arguments, which goes something like this: "Evolution seems to have occurred; therefore, evolution has occurred."[2]

We wonder if Dawkins would agree that blind faith in evolutionary theory is also "one of the world's great evils." Probably not.

Wipond is not alone in noting the absence of any proof for evolution. One of the nation's most eminent biologists, Keith Stewart Thomson, has recently discussed this curious fact.

As long as there have been theories of evolution (and certainly before Darwin), critics have complained that "the hypothesis remains destitute of satisfactory evidence"

(Rev. William Paley, 1802). . . . That the charge applies equally against creation theorists is of little comfort.

Thompson has noted the same problem that creationists have often emphasized. No one in all human history has documented an example of real evolution taking place. Evolution is not empirical science; it is a set of "just-so stories." He goes on to say:

> Perhaps the most obvious challenge is to demonstrate evolution empirically. There are, arguably, some two to ten million species on Earth. The fossil record shows that most species survive somewhere between three and five million years. In that case, we ought to be seeing small but significant numbers of originations and extinctions every decade. [3]

But, of course, we don't! Not even in the laboratory, where many attempts have been made to speed up the "evolutionary process." There have been great numbers of extinctions during the period of human history, but no documented originations.

Furthermore, the problem cannot be solved by stretching the imaginary process out over millions of years. The fossils also say no! There are no fossil records of actual evolutionary transitions anywhere, although billions of fossils are there still preserved in the rocks.

> One of the outstanding problems in large-scale evolution has been the origin of major taxa, such as the tetrapods, birds, and whales, that had appeared to rise suddenly, without any obvious answers, over a comparatively short period of time. [4]

Professor Carroll, an eminent Canadian paleontologist, is well aware of such highly publicized fossils as *archaeopteryx* (the alleged half-reptile, half-bird) and the so-called "walking whale," and he discusses the recently publicized fossils that have been claimed as transitional birds and whales, but these are still highly controversial. It is still obvious that birds and whales arose suddenly without obvious ancestors. As a matter of fact, it is well known by paleontologists that literally *all* phyla, classes, orders, and families of plants and animals have arisen suddenly without obvious transitional ancestors, as far as the fossil record shows.

Nor will it do to attribute these ubiquitous gaps in evolution to the popular new theory of "punctuated equilibrium," being promoted by Harvard's Stephen Jay Gould. If there is minimal evidence for the slow-and-gradual evolutionary process of neo-Darwinism, there is far less evidence for the invisible process of sudden evolution postulated by Gould and his followers. A very interesting and cogent comment about Gould has appeared recently.

> Even his critics grant that Dr. Gould is popular with lay readers, but this has also made him a favorite target of attack. In the *New York Review of Books* last year, John Maynard Smith, a prominent British evolutionist, said of him that "the evolutionary biologists with whom I have discussed his work tend to see him as a man whose ideas are so confused as to be hardly worth bothering with, but as one who should not be publicly criticized because he is at least on our side against the creationists.[5]

Let's stay united against the creationists, they say, no matter how we argue among ourselves, and no matter how flimsy is our evidence for evolution.

Dr. Thomson courageously has recently tried to define just what they should look for that could constitute genuine evidence of evolution.

> All evolution is change but not all change is evolution. . . . I would argue that in order to constitute evidence of true evolution, a phenomenon must meet three simple criteria: it must be shown to be genetically based, it must be irreversible, and it should result in reproductive isolation of populations.[6]

That sounds quite reasonable, but no "change" observed thus far in nature, or in the laboratory, has been shown to meet these criteria. Mutations take place, but they are either reversible, deteriorative, or neutral. Recombinations of existing genes take place, but are "horizontal" changes that do not result in reproductive isolation. Natural selection takes place, but this is a conservative phenomenon, which weeds out defective mutants and keeps the population stable. Adaptations take place, but these are horizontal changes which conserve the species against extinction, but do not produce new species. Thomson concludes:

The million-dollar question is: What mechanisms lie between the short-term, low-scale and wholly reversible results so far obtained, and the origin of a new species? What conditions and mechanisms are required to feed back from a given level of phenotypic plasticity to a new genetic or phenotypic constitution? Stay tuned.[7]

Evolutionists must, therefore, simply "keep the faith." Somewhere, someone may find a real empirical proof of evolution. In the meantime, most everything they say (other than mere recitals of facts on which both creationists and evolutionists agree), seems potentially something that can be used against them.[8] One of their own has said it well.

So if we want to compare science and religion fairly and objectively, let us not compare science the fantasized ideal to religion in human reality but, rather, science in human reality to religion in human reality. And this is where the role of science as spinner of myths, as deluder of the masses, as intensely repressive force, must be confronted.[9]

The Bible Versus Evolutionary Biology

Although evolutionism today is the "politically correct" world view, most people associate it particularly with biology. The origin of life, of different kinds of living creatures, and especially the origin of human life, are taught almost everywhere today in terms of evolution. This is not what God has revealed about life in His inspired Word, the Bible.

Biology, a word derived from two Greek words, *bios* ("life") and *logos* ("word") is "the study of life." The Bible is the written word of God, according to its own claims and an abundance of evidence.

The Bible encourages — in fact, commands — the study of biology and all other factual science. The very first divine commandment given to man was: "Be fruitful and multiply, and replenish the earth, and subdue it: and have dominion over the fish of the sea, and over the fowl of the air, and over every living thing that moveth upon the earth" (Gen. 1:28).

This "dominion mandate," as it has been called, is in effect a command to "do science," for Adam and his descendants could only "subdue" the earth and "have dominion" over all its living creatures by learning their nature and functions. This clearly implies the establishment of a "science" of biology, so that mankind could properly care for and utilize the world's resources of animal and plant life as created by God.

There is thus no conflict at all between the Bible and biological *science*. But "evolutionary biology" is another matter. It is a philosophy, not science, an attempt to explain the origin and developmental history of all forms of life on a strictly naturalistic basis, without the intervention of special creation by the Creator.

The Bible is opposed to evolutionary biology in that sense. Ten times in its opening chapter, it stresses that the various created forms of life were to reproduce only "after their kinds" (see Gen. 1:11–12, 21, 24–25). This restriction does not preclude "variation," of course, since no two individuals of the same kind are ever exactly alike. Such "horizontal" variations, or recombinations, within the created kinds are proper subjects of scientific study and so do not conflict with the Bible.

There are many fully credentialed professional biologists who are Christian creationists (plus a good number of Jewish and Muslim creationist scientists) who have no problem with this biblical stipulation. The Institute for Creation Research, for example, has at least 30 such professionals in the life sciences on its own faculty (regular and adjunct) and boards (governing and advisory), and there are hundreds more in the Creation Research Society and other creationist organizations.

However, it is sadly true that *most* biologists and other life scientists are thoroughly committed to evolutionism. This is especially true of the biological "establishment." A recent poll of the members of the National Academy of Sciences found that, although commitment to atheism was predominant among the leading scientists in all fields, biologists were more so than others.

> Biologists had the lowest rate of belief (5.5% in God, 7.1% in immortality), with physicists and astronomers slightly higher (7.5% in God, 7.5% in immortality).[10]

In fact, probably most of this small minority who *do* believe in God are theistic evolutionists, not creationists.

Lest such statistics intimidate Christians, however, it should be emphasized that this overwhelming commitment to evolutionism is *not* because of the compelling nature of the scientific evidence, but rather because of strong antipathy to biblical Christianity. Even Charles Darwin, the "patron saint" of evolutionary biology, converted to evolutionism and atheist-leaning agnosticism because of his emotional rejection of the biblical doctrine of divine punishment on unbelievers.[11]

If one probes deeply enough, he will usually find that people believe in evolution either because of passive acceptance of majority opinion or else because of emotional antipathy to biblical Christianity — not because of scientific evidence.

Scientific evidence for biological evolution is very weak, at best. In all recorded history, there is no example of real evolution having occurred. The tremendous complexity of even the simplest forms of life is seemingly impossible to explain by natural processes of evolution. Yet they believe it anyway. The genetic code, which governs the reproduction process in all creatures, is extremely complex, clearly implying intelligent design by the Creator. Yet it is attributed to natural selection. Note the following statement.

> The genetic code is the product of early natural selection, not simply random, say scientists in Britain. Their analysis has shown it to be the best of more than a billion billion possible codes. . . . Roughly 10^{20} genetic codes are possible, but the one nature actually uses was adopted as the standard more than 3.5 billion years ago.[12]

However, instead of coming to the obvious conclusion that an intelligent agent must have done the "adopting," the politically correct explanation that it happened naturally is simply assumed.

> It is extremely unlikely that such an efficient code arose by chance — natural selection must have played a role.[13]

Natural selection thus takes the place of God, not only in the origin of species, and in the origin of life, but even in the origin of the remarkable code which governs life, so they say.

However, a number of evolutionary biologists have, in recent years, recognized the absurdity of relying on *natural* selection alone

to accomplish such marvelous feats. Two very prominent evolutionists say it this way.

> Neo-Darwinian language and conceptual structure
> itself ensures scientific failure. Major questions posed by
> zoologists cannot be answered from inside the neo-Dar-
> winian strait-jacket. Such questions include, for example,
> "How do new structures arise in evolution?" "Why, given
> so much environmental change, is stasis so prevalent in
> evolution as seen in the fossil record?" "How did one group
> of organisms or set of molecules evolve from another?"
> The importance of these questions is not at issue; it is just
> that neo-Darwinians, restricted by their presuppositions,
> cannot answer them.[14]

These are the same unanswered questions that creationists have
been posing to evolutionists for years. The obvious *true* answer
(though politically incorrect) is that of biblical creation.

This answer is not acceptable to evolutionists, of course, so
they invent "just-so stories" or mysterious "order out of chaos" scenarios.

> Fanciful abstractions have been invented by the neo-
> Darwinists, many of whom are scientists who, beginning
> as engineers, physicists and mathematicians, found biol-
> ogy "easy." Several of them (for instance, Richard
> Dawkins of Oxford . . .) have become famous darlings of
> life scientists today.[15]

The co-authors of the book cited above are ardent anti-creationists Lynn Margulis and Dorion Sagan (son of Carl Sagan and
Margulis). While vigorously opposing the neo-Darwinian concept
of gradual evolution by random mutation and natural selection, they
are not endorsing the "punctuated equilibrium" hypothesis of Gould
and others, and certainly not creationism. Rather, they think the answers must lie in *Gaia*, the ancient pagan idea that the earth is a giant
organism itself, growing and developing over the ages, all by its own
quasi-intelligence — Mother Earth, as it were.

Richard Dawkins is the best-known neo-Darwinist in England,
with Edward O. Wilson of Harvard probably filling that role in
America. A reviewer of Wilson's latest book notes the following about

Wilson (best known as the leading advocate of sociobiology):

> . . . alludes in several passages to the problem of complexity as the greatest challenge facing all science.[16]

His co-Darwinian, Dawkins, thinks it can all be solved somehow in terms of computer simulations and his "blind watchmaker." However, in trying to understand the origin of the human brain by natural selection, Wilson seems to have come to an impasse.

> Evolution of the brain occurred over the three million years between our simian ancestors and the advent of *Homo sapiens* about a million years ago. The strangest feature of the process is that the capacity of the brain should far exceed the needs of mere survival. A further curiosity is that, once the brain was fully formed, the enormous differentiation of cultures occupied mere millennia, while only the twinkling of an evolutionary eye separates us from the earliest records of any civilization.[17]

Of course, none of this is strange or curious if one is willing to accept the biblical record of the origin of the human brain and the origin of civilization.

Instead of such a simple solution as primeval divine creation, however, evolutionary biologists argue violently among themselves about the relative merits of neo-Darwinism, punctuated equilibrium, and Gaia in explaining man. Stephen Jay Gould of Harvard, the leading advocate of punctuationism, has participated in debates with Dawkins and others over the issue, although he refuses to debate a bona fide creationist scientist such as Duane Gish. More recently he had a widely publicized debate with evolutionary anthropologist/linguist Steven Pinker, arguing over whether human psychology is a product of Darwinian selection or punctuated equilibrium. The comments by science writer Brookes are fascinating and relevant.

> Gould is an inevitable by-product of an age-old controversy, which most scientists now acknowledge to be simplistic and well past its sell-by-date. It has no apparent function other than intellectual one-upmanship. It is precisely because there is so little evidence for either of their views that they can get away

with so much speculation and disagreement.[18]

This particular debate was about evolutionary psychology, but the same comments could apply to any other component of evolutionary biology. Neither side can offer any observational evidence. With respect to neo-Darwinism, evolutionist G. A. Dover says:

> The study of evolution should be removed from teleological computer simulations, thought experiments and wrong-headed juggling of probabilities, and put back into the laboratory and the field. . . . Whilst there is so much more to learn, the neo-Darwinist synthesis should not be defended to death by blind watchmakers.[19]

As far as the field is concerned, the punctuationists find their main evidence in the ubiquitous evolutionary gaps in the fossil record. In spite of these gaps, the fossil record is usually presented as evidence that evolution *has* occurred in the past, even though we cannot see it in either the field or lab in the present.

But the fossils don't really provide any solid evolutionary evidence either, for either gradualism or punctuationism.

> Fossil discoveries can muddle our attempts to construct simple evolutionary trees — fossils from key periods are often not intermediates, but rather hodgepodges of defining features of many different groups. . . . Generally, it seems that major groups are not assembled in a simple linear or progressive manner — new features are often "cut and pasted" — on different groups at different times.[20]

Not only are there no transitional series of fossils among the billions of known fossils in the rocks, but also there are no unequivocal evolutionary sequences.

> This poses a "chicken and egg" problem for paleontologists: if independent evolution of key characters is common, how is phylogeny to be recognized?[21]

The real bottom line of the entire question of biological origins is that the biblical record fits all the real scientific facts, and evolution does not.

Evolutionary Bombast

Instead of presenting real observational evidence that life forms are evolving toward organisms of greater complexity (which must have happened if evolution is true), evolutionary biologists and their followers tend to rely on rhetoric and dogmatic assertion.

A typical example of evolutionary rhetoric appeared in a 1996 newspaper article written by Dr. Joseph D. McInerney in reaction to discussions in the Colorado schools about an evolutionist video to which a student took exception. Dr. McInerney is director of the notorious Biological Sciences Curriculum Study Center, whose government-financed biology textbooks dogmatically promoting evolution have been used by many, many millions of school children since they were first published in the 1960s following the 1959 Darwinian Centennial celebrations — used not only in this country, but also in 50 other countries.

With so much at stake, it is not surprising that evolutionists such as Dr. McInerney rise up in fury whenever their monopoly on public education is threatened or even questioned. The article mentioned above was published in the *Arvada Jefferson Sentinel* on August 8, 1996, and had the provocative title, "Shall School Administrators Be Ruled by Reason or Rhetoric?"

Alarmed that the Jefferson County School Board might be persuaded to tolerate the views of creationist students, Dr. McInerney pontificated as follows:

> Ignorance and zealotry are the twin towers of creationism, structures deeply rooted in the rejection of reason, and in rhetoric devoid of scientific substance.

He went on to describe creationists as ". . . scientific illiterates who call the cadence on a march toward ignorance."

Talk about rhetoric! Bombast would be a better word. Dr. McInerney seems quite adept at inflammatory "rhetoric," but one can search in vain for any "scientific substance" in his article.

One wonders whether he may have studied at the feet of the late Dr. Isaac Asimov who, in a fund-raising letter for the American Humanist Association back in 1982, called creationists ". . . religious zealots . . . marching like an army of the night into our public schools with their Bibles held high."

Asimov wrote hundreds of books on many fields of science, so he presumably was quite familiar with any scientific evidences for evolution if such evidences exist, but he always refused invitations to debate the subject with me or any other creationist scientist.

Dr. McInerney has an interesting explanation as to why evolutionists generally elect not to debate the scientific evidences for and against evolution and creation. He says, ". . . creationism has no scientific basis and therefore cannot occupy any side in a scientific debate."

One suspects, however, that Dr. McInerney's real reason may be that the evolutionists practically always lose such debates! The fact is that all genuine scientific evidence fits the creation model of origins much better than the evolution model. The fact that creationists generally win these debates is not at all because creationists are better debaters, but simply because there is no real scientific evidence for evolution. In fact, the National Center for Science Education, whose specific function is to monitor and oppose activities of creationists, recommends that evolutionists should always decline invitations to debate creationists, acknowledging that they will probably lose the debate.

Dr. McInerney's article reminds me of an exchange I had back in 1973 with his predecessor at the BSCS Center, the late Dr. William V. Mayer. As a result of an inflammatory article he had written against creationists in his monthly *BSCS Newsletter*, I wrote and challenged him to a scientific debate on the subject.

As far as I can recall, this is the only time any of us here at ICR ever tried to arrange a debate on our own initiative. Although we have been involved in over 300 such debates (with Dr. Duane Gish doing the debating in most of them — and always winning, of course), these have always been in response to invitations by others, usually by student organizations on various campuses.

Anyway, this led to a rather fascinating interchange of personal letters between Dr. Mayer and me. Most of these were published in the May 1973 *Acts & Facts* and later reprinted in our book, *Creation — Acts, Facts, Impacts* (both of these are now out of print). The bottom line, however, was that Dr. Mayer flatly refused to debate the scientific aspects of the issue before a general audience.

Several years later, however, he did finally agree to a public debate in Evansville, Indiana, this time with Dr. Gish. Dr. Mayer's presentation was, characteristically, mostly insulting "rhetoric, devoid of scientific substance," and Dr. Gish clearly won the debate.

Another statement in Dr. McInerney's article was "that all scientists accept the reality of evolution." This, of course, is not true, and it is hard to believe that he did not know this. There are literally thousands of qualified scientists — including scores of biologists — who are creationists. ICR alone has some 40 Ph.D. scientists on its resident faculty, adjunct faculty, and advisory board, with at least 15 having terminal degrees in one of the biological sciences. If the distinguished BSCS director is really unaware of this fact, then he ought not to be writing articles on this subject.

It is very frustrating to encounter so many books, articles, talks, etc., repeatedly proclaiming that creationism is nothing but religion, while so many scientists continue to insist that evolution is a scientific fact. Fifty or more anti-creationists books have been published echoing this theme, and even the courts have been persuaded. Every time a school board — such as this one in Colorado — even thinks about letting creation in the classroom, evolutionists demonstrate at the meetings, write indignant letters to the editor, and get the ACLU to threaten an expensive lawsuit, and the intimidated school board quickly backs off. We can't mix "science" and "religion," they whimper.

Why do evolutionists go to all this trouble and expense? All they would have to do to destroy creationism once and for all *is to provide just one scientific proof that macroevolution is true*! Arguments against flood geology or the young earth are irrelevant, because — even though these are important subjects in their own right — they do not treat the basic issue, which is special creation or macroevolution. Citing Darwin's finches or mutations on fruit flies or other such phenomena won't do either, because such "horizontal" or "downward" minor changes (microevolution, if they wish) are all accepted by creationists anyway.

Macroevolution is the issue, and for this there is no proof whatever, or even any good evidence that can't be better explained in terms of the creation model. No true evolution has ever been observed during human history, there are no true transitional structures in the billions of fossil remains from the past, and vertically upward macroevolution seems flatly impossible in terms of the universal (even for open systems!) second law of thermodynamics. Furthermore, these very phenomena are actual "predictions" from the creation model. It seems that creationism is the system that is based on sound science while evolutionism relies solely on faith.

Why, then, do evolutionists perpetually insist that their evolutionary paradigm is science and must be taught exclusively in science classes, textbooks, and media?

"Why?" questions cannot be answered scientifically, of course. They require a philosophical answer, or a theological answer, or — best of all — a biblical answer! So how does the Bible explain such unbelief? It does so in fiery rhetoric based on divine reason!

> For the invisible things of him from the creation of the world are clearly seen, being understood by the things that are made, even his eternal power and Godhead; so that they are without excuse. . . . Professing themselves to be wise, they became fools. And changed the glory of the uncorruptible God into an image made like corruptible man, and to birds, and four-footed beasts, and creeping things. Wherefore God also gave them up. . . . Who changed the truth of God into a lie, and worshipped and served the creature more than the Creator . . . even as they did not like to retain God in their knowledge (Rom. 1:20–28).

Thus, they insist on evolution because they, like Satan, don't want God to be God. It is not because of science that they reject God and his word, but because of sinful unbelief, and they are without excuse. They may well be brilliant scientists in everything but this. They may not believe there is a devil, but the fact is:

> The god of this world [that is, Satan] hath blinded the minds of them which believe not, lest the light of the glorious gospel of Christ, who is the image of God, should shine unto them. . . . For God, who commanded the light to shine out of darkness, hath shined in our hearts, to give the light of the knowledge of the glory of God in the face of Jesus Christ (2 Cor. 4:4–6).

If any reader of these lines is trying to straddle the fence between evolution and creation — young person, parent, teacher, school board member, or whoever — we would urge him or her not to be intimidated by those who speak "great swelling words, having men's persons in admiration, because of advantage" (Jude 16). The empty rhetoric of evolutionary humanism cannot compare with the sound "reason of the hope that is in you" (1 Pet. 3:15) through the omnipotent person and saving work of our great Creator/Redeemer, the Lord Jesus Christ.

Evolutionary Paranoia

Most of the leaders in the bureaucracies that control the scientific and educational establishments are becoming increasingly paranoid concerning the creation model. Perhaps they are feeling a bit guilty about their long censorship of the scientific evidence supporting creation. Or maybe they are sensing an imminent breakup of the humanistic monopoly over our education system.

In any case, their leaders are sounding the alarm. Dr. Eugenie C. Scott is executive director of an organization (founded by the Carnegie Foundation) euphemistically called the National Center for Science Education — which (being translated) means the mission control center for keeping scientific creationism out of the schools. In a widely circulated fund-raising letter to her fellow evolutionary scientists (the NCSE is affiliated with the American Association for Advancement of Science, in which I hold the rank of Fellow and am thus on the mailing list), she recites what to her is an alarming litany of recent inroads made by creationists in various school systems, and then pleads:

> Please consider joining NCSE at the highest level you can — help NCSE keep that light [i.e., the light of evolutionism] as part of the curriculum of our nation's children.[22]

Don't be so upset, Dr. Scott. We creationists do not propose to take evolution out of the curriculum. We realize that roughly half the taxpaying parents of children and young people in our schools want evolution taught, and they have that right.

But remember that the other half are creationists, and they also pay taxes.

> Poll after poll shows our country almost equally divided between those who accept and those who reject the theory that all the earth's flora and fauna descended from a common ancestor.[23]

In fact, the polls also show that even most parents who are evolutionists agree that both models should be taught.

But doctrinaire evolutionists are passionately afraid that this would bring "religion" back into the schools. Even if creationists offer not to use the Bible or even to mention God, but only to use scientific evidence, evolutionists fear that it would still support "religion." Dr. Scott deduces that: "Other creationist aliases include 'abrupt appearance theory' . . . and 'intelligent design theory' " and that these might cause students to attribute such sudden appearances and intelligent design to (perhaps this should be whispered) "The God of the Bible."[24]

Well, how about merely including a brief discussion of the scientific evidences against evolution, with no reference at all to God, creation, the Bible, design, sudden appearance, or anything like that. The dissenting opinion of Justice Scalia in the 1987 Supreme Court decision to strike down Louisiana's two-model law, said that Christians "are quite entitled, as a secular matter, to have whatever scientific evidence there may be against evolution presented in their schools, just as Mr. Scopes was entitled to present whatever scientific evidence there was for it."

But evolutionists are wary of this also. Dr. Scott, expressing the paranoid fear felt by most evolutionary leaders at such a suggestion, complains that such an approach would be "virtually guaranteed to confuse students about evolution and may lead them to reject one of the major themes of science."[25]

It does seem unnaturally strange for evolutionists to be so afraid that students may reject evolution if they hear any scientific evidence on the other side. They insist repeatedly that evolution is a proved fact of science, and they are quite free to present all the positive evidence for evolution that they can, so what are they afraid of?

Instead of giving the scientific evidence for real evolution (not small horizontal variations, of course, but vertical evolution from amoeba to man), they resort to authoritarianism ("all we scientists believe it, so it must be true"). As far as the scientific evidence for creation is concerned (which they assume is really the same as the scientific evidence against evolution), they deal with that mainly by name-calling.

> Creationism is an incredible pain in the neck, neither honest nor useful, and the people who advocate it

have no idea how much damage they are doing to the credibility of belief.

So says Sir John Houghton, a physicist who professes to believe in God. Richard Dawkins, the atheistic zoologist who is probably the most influential evolutionist in Great Britain, "now goes so far as to say that anyone who believes in a Creator God is 'scientifically illiterate.' "[26]

Another recent article says that the reason so many students and people in general are turning to creationism is because "we [that is, we biology professors] are doing a poor job of educating our biology students about Darwin, evolution, and the nature of science."[27]

No doubt he is right. I have often told evolutionists that they are going to a tremendous amount of trouble trying to stop the creationism revival, when all they would have to do is to present *one real proof* of true evolution. If they would just take the time to give one single definite scientific proof of macroevolution instead of fuzzy generalities, then we might all become evolutionists.

But this they will not do because they have no such proof. There is no scientific proof of evolution. They can recite certain supposed scientific evidences for evolution (humans and chimpanzees have many similarities) but creationists can also cite scientific evidences against it (there are many even greater differences between humans and chimpanzees).

As a matter of fact, in all human history, no one has ever seen any real evolution take place (horizontal variation within kinds is not macroevolution), although thousands of species have become extinct during human history. Furthermore, out of the billions of known fossils in the earth's rock record of the past, no true intermediate evolutionary transitional form between kinds has ever been discovered, whereas there ought to be large numbers of such intermediate forms if evolution had really happened.

No wonder evolutionists become paranoid when asked to allow both sides of the creation-evolution issue to be heard. They cannot respond with real scientific evidence, because there is none — no evolution in the present, none in the past. This has become painfully obvious in the hundreds of scientific debates between evolutionists and creationists during the past 25 years.

Consequently, Eugenie Scott, from her strategic position as director of the main anti-creationist organization, is now warning her fellow evolutionists not to debate the issue at all. *"Avoid debates,"* she says. "If your local campus Christian fellowship asks you to 'defend evolution,' please decline . . . you probably will get beaten."[28]

It is easier to deal with creationism with bombast than with evidence and by *ad hominem* arguments rather than by scientific arguments. And, of course, this approach works quite well in most cases, since many people by nature would rather keep God and His control over their lives as far off as possible anyway. Even many Christian leaders are intimidated and would rather go along with them (or even to ignore the whole subject) than to take a clear and knowledgeable stand for true biblical creationism. Note the widespread euphoria over the Pope's statement in 1997 seeming to endorse evolutionism. Not only Catholic intellectuals and liberal Protestants are going along with evolutionism, but so are many evangelicals.

> Later this year, the Fuller Theological Seminary in Pasadena, California (the intellectual hub of conservative Protestant denominations), will publish a book acknowledging a natural origin for the human family tree.[29]

In spite of all this, however, there are now thousands of well-trained scientists who have become creationists, as well as a growing number of solidly biblical churches and schools. Many people are *not* afraid to consider the biblical and scientific evidences for creation — even *recent creation*! And when they do, many do reject the entire evolutionary system with all its humanistic baggage.

That is why so many evolutionary leaders seem to become paranoid about this. My Webster's dictionary defines "paranoia" as a mental attitude "characterized by systematized delusions of persecution and of one's own greatness."

We Christian creationists are not the least bit afraid to have people consider the evidences (if there are any) for evolution, so why are they so afraid to let them hear the evidences for creation?

In the meantime, the Bible assures *us* that "God hath not given us the spirit of fear, but of power, and of love, and of a sound mind" (2 Tim. 1:7).

Scientific Bigotry

Scientists like to be accepted as clear-thinking, objective scholars who observe and measure natural processes as they actually occur, documenting and confirming experimentally the physical phenom-ena of the real world. Their scientific method involves careful test-ing and replication of experimental data, without regard to personal beliefs.

Such ideals are not always attained, unfortunately. Scientists are fallible, sinful human beings, just like everyone else. Often they are downright bigoted, especially when asked to consider a concept outside their naturalistic world view. Their process of "peer review" screens out all other world views and any data which support them.

For example, consider the complaint of one of their number, Dr. Lynn Margulis:

> More and more . . . today's universities and profes-sional societies guard their knowledge. Collusively, the university biology curriculum, the textbook publishers, the National Science Foundation review committees, the Graduate Record examiners, and the various microbio-logical, evolutionary, and zoological societies map out domains of the known and knowable; they distinguish required from forbidden knowledge, subtly punishing the trespassers with rejection and oblivion; they award the faithful liturgists by granting degrees and dispersing funds and fellowships. Universities and academies . . . deter-mine who is permitted to know and just what it is that he or she may know. Biology, botany, zoology, biochemis-try, and microbiology departments within U.S. universi-ties determine access to knowledge about life, dispensing it at high prices in peculiar parcels called credit hours.[30]

One might almost think that the above had been written by a committee of creation scientists complaining about their ostracism by the evolutionary establishment. The fact is, however, that Dr. Margulis is a doctrinaire evolutionist herself, strenuously opposed to creationism. She has impeccable credentials (a Ph.D. from the Uni-versity of California at Berkeley) and is Distinguished Professor of Biology at the University of Massachusetts.

Note also the complaint of one of the world's most distinguished evolutionary astrophysicists. Referring to his own theory of the ori-gin of the universe which differs from the orthodox "big-bang" theory, Dr. Hannes Alfvèn, says:

This has been a great advantage because it gives me a possibility to approach the phenomena from another point than most astrophysicists do, and it is always fruitful to look at any phenomenon under two different points of view. On the other hand, it has given me a serious disadvantage. When I describe the phenomena according to this formalism, most referees do not understand what I say and turn down my papers.[31]

Margulis is unhappy that she cannot get a good hearing for the Gaia hypothesis by the Darwinist-controlled scientific establishment, and Alfvèn is complaining that the "Big Bang" evolutionary cosmologists conspire to prevent studies and publications on his own evolutionary cosmology. Neither Margulis nor Alfvèn are creationists and both would undoubtedly be opposed to publishing creationist articles in any scientific journal.

Nevertheless, they do highlight a problem that creationists encounter almost universally. People who criticize creationists for not publishing their articles in the standard scientific journals should realize that this door is closed tight. *We have tried, and we know!*

Scientists can be plain bigots when considering concepts they don't favor. We are not the first to recognize this. Another top scientist, Dr. Philip Abelson, noted this fact years ago.

One of the most astonishing characteristics of scientists is that some of them are plain old-fashioned bigots. Their zeal has a fanatical egocentric quality characterized by disdain and intolerance for anyone or any value not associated with a special area of intellectual activity.[32]

At the time he wrote this editorial, Dr. Abelson was editor of *Science*, the official journal of the American Association for Advancement of Science, so he surely knew what he was talking about! Yet he would have been as adamant as anyone else against giving creationists a hearing in his journal.

It is not that creationist scientists have not published in their own scientific fields. For example, before coming to ICR, Dr. Duane Gish had published at least 25 articles on biochemistry in secular science journals; Dr. Ken Cumming, over 18 articles in biology; and Dr. Larry Vardiman, at least 10 articles in atmospheric physics. My own publications in engineering include five books and 20 articles.

One of the books, *Applied Hydraulics in Engineering*, has been continuously in print since 1963 and has been used as a textbook in scores of universities.

But none of us can get a scientific article promoting creationism published in the secular journals, whether technical journals or popular magazines such as *Reader's Digest* or *National Geographic*. In fact, very few religious magazines will accept an article on creationism, especially one that promotes six-day creation and a global flood.

On one occasion, a member of the Society of Exploration Geophysicists was able to get an invitation for me to speak at their convention, with an agreement that the Society would publish the paper in its journal. When they saw my paper, however, they quickly reneged, even though the article had no religious material in it at all, only science. It was later published by ICR as the small book, *The Scientific Case for Creation*. It was translated into Russian and was instrumental in the conversion of a significant number of Russian scientists and science students to creationism and then to Christ, prior to the fall of communism there.

Such evolutionist bigotry has been encountered many times here at ICR, as well as by other creationists. Most readers may remember the failed attempt of the California Department of Education to close the ICR Graduate School, for example. The rationale behind such bigotry was indicated by the State Superintendent of Education, Bill Honig, when he told me verbally that science is not science without evolution, and therefore we could not teach science. As a lawyer, he had been indoctrinated by the scientists at Berkeley and other state universities into this ideology.

Lynn Margulis (not arguing for the right of students to learn the scientific evidence for creation, but rather her own Gaian theory of evolutionary pantheism) has expressed her concerns rather colorfully.

> Yet the Academy guards, using neo-Darwinism as a tool, superimpose a gigantic superstructure of mechanism and hierarchy that protects the throbbing biosphere from being directly sensed by these new scientists — people most in need of sensing it. The dispensers of the funds for scientific research and education and other opportunity makers, herd the best minds and bodies into sterile laboratories and white-walled university cloisters to be catechized with dogmatic nonsense.[33]

Now if Margulis finds it frustrating to try to get the scientific evolutionary theory of Gaia (i.e., "Mother Earth") taught in the classrooms and laboratories and textbooks of science (along with Darwinian evolution), she ought to try to get a hearing for scientific creationism!

All of this is why creationists have to publish their own books and journals and establish their own schools if they want their young people to learn the truth about origins. The bigotry of the scientific and educational establishments has forced us to this position, even in a once-free country like our own.

And if our youth never learn the great truths about creation, the Fall, and the Curse, how can they ever *really* understand the meaning of salvation through Christ?

Somehow I can't help thinking about Christ's words to the intellectual leaders of the time when He walked the earth:

> Woe unto you, scribes and Pharisees, hypocrites! for
> ye compass sea and land to make one proselyte, and when
> he is made, ye make him twofold more the child of hell
> than yourselves (Matt. 23:15).

The Postmodern Agnostics

A new dimension of the evolution/creation question has emerged recently in what is called "postmodernism." However, this system involves, if anything, still more rhetoric and still less scientific substance than old-fashioned evolutionary agnosticism.

The term "agnostic" is generally believed to have been coined by Thomas Huxley, "Darwin's bulldog." It is supposedly a less dogmatic position than that of atheism, holding that one can neither prove nor disprove the existence of God.

Charles Darwin, as well as Huxley, professed to be an agnostic, although both seemed to waiver back and forth between agnosticism and atheism in their writings and correspondence.

Actually, the word is derived from two Greek words, *a* ("no" or "against") and *gnosis* ("knowledge"). When combined as *agnosia*, it is translated as "ignorance." For example, it is used in 1 Peter 2:15: "For so is the will of God, that with well doing ye may put to silence the ignorance [read "agnosticism"] of foolish men."

But now a strange new form of agnosticism is making inroads among left-leaning intellectuals, associated with the "postmodernism" of the so-called "Generation X." The new agnosticism holds that one cannot really know anything at all!

> Only recently have we been using this term [i.e., "postmodernism"], but this many-headed monster has been growing for some time among us. Most prominent in the children of "baby-boomers," this new cultural pattern refers to the *complete loss of values, beliefs, and traditions*. At its core is the loss of belief in any kind of Truth, and therefore the loss of belief that Right and Wrong exist.[34]

To the postmoderns everything is relative. What may be true or right for one person may not be true or right for the next. Ethics is a matter of taste, and what's right is merely a pragmatic question of what works.

This attitude even is starting to affect the teaching of evolutionary biology. Anthropologist Matt Cartmill complains, "Now we find ourselves defending Darwin against attacks not only from the religious right but from the academic left as well."[35]

It seems that these postmodern liberals not only reject Christianity, but science as well, especially when its findings and theories are presented as objective truth.

> Although these notions are often expressed in a mind-numbing "postmodern" jargon, at bottom they're pretty simple. We can sum them up in one sentence. Anybody who claims to have objective knowledge about anything is trying to control and dominate the rest of us.
>
> And though all fields of science are suspect, what most left-wing anxiety centers on is biology.[36]

In a well-reported example, social psychologist Phoebe Ellsworth encountered an unexpected reaction when giving an interdisciplinary seminar lecture on human emotions. When she first mentioned "experiments," audience members objected that the experimental method was merely a power-grabbing device by white Victorian males. Then, when she countered by reminding them that this scientific method had led to the discovery of DNA, the dialogue was terminated when the audience expressed strong disapproval of anyone who "believed" in DNA!

In commenting on this experience, Ehrenreich and McIntosh

somehow manage to equate this unscientific attitude of the postmoderns with creationism, although they call it "secular creationism," since they are well aware that these protagonists have no commitment at all to either biblical creationism or scientific creationism.

> It was only with the arrival of the intellectual movements lumped under the term "postmodernism" that academic antibiologism began to sound perilously like religious creationism. . . . Glibly applied, postmodernism portrays evolutionary theory as nothing more than a sexist and racist story line created by western white men.[37]

To the postmodern, human behavior and human societies are functions only of their respective group cultures. They are not to be explained in terms either of ancestral animal characteristics or of any cross-cultural commonalities.

In fact, it is hard to pinpoint just what they *do* believe. As noted above, Thomas Johnson (a professor teaching in the Czech Republic) calls it a "many-headed monster." They are against Darwinism and against capitalism and against Christian moral constraints, but they all seem to favor feminism, multi-culturalism, and situational ethics. Otherwise they are an extremely heterogeneous group.

> The academic left is a diverse group. It includes all shades of opinion from the palest pink liberals to old-fashioned bright red Marxists. Probably no two of them have the same opinions about everything. But a lot of them have bought into some notions that are deeply hostile to the scientific enterprise in general and the study of evolution in particular.[38]

These postmodern secular "creationists" are certainly not Bible-believing creationists, or creation scientists, however, so they necessarily must believe in some form of evolution if they delve into the subject of origins at all.

There is undoubtedly a wide variety of opinions on this subject among these latter-day agnostics, but most or all of them (if not frankly atheistic) would favor some form of "New Age" pantheistic evolution. Of these, the most highly developed is probably the Gaia hypothesis, Gaia being the name of the ancient Greek goddess of earth.

> Scientific evidence for the idea that the Earth is alive

abounds. The scientific formulation of the ancient idea goes by the name of the Gaia hypothesis. . . . In its most elegant and attackable form, the hypothesis lends credence to the idea that the Earth — the global biota in its terrestrial environment — is a giant organism.[39]

The so-called "scientific evidence" for Gaia, however, consists of the "fitness of the environment" and the many symbiotic relationships in the living world — evidences which, to the true creationist, are beautiful evidences of God's design of the natural world.

In any case, this secular creationism (or postmodern agnosticism concerning Darwinian evolution and biology) has no real resemblance to true scientific biblical creationism at all.

This climate of intolerance, often imposed by scholars associated with the left, ill suits an academic tradition rhetorically committed to human freedom. What's worse, it provides intellectual backup for a political outlook that sees no real basis for common ground among humans of different sexes, races, and cultures.[40]

The above assessment of secular creationism was written by traditional neo-Darwinists, but it could just as well have been an assessment of academic evolutionism by a Bible-believing creationist. Biblical creationism does provide real common ground between all sexes, races, and cultures, for the inspired account in Genesis assures us that we are all descended from Adam and Eve, who were both created in the image of God!

But evolutionism in any form — that is, any world view other than solid biblical literal creationism — provides no such foundation.

Furthermore, scientific biblical creationists are not opposed to experimental observational science, as are these new agnostics. We strongly support all fact-based science. Our concerns are with speculative evolutionary philosophy masquerading as science.

There is really no place for agnosticism among those created in God's image, whether that agnosticism is of either the Huxleyan or the postmodern variety, for we have God's inspired and completed inscripturated word to guide us in our beliefs and behavior.

The world, represented in the governor who delivered the world's Creator to be crucified, may ask sarcastically: "What is truth?"

(John 18:38). But we can answer back, with Christ "Thy word is truth" (John 17:17). Christ also claimed: "I am the truth" (John 14:6).

And we can say with the Psalmist: "Thy word is true from the beginning: and every one of thy righteous judgments endureth for ever (Ps. 119:160). "Therefore I esteem all thy precepts concerning all things to be right; and I hate every false way" (Ps. 119:128).

Evolutionary Hydraulics

"I must go down to the sea again — to the lonely sea and the sky." This famous poem by John Masefield, former Poet Laureate of England, was one I had to memorize in school many, many years ago. It is a beautiful and moving poem, but I could never identify with it myself. My early boyhood had been spent in El Paso, Texas, in a region of mountains and deserts, far from the sea, and I never felt any such compulsion at all. Even though my major field was water engineering, I never even liked swimming.

But now I learn, from a fascinating article in the *New Age Journal*, that we have all evolved from aquatic apes! This is the theory proposed by Elaine Morgan in her popular book, *The Scars of Evolution*, which proposes still another strange new theory of evolution.

> Ever wonder why we love water? Why we head for the beach at the first opportunity, stay in the shower long after we're clean, even ponder water births for our babies? According to Welsh author Elaine Morgan, this urge to submerge may have an evolutionary explanation — one that holds some surprising implications for our health today.
>
> Traditional evolutionary theory posits that humans separated from monkeys when our ancestors dropped from trees to hunt animals on the dry African plains. In contrast, Morgan argues that the first humans evolved in a flooded wet region of northeast Africa where they spent much of their time swimming or wading hip-deep in water.[41]

This new theory of human origins does have the merit of explaining why fossil remains of ape-men are so scarce. One would think, if man has been in the process of evolving on land for a million years, and with so many paleoanthropologists searching for these remains, there would now be an abundance of such remains available everywhere to document our human evolution. As another advocate of the aquatic ape theory reminds us, however, in his article, "The Water People":

> The fossils that decorate our family tree are so scarce that there are still more scientists than specimens. The remarkable fact is that all the physical evidence we have for human evolution can still be placed, with room to spare, inside a single coffin. . . . And the true origin of modern humans — of upright, naked, toolmaking, big-brained beings — is, if we are to be honest with ourselves, an equally mysterious matter.[42]

This extreme scarcity of authentic hominid fossils is probably why paleoanthropologists feud so vigorously among themselves as to whose fossils are the best and oldest. Some evolutionists think the time is ripe for promoting aquatic apes as the real key.

> While largely ignored by many mainstream anthropologists, the aquatic ape theory has been attracting increasing scientific interest. Last summer, a symposium on the subject at the California Institute of Integral Studies (CIIS) attracted researchers from around the world. When earlier published in England, *The Scars of Evolution* was positively reviewed in scientific journals.[43]

Here, then, may be the solution to the extreme scarcity of hominid fossils. They are all under water somewhere!

Now we creationists should usually be very cautious about anything published in a "New Age" journal. However, the aquatic-ape theorists are probably right about this particular aspect. The reason why anthropologists can find so few fossils of primitive people is that they were all drowned and their remains, if they survived scavengers and decay processes after drowning, are now buried in the sediments at the bottom of the sea.

Those who are skeptical of the biblical record of the global flood, in which "the world that then was, being overflowed with water, perished" (2 Pet. 3:6), often raise this question (so do believers, for that matter). If there were so many wicked people in the antediluvian world, why is it so hard to find human remains and artifacts from that period?

They drowned in the flood — that's why. The flood waters now comprise the world's oceans, which cover two-thirds of the earth's surface, reaching deeper depths than the highest mountains. The day will come, the Bible says, when "the sea gave [gives] up the dead which were in it; and death and hell delivered [deliver] up the dead which were [are] in them" (Rev. 20:13). Their bodies and spirits thus will be reunited with all others who have since died as unbelievers, "And whosoever was [is] not found written in the book of life was [is] cast into the lake of fire" (Rev. 20:15).

Even before Morgan developed her theory of the aquatic evolution of people, many other evolutionists had long been claiming that the origin of life itself was in the primeval sea. That is why, they explain, that human flesh is still 90 percent water and why blood has almost the same chemical composition as sea water.

The Bible, of course, says otherwise. "The Lord God formed man of the dust of the ground" (Gen. 2:7). "The first man is of the earth, earthy" (1 Cor. 15:47).

However, it is intriguing to note that God created the angels when there was only water all around them, probably on the first day of creation week. "Who coverest thyself with light as with a garment: who stretchest out the heavens like a curtain; who layeth the beams of his chambers in the waters: who maketh the clouds his chariot: who walketh upon the wings of the wind [same word as 'Spirit']: Who maketh his angels spirits" (Ps. 104:2–4). "And the Spirit of God moved upon the face [same word as 'presence'] of the waters. And God said, Let there be light" (Gen. 1:2–3). In that majestic all-pervasive heavenly ocean, He made "His angels spirits; his ministers a flaming fire" (Ps. 104:4; Heb. 1:7).

Among all these "angels of light" (note 2 Cor. 11:14), none was more glorious than "Lucifer, son of the morning" (Isa. 14:12), who was evidently the "anointed cherub," hovering over the "holy mountain of God" in the heavenly "garden of God" (see Ezek. 28:13–14).

But Lucifer rebelled, aspiring to rule over creation himself, thereby becoming Satan (the "adversary"), and so he was cast out of heaven to the earth (Ezek. 28:15–17). The root of all sin, including that of Lucifer, is unbelieving pride. He rejected God and His Word, assuming that he could defeat God, refusing to believe that he had been "created" in any way different from the way God himself had been created.

Since his first consciousness had been of the pervasive waters surrounding him and the other angels, as well as the throne of God, he must have assumed they all had in some mysterious way been "created" by the waters themselves. It was perhaps by such reasoning that he could rationalize his otherwise completely irrational rebellion against his Creator, a rebellion which is still continuing today.

It is probably no coincidence that all the ancient pagan cosmogonies — most notably those of Sumeria, Egypt, Babylonia, and Greece, as well as others — taught that the world, with all its systems and inhabitants, evolved out of an eternal primeval watery chaos. The "deceiver of the whole world" (Rev. 12:9) has deceived himself most of all.[44]

And one can wonder whether this is why and how he has also deceived modern intellectuals into thinking that earthly life, as well as heavenly life, "evolved" out of primeval waters.

Water is, indeed, essential for physical life, and earth is uniquely the "water planet." God even uses water as a symbol of His lifegiving Word (e.g., Isa. 55:10–11), but it is idolatry to consider it the source of life. It is vital that we understand as much about water as we can, and my own field of science was particularly the study and control of water (hydraulic engineering), but water did not create life. Instead, God used it to destroy life in the great flood (in fact, my own main purpose in doing graduate work in hydraulics and hydrology was to understand better the significance of the flood in opposing evolutionism).

In the new earth, there will be "no more sea" (Rev. 21:1), but there will be forever flowing "a pure river of water of life, clear as crystal, proceeding out of the throne of God and of the Lamb" (Rev. 22:1), and that will be all the water we shall ever need. In the meantime, the final invitation of the Bible is: "Whosoever will, let him take the water of life freely" (Rev. 22:17).

Endnotes

1   Richard Dawkins, "Is Science a Religion?" *The Humanist*, vol. 57, Jan/Feb 1997, p. 26.
2   Rob Wipond, "The World Is Round (and Other Mythologies of Modern Science)," *The Humanist*, vol. 58, March/April 1998, p. 10–11.

3   Keith Stewart Thomson, "Natural Selection and Evolution's Smoking Gun," *American Scientist*, vol. 85, Nov/Dec 1997, p. 516.

4   Robert L. Carroll, *Patterns and Processes of Vertebrate Paleontology* (Cambridge, UK: Cambridge University Press, 1997), p. 391.

5   David L. Wheeler, "An Eclectic Biologist Argues that Humans Are Not Evolution's Most Important Results: Bacteria Are," *Chronicle of Higher Education*, vol. LXIII, Sept. 6, 1996, p. A-23.

6   Thomson, "Natural Selection and Evolution's Smoking Gun," p. 518.

7   Ibid.

8   See Henry M. Morris, *That Their Words May Be Used Against Them* (Green Forest, AR: Master Books, 1997), 487 pages, for almost 3,000 quotes of this nature from evolutionists.

9   Robert Wipond, "The World Is Round (and Other Mythologies of Modern Science)," p. 9.

10 Edward J. Larson and Larry Witham, "Leading Scientists Still Reject God," *Nature*, vol. 394, July 23, 1998, p. 313.

11 Christopher Rawlings, editor, *The Voyage of Charles Darwin* (BBC: UK, 1978), Charles Darwin autobiography reprinted. See "A Scientist's Thoughts on Religion," *New Scientist*, vol. 158, April 18, 1998, p. 15.

12 Jonathan Knight, "Top Translator," *New Scientist*, vol. 158, April 18, 1998, p. 15.

13 Ibid.

14 Lynn Margulis and Dorion Sagan, *Slanted Truths: Essays on Gaia, Symbiosis and Evolution* (New York: Springer-Verlag, 1997), p. 100.

15 Ibid., p. 270.

16 Charles C. Gillispie, "E. O. Wilson's Consilience: A Noble Unifying Vision, Grandly Expressed," review of *Consilience: the Unity of Knowledge* by Edward O. Wilson (New York: Alfred Knopf, 1998), in *American Scientist*, vol. 86, May/June 1998, p. 282.

17 Ibid., p. 281.

18 Martin Brookes, "May the Best Man Win," *New Scientist*, vol. 158, April 11, 1998, p. 51.

19 G. A. Dover (1988), cited in Margulis and Sagan, *Slanted Truths: Essays on Gaia, Symbiosis and Evolution*, p. 271.

20 Neil Shubin, "Evolutionary Cut and Paste," *Nature*, vol. 394, July 2, 1998, p. 12.

21 Ibid., p. 13.

22 Eugenie C. Scott, letter to "Fellow Scientists: National Center for Science Education, Inc.," April 1997, p. 4.

23 Rebecca Zacks, "What Are They Thinking?" *Scientific American*, October 1997, p. 34.

24 Eugenie C. Scott, "Monkey Business," *The Sciences*, January/February 1996, p. 21.

25 Ibid., p. 24.

26 Quoted in "Science and God: A Warming Trend?" by Gregg Easterbrook, *Science*, vol. 277, August 15, 1997, p. 891–892.

27 Richard Storey, "A Plea to College Biology Professors," *American Biology Teacher*, vol. 59, February 1997, p. 69.

28 Scott, "Monkey Business," p. 25.

29 Easterbrook, "Science and God: A Warming Trend?" p. 890.

30 Margulis and Sagan, *Slanted Truths: Essays on Gaia, Symbiosis, and Evolution*, p. 265.

31 Hannes Alfvèn, "Memoirs of a Dissident Scientist," *American Scientist*, vol. 76, May/June 1988, p. 250.

32 Philip H. Abelson, "Bigotry in Science," *Science*, vol. 144, April 24, 1964, p. 373.

33 Margulis and Sagan, *Slanted Truths: Essays on Gaia, Symbiosis, and Evolution*, p. 279. Although Dorion Sagan is listed as co-author of this book, Dr. Margulis was author of the chapter containing the quotes cited in this article. She is the mother of Dorion Sagan and the first wife of the late Carl Sagan.

34 Thomas Johnson, "Abortion, the Sexual Revolution and Post-modernism," *The Outlook*, vol. 48, February 1998, p. 3. Emphasis is his.

35 Matt Cartmill, "Oppressed by Evolution," *Discover,* March 1998, p. 78.

36 Ibid., p. 80–81.

37 Barbara Ehrenreich and Janet McIntosh, "Biology under Attack," *The Nation*, June 9, 1997, p. 13.

38 Cartmill, "Oppressed by Evolution," p. 80.

39 Margulis and Sagan, *Slanted Truths: Essays on Gaia, Symbiosis, and Evolution*, p. 190, section by Dorion Sagan, son of atheist Carl Sagan and Gaian evolutionist Lynn Margulis.

40 Ehrenreich and McIntosh, "Biology under Attack," p. 16.

41 Meryl Davids, "An Evolutionary Urge to Submerge?" *New Age Journal,* January/February 1995, p. 19.

42 Lyall Watson, "The Water People," *Science Digest*, vol. 90, May 1982, p. 44.

43 Davids, "An Evolutionary Urge to Submerge?" p. 20.

44 For more detailed treatment of this intriguing topic, please see my book, *The Long War Against God* (Grand Rapids, MI: Baker Book House, 1989), chapter 5.

Chapter V

The Bondage of Corruption

here is a strange and dark contrast between the world created by God in the beginning and the world in which we live today. When God finished His creation, the record says that "God saw everything that he had made, and behold, it was very good" (Gen. 1:31). Today, however, as the apostle Paul says: "We know that the whole creation groaneth and travaileth in pain together until now" (Rom. 8:22), and he even calls it "this present evil world" (Gal. 1:4).

As discussed in chapter 3, the reason why there is evil and suffering and death in the world is because there is sin in the world and God's curse is upon the world. It is enchained in "the bondage of corruption" (Rom. 8:21) and old Lucifer has become "the god of this world" (2 Cor. 4:4).

The divine curse extends throughout the whole creation, even to the very elements, "the ground" (Gen. 3:17), out of which God had formed all things, even the flesh of the animals and man (Gen. 2:7, 19). God had formed man out of "the dust of the ground," but now, under the curse, everything including man, is in the process of returning back to "the dust of the ground" (Gen. 2:7; 3:19). Man had been placed in dominion over the whole creation, so now his sin has caused God's curse to fall on that dominion, and the bondage of corruption (meaning "decay," "disintegration," drifting down toward death) permeates everything.

This downward tendency is so pervasive that it eventually became recognized as a universal law of nature. Every system, every process, and the entire creation itself are all heading downhill toward disintegration and death.

The Bible and Thermodynamics

This phrase may seem at first almost like an oxymoron. What does the Bible have to do with thermodynamics? Thermodynamics is a particular field of science, along with engineering, physics, and chemistry, and one might justifiably wonder what possible bearing it could have on the Bible. However, thermodynamics is not merely an isolated branch of science, but actually provides the basic framework within which we must study every science. Since the Bible deals with God's purpose in creation and describes that creation, it really is quite natural that there is a very real correlation between the Bible and thermodynamics.

The word "thermodynamics" comes from two Greek words meaning "heat" and "energy." Technically speaking, thermodynamics is the study of energy relationships, especially heat energy. The terms and the laws of thermodynamics were developed beginning about 200 years ago in connection with the study and development of the steam engine. Although these laws originated in a particular field of technology, it was soon realized that they are universal laws and that the science of thermodynamics is really a universal science.

The word "energy" is a somewhat obtuse term, but it has the connotation of the capacity for accomplishing work, for making things happen, or for keeping processes going. There are many different kinds of energy — electrical, magnetic, heat, light, sound, chemical, nuclear, and others. Each of these different types of energy is measured in a certain way, but about 150 years ago it was realized that basically all the different kinds of energy are essentially equivalent. This was worked out by such scientists as Kelvin, Joule, Carnot, Clausius, and others, when it was found that heat energy could be converted into work and other forms of energy.

The First Law of Thermodynamics

It is now accepted as a universal axiom of science, indeed as the very first law of science, that all forms of energy are basically the same and can be converted one into another, and that in the process of conversion from one into another, no energy is created or destroyed. This is the law of the conservation of energy, also known as the "first law of thermodynamics." Every process, whether it is a natural or an artificial process, involves energy conversion. Everything that happens, physically speaking, is simply a conversion of energy from one type into another. For example, electrical energy in the wires is converted into light energy in the bulb. Chemical energy stored in the gasoline is transformed into mechanical energy in the wheels of the automobile. And so on.

We know, furthermore, that even matter itself is basically a form of energy, for we can convert matter into other forms of energy, as in such processes as nuclear fission. Now we have these tremendous reservoirs of energy in the earth, exchanging with one another, and keeping the various processes of life and the physical world going. Yet all of it is being conserved — none is being created and none is being destroyed.

Physically speaking, essentially all the earth's energy (except radioactivity) comes originally from the sun. In the processes of thermo-nuclear fusion presumably taking place on the sun, the sun radiates energy and liberates tremendous quantities of heat, light, and radiation. Some of this reaches the earth. This radiant energy from the sun causes ocean waters to evaporate, later to return as rain on the land, sets the air in circulation in the atmosphere, through the process of photosynthesis causes plants to grow, and in general is responsible for almost all of earth's biological and geological processes.

All of this is implied in that great creation chapter, Psalm 19. This psalm starts out by proclaiming that "The heavens declare the glory of God; and the firmament showeth his handiwork." It continues, "In them hath he set a tabernacle for the sun, Which is as a bridegroom coming out of his chamber, rejoicing as a strong man to run a race. His going forth is from the end of the heaven, and his circuit unto the ends of it" (Ps. 19:4–6).

Some critics have called this "pre-scientific" language. However, since all motion is relative, it is just as scientific to write in terms of the earth standing fixed and the sun moving, as vice versa. Actually, the sun does have a vast "circuit," if one really wishes to press the point, a circuit that would require 230 million years to complete. The sun does move through the heavens, and its radiant energy completely inundates the earth. The Psalmist also says, "There is nothing hid from the heat thereof" (Ps. 19:6). One might properly paraphrase this as saying, "There is nothing on earth unaffected by the radiant heat energy from the sun." The Bible here surely speaks of thermodynamics!

The Psalmist then compares the written revelation in Scripture to the natural revelation contained in the heavens and in the thermodynamic processes. The next verse says "The law of the Lord is perfect, converting the soul: the testimony of the Lord is sure, making wise the simple. The statutes of the Lord are right, rejoicing the heart: the commandment of the Lord is pure, enlightening the eyes. The fear of the Lord is clean, enduring for ever: the judgments of the Lord are true and righteous altogether" (Ps. 19:7–9). Here we have six different names for the Word of God, the emphasis being on its utter perfection and completeness. As the sun provides all the earth's energy for its physical processes, so the Word of God provides all the spiritual energy needed for everlasting life.

Thus, the earth's energy comes from the sun's heat, which maintains all the multitudinous geological, biological, chemical, and physiological processes. In the study of these processes (which is what science is) we find that all of them can be included under the concepts of thermodynamics, of heat, of energy, and of power.

The first and most basic law of science is the law of energy conservation, the first law of thermodynamics, which states that no energy is being created or annihilated in the present world. In every process the energy which goes in and the energy which comes out, and the changes taking place in between, all add up algebraically to zero. There is no change in the total. The energy of the universe, as far as we can tell, is a constant.

Now the question is: why is this so? This is not merely a mathematical generalization. This first law has always proved to be true experimentally: in observations it always works this way. It is an empirical law, and no exception has ever been found. Scientifically, we know it is true, but don't know why. The only explanation is given in the Bible. The first law of thermodynamics is found in the Bible, not in scientific terminology, of course, but nevertheless it is there.

There are tremendous reservoirs of energy and matter in the physical universe, and according to the first law they are not now being created. If they were created in the past, if ever there was a beginning, it must have been by processes that are not now in existence. Thus, science in its study of these present processes cannot possibly tell us anything about creation. These processes are all conservative processes — none of them are creative processes.

This is exactly what the Bible says. It describes the events of creation in the first chapter of Genesis, giving the order of things created, and then in Genesis 1:31, it stresses the completed perfection of the entire creation.

Then, in Genesis 2:1, we read, "Thus the heavens and the earth were finished, and all the host of them." The heavens, the earth, and everything in them were finished in six days. "On the seventh day God ended his work which he had made; and he rested on the seventh day . . . from *all* his work which God created and made" (Gen. 2:2–3). Whatever distinction may exist between His work of "creating" and His work of "making," we note that all of it was accomplished and completed in the six days.

We read also in Exodus 20:11, "For in six days the Lord made heaven and earth, the sea, and all that in them is, and rested the seventh day." Whatever processes God used for bringing into existence all these tremendous reservoirs of power and energy in the universe, He stopped using and He rested. The processes He now uses are processes of providence, maintenance, and sustenance — processes of *conservation*. He is now "upholding all things by the Word of his power" (Heb. 1:3). He is now conserving all things, but He is not creating anything except through occasional miraculous acts. This is the first law of science — that nothing is now being created!

The Second Law

One might still say, however, that the universe has always existed, that it never had a beginning. Basically, this is the premise of evolution. All ancient pagan systems, as well as modern Darwinism evolution, begin with the premise of the eternity of matter in one form or another. All non-biblical systems are thus fundamentally evolutionary systems. It does seem possible, on the basis of the first law, to say there was never a beginning and that the universe has always been as it is now.

However, we then run into the law of the increase of entropy, and this law is equally universal. This is the second law of thermodynamics. So far as we know, there is no exception to either law. They do not follow from mathematical proof, but they are universal facts of observation, and have been verified many thousands of times. From the smallest scale to the largest, no exceptions have been found. If there can be defined such a thing as a "law" in science, these two laws would meet that definition.

The second law states not only that the universe is being conserved, but also that it is decaying. Every process operates in such a way that to some degree the system decays, or runs down. Every system tends to become disordered. Speaking in thermodynamic terms, the quantity called "entropy" tends to increase. This entity can be defined in various ways. In applied thermodynamics it has to do with the irreversible flow of heat, but more broadly speaking, it is basically a probability function which describes the state of disorder of a system or process. And the second law says that disorder or randomness tends to increase. Speaking in terms of energy, the availability of energy to do further useful work decreases. This is true of every system and every process without exception. Ultimately everything will run down to a uniform temperature level, and the universe will die a "heat death." As this has not yet happened, the universe in its present form cannot possibly be infinitely old. Therefore, there must also have been a beginning.

The first law thus tells us the universe cannot have created itself: the second law tells us it must have been created. The only reasonable conclusion scientifically is that there must have been a creation at some time in the past by processes that are not now operating. The only way to account for such a creation is to allow for a Creator. Philosophically one might hypothesize that these present processes did not exist in the past, or that the universe is oscillating back and forth, or that there is a continuous generation of hydrogen from nothing out in space, or some other speculative suggestion. But such ideas are certainly not *science*! Scientifically, the inexorable conclusion of the two basic laws of science is that there must have been a creation at some time in the past.

The Triune Creation

These two laws of thermodynamics, and the concepts of energy and entropy, also have other implications. We shall briefly consider some of them under a three-fold category — the three basic types of science: physical, biological, and social.

It is significant that the three acts of creation recorded in Genesis 1 fall into these three categories. There is a slight distinction between God's work of "creating" and His work of "making." By "creating" is meant calling into existence from nothing by His own infinite power. The process of "making," on the other hand, means taking a created entity and organizing it into a higher state or order. God not only called things into existence out of nothing except His own omnipotence, but also He took this created material and organized it to its final perfect state.

Three definite acts of creation are mentioned, as marked by the use of the Hebrew verb, *bara*, "to create." One has to do with the physical world. "In the beginning God created the heavens and the earth." This is nothing less than the space-mass-time continuum that is our universe. The "beginning" is time, the "heavens" are space, and the earth in its original "without form and void" state was basically matter. Since the stars were made only on the fourth day (Gen. 1:14), the physical universe originally consisted only of the earth in its primitive form. In the first verse of Genesis, we thus have the statement of God's creation of the physical cosmos. Physical science is the study of the physical world.

The second act of creation is mentioned in the statement that God created great whales and every "living creature" (Gen. 1:21). Here God created animal life, or one might say "sentient" life. This is studied in the biological science.

God's third act of creation was to create man in His own image. This is different from biological life. This is spiritual life, and this also required God's direct creative power. We study man — his behavior, thoughts, acts, etc. — in the social sciences. Man, being made not only of the common physical substance and the common biological life but also being created in God's image, possesses a spiritual life. Man thus has a physical aspect, a biological aspect, and a spiritual aspect. In the complete study of man we need all three sciences, or fields of science — the physical, biological, and social sciences.

When man sinned, not only did God pronounce a curse on man himself but also on man's whole dominion (Gen. 3:17) — the physical universe, the biological universe, and the spiritual or social universe. This means that the study of the processes of nature under the concepts of thermodynamics must, at least to some extent, be controlled by the fact that this whole creation and all of its processes have been brought under the curse of God. Romans 8:21 says it is under the "bondage of corruption" (literally, "decay").

As we study these different fields of science, we find that the laws of thermodynamics, the first of which has to do with a finished creation and the second with disorder entering that creation, have universal applicability.

Physical Sciences

Let us take the physical sciences first. Psalm 102:25–27 is quoted in Hebrews 1:10–12: "Thou, Lord, in the beginning hast laid the foundation of the earth; and the heavens are the works of thine hands: They shall perish; but thou remainest; and they all shall wax old as doth a garment; And as a vesture shalt thou fold them up, and they shall be changed: but thou art the same, and thy years shall not fail." There are numerous other references in the Bible to the same effect. This whole physical creation, the heavens and the earth, are now in the process of getting old. They are wearing out. The sun is sending out great quantities of energy, but someday it will burn out. So will all the other stars. Heaven and earth are passing away, but Jesus says His Word will not pass away (Matt. 24:35).

This phenomenon of decay, of increased entropy, of increased probability, proceeding from a state of high organization and complexity to a state of low organization and complexity, is essentially the condition that the second law of thermodynamics describes. It has universal applicability in every field of physical science.

That is why, for example, in engineering, it is impossible to make a perpetual motion machine. Many people have tried, and large numbers of ingenuous devices have been sent to the patent office. Without exception they are thrown out, however, because perpetual motion machines are known to be impossible according to the second law of thermodynamics. One cannot get something out of nothing: in fact, he cannot even keep what he has, for it will eventually run down or wear out.

This is also why we cannot design a machine that is 100 percent efficient. We try to design our processes and our machines to be as efficient as possible, in an attempt to approach that 100 percent, but we can't make it. Inevitably, some of the energy that goes into the process will be degraded through friction into low-level heat energy, no longer available for useful work.

Not only is this principle true in the processes of energy conversion, but it is even true in the structure of matter itself. Here the term "configurational entropy" is used. The crystal structure of solids, for example, steel or a similar substance, ideally should be perfect in its structure. We normally visualize a crystal as being of an ideal geometric shape. Actually, however, there is no such thing as a perfect crystal; all of them have defects. In terms of God's perfect creation, it is hard to understand why every material in the world is defective. There are many kinds of defects: impurities enter, or there are vacancies where an atom ought to be, or something else. Inevitably, there are defects in every solid, and the location and character of these defects determine the particular strength or other properties of the material. The configurational entropy is simply a measure of the degree of disorder in such a structure.

Sometimes people say the second law of thermodynamics really is statistical; it is possible in a particular instance for the entropy to decrease; it need not always increase. It can indeed be defined that way, particularly in dealing with atomic structure. There are so many different particles that one can define the total entropy as the sum of the entropies of all the individual particles; thus maybe the entropy of one is decreasing while the rest are increasing. It may even be theoretically possible under certain rare conditions to have a decrease of entropy of the whole system.

But when we try to put numbers on these probabilities, we find they are so infinitesimally small, they are quite negligible. No one has actually seen or measured an automatic increase in organization, or functioning complexity. This is strictly in the realm of statistical theory.

And now modern nuclear physicists are finding evidence that the very protons of matter itself are decaying. As the Scripture says, "the whole creation . . . travaileth in pain" (Rom. 8:22).

Biological Sciences

People occasionally object that the laws of thermodynamics apply only to physical systems and therefore have no applicability to biology. But of course they do apply to biology. As a matter of fact, the biologist is the one who is most insistent in saying that all life processes ultimately can be understood in terms of physics and chemistry. He eschews the concept of vitalism quite vigorously. Chemistry and physics are certainly controlled by thermodynamics, and therefore so are biological processes.

There is a sense of course in which the biological system is not merely a physical system. The "soul" or the consciousness is a factor of life which is a separate created entity according to Genesis 1:21. This aspect of life cannot be brought into equivalence with the other types of energy as some have tried to do. As far as the actual structure and processes of animal bodies are concerned, however, they very definitely obey the laws of thermodynamics. This appears in many different applications. The most obvious example is that every individual eventually dies.

Sometimes the growth of an organism is erroneously used as an illustration of evolution. Thus, a human develops all the way from an embryo to an adult, showing an innate principle of growth and development. But this really doesn't refute the second law because this growth of the structure of a baby is predicated on the very high organization and complex structure of the germ cell that it has to begin with. It is all sort of an automated arrangement, built up from the template and feedback mechanisms received from the parents. It is implicit from the very start.

The same thing is true in the growth of a crystal. It is basic in the atomic structure to begin with. Even this apparent superficial growth and development is only local and temporary. Though the crystal tends to grow, if it contains defects (and it will), it will eventually disintegrate and crumble and return to the dust. Whenever there is apparent growth of order, there must be a source for that growth to begin with. There must be an outside ordering source of energy or information that causes the apparent growth, and even then it is only local and temporary. Eventually it passes away.

So it is with an individual — he ages and finally dies. From the time he is born, he begins to die. One can also extend this principle to larger biological categories, not to just an individual, but to an entire species. The process by which species change and which supposedly explains evolution, namely mutations, is basically a process which operates very definitely within the second law of thermodynamics. This law, as we have noted, states that all systems left to themselves tend to become disordered.

A mutation is basically just that. We have a wonderful highly organized system in the genetic structure of the germ cell, but when that system is penetrated by a disturbing agent, such as radiations or mutagenic chemicals, then a random change in the order of the system may occur. It can be shown, and it is also intuitively obvious, that any highly ordered system subjected to a random change will, to an exceedingly high degree of probability, be less ordered after the change than it was before. A mutation, which is a sudden random change in the germ cell, will naturally cause a decrease in order in that system, and this will show up in the form of deleterious characteristics in the organism which experiences it. Probably it will cause its death. It almost certainly will be harmful or at best neutral.

This is why geneticists have such an exceedingly difficult time showing any kind of mutation which is favorable to the creature which experiences it in its natural environment. Even the most insistent evolutionist will recognize and admit that 99.9 percent of all known mutations are harmful. A mutation represents a random change in a highly ordered system, and this is in accord with the second law of thermodynamics, that an increase in entropy will decrease the order of that system.

But then to say this is the mechanism by which evolution occurred is wishful thinking at best. There certainly is no proof for it. If by the rarest chance one of these mutations did cause a higher order in the genetic system experiencing it, so that it became better equipped than before (in other words, "evolved"), then the probability that the next mutation will cause a still higher order, is even lower. This follows because the probability that a random variation will increase the order of a system decreases as its initial degree of order increases. This can be shown both logically and statistically. To say that the tremendous complexity of the ordered world of life has arisen from a common ancestor by chance mutation and natural selection is thus utterly fantastic. The evolutionist must believe in magic to believe this!

The only real evidence for evolution is the geological record of the fossils. Biologically, mutations and genetics certainly do not prove evolution. There is some biological variation, of course, but all the evidence of biological change that we actually observe can easily be explained in terms of variation within the created kind. God has provided, in the genetic system, a tremendous potential for adaptation to new environmental situations. We have different varieties of dogs and different varieties of cats. But we have nothing between a dog and cat, or between a horse and elephant, or between an ape and man. When a real change does take place, such as a genuine mutation, this is always in a downward direction, in accordance with the law of entropy.

This is why even in the record of the fossils, we have many kinds of animals that have become extinct. We never find evidence of the gradual development of a new basic kind, but we do have many evidences of extinct kinds. Even in historic times, many animals have become extinct. In the fossil record we have such animals as the dinosaurs, the sabre-tooth tigers, and the great cave bears. All these lived and thrived once, but because of decay processes of some form or another, they died out. There is also the evidence of alleged vestigial organs in animals still living. These are all indications of the universal reign of the second law of thermodynamics.

Social Sciences

Let us consider also the social sciences. It seems this law of decay and death can even be applied to man's culture and behavior. Again and again we find evidence in history of an outside source of spiritual or moral power coming into a society and civilization, causing its development for a time. Then it begins to feed on itself and goes downward. So we have the rise and fall of one civilization after another.

Language has decayed. One may argue about this, but there is a compelling case for holding that the English of the King James Bible, for example, is of a higher order of complexity and applicability than our modern English. People working with savage tribes tell us the structure of the language of these jungle tribes is much more complex than that of our civilized languages.

One can make, of course, quite a case for the decay of religion and morals. Everywhere in the realm of society are found indications of this law of decay and death. Everyone knows from experience that if he lets himself go naturally, he will go downward. One does not automatically improve. To go up, one must take hold of himself and work and make an effort, drawing on information and energy outside himself. Paul in fact calls this a "law," when he says in the Book of Romans, "I find then a law, that, when I would do good, evil is present with me. . . . But I see another law in my members, warring against the law of my mind" (Rom. 7:21–23). He describes a law of sin and death that is in his very being. These are the spiritual and moral implications of these laws of conservation and decay.

Remember, however, that in all these references (and many others to which we could point) in Scripture, that although the testimony uniformly is that the world is getting old and running down, and that all flesh is like grass, God himself is not bound by these laws. He established them and His Word shall endure. God can still create new energy and new order and can still arrest and reverse the processes of disintegration, when he so wills.

It is interesting to study the miracles of the Bible. It seems there are two kinds of miracles — the miracles of providence and the miracles of creation. Miracles of providence are rare statistical fluctuations of natural processes, but still in conformity with the basic laws (such as Elijah's three-year drought, for example). But miracles of creation set aside one or both of the two laws. Thus, God creates wine from water; He creates thousands of servings of bread from a few small loaves; or He restores the dead to life. Such creative miracles testify to the fact that Jesus is the Christ, the Son of God, because only God can create (John 20:30–31).

It is a true miracle when a person who is going ever downward suddenly is regenerated and given a new life, and through the power of God now goes in a completely different direction. This regeneration is a miracle of creation (2 Cor. 5:17). It is directly opposed to the second law of thermodynamics and thus testifies to the presence and power of God.

Finally, the whole physical creation, as Paul says in Romans 8:19–22, will be regenerated: "For the earnest expectation of the creation waiteth for the manifestation of the sons of God. For the creation was made subject to vanity, not willingly, but by reason of him who hath subjected the same in hope, Because the creation itself also shall be delivered from the bondage of corruption into the glorious liberty of the children of God. For we know that the whole creation groaneth and travaileth in pain together until now."

When Christ comes, He will set all things right and make all things new. The law of sin, decay, and death will be replaced with a law of everlasting righteousness and endless life. Then His purpose in creation will finally be accomplished.

The Strange Science of Chaos

However this wonderful inference from thermodynamics when understood in light of Scripture is very unwelcome to doctrinaire evolutionists. Consequently, there has recently arisen an attempt to negate this conclusion by means of a new science abroad in the land — the science of chaos! This science has spawned a new vocabulary — "fractals," "bifurcation," "the butterfly effect," "strange attractors," and "dissipative structures," among others. Its advocates are even claiming it to be as important as relativity and quantum mechanics in 20th-century physics. It is also being extended into many scientific fields and even into social studies, economics, and human behavior problems. But as a widely read popularization of chaos studies puts it:

Where chaos begins, classical science stops.[1]

There are many phenomena that depend on so many variables as to defy description in terms of quantitative mathematics. Yet such systems — things like the turbulent hydraulics of a waterfall — do seem to exhibit some kind of order in their apparently chaotic tumbling, and chaos theory has been developed to try to quantify the order in this chaos.

Even very regular linear relationships will eventually become irregular and disorderly, if left to themselves long enough. Thus, an apparently chaotic phenomenon may well represent a breakdown in an originally orderly system, even under the influence of very minute perturbations. This has become known as the "Butterfly Effect." Gleick defines this term as follows:

Butterfly Effect: The notion that a butterfly stirring the air in Peking can transform storm systems next month in New York.[2]

There is no doubt that small causes can combine with others and contribute to major effects — effects that typically seem to be chaotic. That is, order can easily degenerate into chaos. It is even conceivable that, if one could probe the chaotic milieu deeply enough, he could discern to some extent the previously ordered system from which it originated. Chaos theory is attempting to do just that, and also to find more complex patterns of order in the overall chaos.

These complex patterns are called "fractals," which are defined as "geometrical shapes whose structure is such that magnification by a given factor reproduces the original object."[3] If that definition doesn't adequately clarify the term, try this one: "spatial forms of fractional dimensions."[4] Regardless of how they are defined, examples cited of fractals are said to be numerous — from snowflakes to coast lines to star clusters.

The discovery that there may still be some underlying order — instead of complete randomness — in chaotic systems is, of course, still perfectly consistent with the laws of thermodynamics. The trouble is that many wishful thinkers in this field have started assuming that chaos can also somehow generate higher order — evolution in particular. This idea is being hailed as the solution to the problem of how the increasing complexity required by evolution could overcome the disorganizing process demanded by entropy. The famous second law of thermodynamics — also called the law of increasing entropy — notes that every system — whether closed or open — at least tends to decay. The universe itself is "running down," heading toward an ultimate "heat death," and this has heretofore been an intractable problem for evolutionists.

> The grim picture of cosmic evolution was in sharp contrast with the evolutionary thinking among nineteenth century biologists, who observed that the living universe evolves from disorder to order, toward states of ever increasing complexity.[5]

The author of the above quote is Fritjof Capra, a physicist at the University of California at Berkeley, one of the prominent scientists involved in the New Age movement, which tends to associate evolutionary advance with catastrophic revolutions. He believes that, in some mysterious fashion, chaos can produce evolutionary advance.

Paul Davies, the prolific British writer on astronomy, is another. He, like Capra, is not an atheistic evolutionist but a pantheistic evolutionist. He has faith that order can come out of chaos, that the increasing disorder specified by the entropy law can somehow generate the increasing complexity implied by evolution.

> We now see how it is possible for the universe to increase both organization and entropy at the same time. The optimistic and pessimistic arrows of time can co-exist: the universe can display creative unidirectional progress even in the face of the second law.[6]

And just how has this remarkable possibility been shown? Capra answers as follows:

> It was the great achievement of Ilya Prigogine, who used a new mathematics to reevaluate the second law by radically rethinking traditional scientific views of order and disorder, which enabled him to resolve unambiguously the two contradictory nineteenth-century views of evolution.[7]

Prigogine is a Belgian scientist who received a Nobel Prize in 1977 for his work on the thermodynamics of systems operating dynamically under non-equilibrium conditions. He argued (mathematically, not experimentally) that systems that were far from equilibrium, with a high flow-through of energy, could produce a higher degree of order.

Many others have also hailed Prigogine as the scientific savior of evolutionism, which otherwise seemed to be precluded by the entropy law. A UNESCO scientist evaluated his work as follows:

> What I see Prigogine doing is giving legitimization to the process of evolution — self-organization under conditions of change.[8]

The assumed importance of his "discovery" is further emphasized by Coveny:

> From an epistemological viewpoint, the contributions of Prigogine's Brussels School are unquestionably of original importance.[9]

Capra elaborates further:

> In classical thermodynamics, the dissipation of energy in heat transfer, friction, and the like was always associated with waste. Prigogine's concept of a dissipative structure introduced a radical change in this view by showing that in open systems dissipation becomes a source of order.[10]

The fact is, however, that except in a very weak and temporary sense, Prigogine has not shown that dissipation of energy in an open system produces order. In the chaotic behavior of a system in which a very large energy dissipation is taking place, certain temporary structures (he calls them "dissipative structures") form and then soon decay. They have never been shown — even mathematically — to reproduce themselves or to generate still higher degrees of order.

He used the example of small vortices in a cup of hot coffee. A similar example would be the much larger "vortex" in a tornado or hurricane. These might be viewed as "structures" and to appear to be "ordered," but they are soon gone. What they leave in their wake is not a higher degree of organized complexity, but a higher degree of dissipation and disorganization.

And yet evolutionists are now arguing that such chaos somehow generates a higher stage of evolution! Prigogine has even co-authored a book entitled, *Order Out of Chaos.*

> In far from equilibrium conditions, we may have transformation from disorder, from thermal chaos, into order.[11]

It is very significant, however, that all of his Nobel-Prize winning discussions have been philosophical and mathematical — not experimental! He himself has admitted that he has not worked in a laboratory for years. Such phenomena as he and others are trying to call evolution from chaos to order may be manipulated on paper or on a computer screen, but not in real life.

Not even the first, and absolutely critical, step in the evolutionary process—that of the self-organization of non-living molecules into self-replicating molecules—can be explained in this way. Prigogine admits:

> The problem of biological order involves the transition from the molecular activity to the supermolecular order of the cell. This problem is far from being solved.[12]

He then makes the naive claim that, since life "appeared" on earth very early in geologic history, *it must have been* (!) "the result of spontaneous self-organization." But he acknowledges some uncertainty about this remarkable conclusion.

> However, we must admit that we remain far from any quantitative theory.[13]

Very far, in fact — and even farther from any experimental proof!

With regard to the claim that the "order" appearing in fractals somehow contributes to evolution, a new book devoted to what the author is pleased to call "the science of self-organized criticality," we note the following admission:

> In the popular literature, one finds the subjects of chaos and fractal geometry linked together again and again, despite the fact that they have little to do with each other. . . . In short, chaos theory cannot explain complexity.[14]

The strange idea is currently being widely promoted that, in the assumed four-billion-year history of life on the earth, evolution has proceeded by means of long periods of stasis, punctuated by brief periods of massive extinctions. Then rapid evolutionary emergence of organisms of higher complexity came out of the chaotic milieu causing the extinction.

> On the other hand, a catastrophic extinction of global biotas might negate the effectiveness of many survival mechanisms that evolved during background conditions. Simultaneously, such a crisis might eliminate genetically and ecologically diverse taxa worldwide. Only a few species would be expected to survive and seed subsequent evolutionary radiations. This scenario requires high levels of macroevolution and explosive radiation to account for the recovery of basic ecosystems within 1–2 m.y. after Phanerozoic mass extinctions.[15]

Such notions come not from any empirical evidence but solely from philosophical speculations *based on lack of evidence*! "Since there is no evidence that evolution proceeded gradually, it must have occurred chaotically!" This seems to be the idea.

If one wants to believe by blind faith that order can arise spontaneously from chaos, it is still a free country. But please don't call it science!

The fact still remains, despite all equivocations, that the scientifically impregnable laws of thermodynamics point, not to evolution, but to God and special creation of all things in the beginning.

Endnotes

1   James Gleick, *Chaos — Making a New Science* (New York: Viking Press, 1987), p. 3.
2   Ibid., p. 8.
3   *McGraw-Hill Dictionary of Scientific and Technical Terms,* 4th ed. (New York: McGraw-Hill, 1989), p. 757.
4   Stan G. Smith, "Chaos: Making a New Heresy," *Creation Research Society Quarterly*, vol. 30, March 1994, p. 196.
5   Fritjof Capra, *The Web of Life* (New York: Anchor Books, 1996), p. 48.
6   Paul Davies, *The Cosmic Blueprint* (New York: Simon and Schuster, 1988), p. 85.
7   Capra, op. cit., p. 49.
8   As quoted by Wil Lepkowski in "The Social Thermodynamics of Ilya Prigogine," *Chemical and Engineering News* (New York, Bantam, 1979), p. 30.
9   Peter V. Coveny, "The Second Law of Thermodynamics: Entropy, Irreversibility, and Dynamics," *Nature*, vol. 333, June 2, 1988, p. 414.
10 Capra, op. cit., p. 89.
11 Ilya Prigogine and Isabelle Stengers, *Order Out of Chaos* (New York: Bantam Books, 1984), p. 12.
12 Ibid., p. 175.
13 Ibid., p. 176.
14 Per Bak, *How Nature Works: The Science of Self-Organized Criticality* (New York, Springer-Verlag, 1996), p. 31.
15 Erle G. Kauffman and Douglas H. Erwin, "Surviving Mass Extinctions," *Geotimes*, vol. 40, March 1995, p. 15.

Chapter VI

The Wild Blue Yonder

volutionary scientists and philosophers in general cannot be content with *organic* evolution. They must have *total* evolution. The very purpose of evolutionism is to explain everything naturalistically, without any supernatural injections into the process by a transcendent agent of any kind. Speculative naturalistic evolutionary processes must explain not only the origin of species but also the origin of life itself and even of the entire cosmos.

So we have theories of cosmic evolution, stellar evolution, galactic evolution, planetary evolution, and finally abiogenesis, all as precursors to organic evolution. If — as noted in chapter 3 — discussion of the origin of species is mainly rhetoric rather than real scientific evidence, then what can we say about theories of inorganic evolution?

It is painfully obvious that no one has ever observed this kind of evolution. Those who wish to have stars evolve or galaxies evolve or life evolve from non-life are, in the very nature of the case, limited to mathematical manipulations, computer simulations, or just plain metaphysical speculation, for they can never observe any such thing happening in the real world.

The biggest question of all is that of the origin of the universe. Various theories exist, none of which can be tested, of course, but the theory in current favor is that of the big bang, which had to precede everything else if it ever really happened. Accordingly, this chapter is centered mainly on this widely accepted theory, which is itself contrary to the laws of thermodynamics, the law of cause-and-effect, and to other scientific laws, as well as being completely contrary to the revealed Word of God. The big bang and all other theories of the origin of the great blue "yonder" are wild indeed.

The Big Bust

The notorious big bang that supposedly started our evolving cosmos was neither "big" nor a "bang." It is said simply to have evolved suddenly out of the primordial "nothing" to become an infinitesimal particle of space/time. This remarkable particle somehow contained essentially infinite energy and unlimited information which enabled it to expand rapidly into our gigantic universe with all its stars and galaxies and animals and people.

Fred Hoyle, who was deriding the whole idea while promoting his own "steady state" concept of the universe, originated the name "big bang" in 1950. Ever since, "big bang" has seemed somewhat inelegant as a name for such a sophisticated mathematical construct, so in the August 1993 issue of *Sky and Telescope* magazine, one of its editors, Timothy Ferris, announced a contest to determine a better name to replace "big bang." The three judges were to be Carl Sagan, Hugh Downs, and Ferris.

The contest proved a great public relations and media event, with over 13,000 entries from persons in 41 countries.[1] Since there are only about 10,000 professional astronomers in the whole world, this subject apparently is of considerable concern to people in general. Many remarkable and ingenious names were submitted. Some of my own favorites include: "Matter Morphosis," "The Bottom Turtle," "Super Seed," "Hubble Bubble," "Bertha D. Universe," "Doink," "Let There Be Stuff," and "Hey Looky There at That!"

With 13,000 names to choose from, it would have seemed that the three very eminent judges could have selected the best and then started an advertising promotion that would have given the great event the dignity it deserves.

But they couldn't decide and finally gave up. Astronomer Sagan explained: "There's nothing that even approaches the phrase 'Big Bang' in felicity. . . . The idea of space-time and matter expanding together and not 'into' anything may be permanently beyond reach in the universe of short and lucid phrases."

I would agree. How does one really name something as esoteric and intangible as this mathematical toy of the cosmo-physicist?

What, exactly, is meant by "quantum fluctuations of empty space," as they are saying by way of explanation? In an article intriguingly titled "Everything for Nothing," a theoretical physicist at the Institute for Advanced Studies in Austin, Texas, notes that Alexander Vilenkin of Tufts University "proposed that the universe is created by quantum tunneling from literally nothing into the something we call the universe. Although highly speculative, these models indicate the physicists find themselves turning again to the void and fluctuations therein for their answers."[2]

Highly speculative indeed! Astronomer Robert Oldershaw of Dartmouth College has some pithy comments about all this. "First, the big bang is treated as an unexplainable event without a cause. Secondly, the big bang could not explain convincingly how matter got organized into lumps (galaxies and clusters of galaxies). And thirdly, it did not predict that for the universe to be held together in the way it is, more than 90 percent of the universe would have been in the form of some strange unknown dark form of matter."[3]

It does seem that science is becoming quite squishy if it has to salvage its theory of cosmic evolution by assuming that 90 percent of all matter in the universe is invisible and unknown and strange. Oldershaw goes on to say: "Theorists also invented the concepts of inflation and cold dark matter to augment the big bang paradigm and keep it viable, but they, too, have come into increasing conflict with observations. In the light of all these problems, it is astounding that the big bang hypothesis is the only cosmological model that physicists have taken seriously."[4]

There are other cosmological models (the steady state theory, the plasma theory, etc.), but these have even more problems, which is why most cosmologists cling to the big bang. Nevertheless, as one of America's most eminent astronomers has said: "Big bang cosmology has become a bandwagon of thought that reflects faith as much as objective truth. . . . This situation is particularly worrisome because there are good reasons to think the big bang model is seriously flawed."[5]

The fact is that astronomers simply do not know *how* the universe evolved, nor do they know how stars evolved, how galaxies evolved, how clusters of galaxies evolved, how anything evolved! They do have mathematical equations that purportedly describe in part how some of these *might* have evolved, but that's a far cry from any experimental proof! It should be remembered that no one has ever actually *observed* the formation of a star or a galaxy or a universe.

In the very nature of things, this type of exercise must always be nothing but sheer speculation. Astronomer Roger Windhorst of Arizona State University has said concerning stellar evolution: "Nobody really understands how star formation proceeds; it's really remarkable."[6]

With respect to galactic evolution, a recent article is even entitled, "Seven Mysteries of Galaxies," indicating how little is really known about such things. Its authors say: "Now, in the 1990s we can still say that we are only on the verge of understanding how galaxies are born, how they work, and what roles they play in the universe at large." Furthermore, "the process by which galaxies clump together poses a significant mystery for astronomers."[7]

Lest anyone misunderstand, none of these authorities whom I have quoted are creationists in any sense of the word; they are all devout evolutionists. Nevertheless, they are honest enough to admit they don't yet have any proof.

And the sad thing about all this is that there are a number of evangelistic scientists and theologians who are willing to give up the straightforward, factual, sensible Genesis record of the creation of the universe in order to accommodate this badly flawed big bang model of evolutionary origins. Some are even trying to convince Christians that the big bang is God's work of creation, as announced in Genesis 1:1.

The leading astronomers, cosmologists, and astrophysicists harbor no such notions, of course. A few may be flirting with New Age pantheism, but not biblical creationism. Note the words of Paul Davies of England, one of the world's most influential astronomers:

> When the Big Bang theory became popular in the 1950s, many people used it to support the belief that the universe was created by God at some specific moment in the past. . . . However, this sort of armchair theology is wide of the mark. The popular idea of a God who sets the universe going like a clockwork toy and then sits back to watch, was ditched by the church in the last century.[8]

Sometimes, Christians refer to Davies or Fred Hoyle or Robert

Jastrow or some other eminent astronomer as believing in God, but their "god" is not the God of the Bible, and it is dangerous to follow them. As Davies says, it is "possible to imagine the universe coming into being from nothing entirely spontaneously. . . ." He sees "no need for an external creator."[9]

Oh, but there is a need! Without a Creator, there is no Savior and no hope for eternity. May God help us to do all we can to tell the world there is a great God who made us for himself and has even, through Christ, given us eternal life in Him!

If the evolutionists want a better name for the "big bang," I would like to suggest the "big bust." That's what it will be in a few years, anyhow, with all the evidence piling up against it.

There is not a fact of science anywhere to keep us from believing that: "By the word of the Lord were the heavens made, . . . and all the host of them by the breath of his mouth. . . . For he spake, and it was done; he commanded, and it stood fast" (Ps. 33:6–9).

In the Beginning, Hydrogen

Evolutionists have a most amazing faith. They believe that people have evolved up from the ape (or something like an ape), that apes and other mammals have evolved from reptiles, that reptiles have evolved from amphibians, amphibians from fish, fish from some unknown phylum of multi-celled invertebrates, that invertebrates in all their phyla evolved from some unknown protozoan, that some other unknown protozoan evolved from complex chemicals, and that the complex chemical elements evolved from the simplest chemical element of all, namely hydrogen.

The operative word in the above sentence is *believe*. There is no evidence for this remarkable chain of events. Apes and reptiles and vertebrates and invertebrates and chemical elements (including hydrogen) still are here in abundance, but none of them are changing into anything else. Neither are there any evolutionary transitions documented in the records of the past (despite olden tales of mermaids and centaurs), not even in the fossils which are purported to represent a billion years of earth history. This remarkable chain of events is in reality nothing but a remarkable statement of faith in the great god "hydrogen," the elemental substance that is supposed to be the father and mother of us all!

Thus, hydrogen, the simplest chemical element, is "a colorless, odorless, tasteless gas which, given ten billion years or so, produces people." That quaint definition, originally suggested by the late creationist astronomer George Mulfinger, is a cogent summary of the faith one must exercise in order to be an evolutionist.

It was that prince of evolutionary astronomers, Harlow Shapley, long-time head of the Harvard University Observatory, who long ago pontificated that people today should rewrite the first verse of Genesis. According to him, it should be something like: "In the beginning, hydrogen created the heavens and the earth." Modern evolutionary astronomers and cosmologists have thus ruled out the idea of a personal, omnipotent, omniscient God as Creator of the universe. A more recent scientist has put it this way:

> Take some matter, heat while stirring and wait. That is the modern version of Genesis. The "fundamental" forces of gravity, electro-magnetism and the strong and weak nuclear forces are presumed to have done the rest.

But this same writer, perhaps not suspecting that some creationist might happen to read his evaluation of this statement of faith, proceeds to make the following admission.

> But how much of this neat tale is firmly established, and how much remains hopeful speculation? In truth, the mechanism of almost every major step, from chemical precursors up to the first recognizable cells, is the subject of either controversy or complete bewilderment.[10]

To unbiased observers it must seem that "every major step" from one degree of organization to the next higher degree is not only speculative, but also impossible — at least in any realistic sense.

The chief problem (among many) is the second law of thermodynamics, which notes that everything at least *tends to go* toward disorganization — not greater organization.

> Presumably the universe began in a very chaotic state. A chaotic state is by definition, a state of high entropy (when we speak of "chaos," we mean that there is a great deal of disorder). On the other hand, numerous kinds of structure have appeared since the universe began. . . . But how can this be, if entropy was so high at the beginning?[11]

Most cosmologists assume that the universe began with the big bang, which would seem to be about the ultimate in chaos. Explosions normally generate disorder, and this primeval explosion of nothing into something must have been the greatest explosion of all, if it really happened.

Cosmologists, however, have devised various curious schemes in their attempts to circumvent the second law. That most prolific of all science writers, Isaac Asimov, assumed the universe was like a cosmic egg (the ancient pagan evolutionists used to think of it in some such way also). He said:

> The cosmic egg may be structureless (as far as we know), but it apparently represented a very orderly aggregation of matter. Its explosion represented a vast shift in the direction of disorder, and ever since, the amount of disorder in the Universe has been increasing.[12]

Just how the cosmic egg could have no structure and yet have a high degree of order is not clear to me, but of course I am an ignorant and biased creationist. Neither is it clear how this vast shift toward disorder somehow produced all the highly ordered systems in the universe, including human beings. To Asimov, however, it was quite simple.

> Within the vast shift toward disorder involved in the big bang and the expansion of the Universe, it is possible for there to be local shifts in the direction of order, so that the galaxies can form and within them individuals stars, including our sun.[13]

Well, perhaps it may be "possible," but no one yet has been able to explain how. Abraham Loeb, a Harvard astrophysicist, says:

> The truth is that we don't understand star formation at a fundamental level.[14]

One of the great successes of evolutionary cosmology is the supposed ability of the big bang to explain the origin of hydrogen gas, and this is always offered as one of the three "proofs" of the big bang (the others are the background radiation and the supposedly expanding universe — both of which, however, have also been explained by certain rival cosmologies).

But that's all. Thus, we are left with hydrogen as the originator of everything else, even though we don't know how it did this. As an article of faith, we are asked simply to intone the evolutionary mantra: "In the beginning, hydrogen."

That belief is supposed to be more credible than "In the beginning God created." One wants to be charitable, but it is hard for the Christian not to recall certain Scriptures at this point. For example:

> . . . because they received not the love of the truth, that they might be saved. And for this cause God shall send them strong delusion, that they should believe a lie (2 Thess. 2:10–11).

> Professing themselves to be wise, they became fools, And changed the glory of the uncorruptible God into an image made like to corruptible man (Rom. 1:22–23).

Perhaps the saddest aspect of this whole scenario is that so many Christians are being taken in by it. For example, a currently popular evangelical scientist seems to be echoing the atheist Asimov when he defends the big bang and the whole system of cosmic and stellar evolution. He says:

> What [Dr. Duane] Gish and others fail to recognize is that the hydrogen which forms (by God's cause and design) one millisecond after the universe began is much more ordered and less entropic than the galaxies, stars, planets, and life-essential elements. The galaxies and stars are broken-up pieces of the primordial gas cloud. The planets and life-essential elements are the burned-up remains — i.e., ashes — of hydrogen gas. Thus, the big bang manifests, rather than violates, the second law of thermodynamics.[15]

I'm not making this up; that paragraph is really quoted verbatim from a recent book! He believes that the obvious conflict of this concept with the second law is resolved simply by the postulated heat energy in the big bang.

The key word, once again, is "believe." He would like for us to believe that stars are "broken-up pieces" of the primordial hydrogen and that our own living bodies with their "life-essential elements" are the "burned-up ashes" of hydrogen gas because that's what the secular astronomers who reject the God of the Bible must believe, and he believes we should not question their (and his) authority.

One cannot help but think of another verse of Scripture here: "For they loved the praise of men more than the praise of God" (John 12:43).

The Incredibly Aging Universe

The subject of cosmology is said by its practitioners to be a science. It does have the trappings of science, encased in a heavy apparatus of relativistic mathematics and esoteric jargon. These experts have Ph.D. degrees in astrophysics or astronomy or perhaps in the philosophy of science, and they regularly send forth a voluminous body of speculative literature on the origin and structure of the universe, with new variations and speculations appearing every month or so.

Although cosmology in many respects is indeed a science, it has many philosophical, political, or even religious overtones. This aspect of cosmology appears in the very titles of the many scientific articles in this field being written for non-cosmologists. Here are some of them in my files — more or less picked at random:

> "Law and Order in the Universe" (*New Scientist*, October 15, 1988).
> "Big-Bang Bashers" (*Scientific American*, September 1987).
> "Down with the Big Bang" (*Nature*, August 10, 1989).
> "Are We All in the Grip of a Great Attractor?" (*Science*, September 11, 1987).
> "Chaos Frees the Universe" (*New Scientist*, October 6, 1990).
> "Is the Universe Made of Froth?" (*New Scientist*, February 13, 1986).
> "Giant Structure Spells Trouble for Cosmology" (*New Scientist*, February 23, 1991).

An article with a particularly intriguing title is "Searching for Cosmology's Holy Grail," a review article by Ron Cowen.[16] The "holy grail," in medieval religious tradition, was supposed to be the cup used by Christ and His disciples at the Last Supper. It was the object of many fruitless searches by the legendary knights of the Middle Ages.

The cosmologists are engaged in a fruitless search for their own "holy grail," by which is meant the age of the universe.

When most scientists still believed the Bible (including Sir Isaac Newton, the greatest of all), they believed the universe to be about 6,000 years old. With the coming of Lyell's uniformitarianism, it became several million years old.

When I was in college, I was taught that the age of the universe had become two billion years. Since then, its age has grown even more, although there is still disagreement as to just how much.

> How old is the universe? After years of fractious debate, astronomers still do not know the answer. Some believe the universe is 10 billion years old, others argue that it is closer to 20 billion.[17]

The two billion years of my college days were supposedly confirmed by about five other independent age calculations — including the uranium/lead age of the earth's oldest rocks. The age of the earth itself has since grown to 4.6 billion years.

I realize it has been a long time since I was in college (1939, to be exact, when I graduated from Rice University with my first degree), but not *that* long!

A recent problem was that measurements, both from the Hubble Space Telescope and from certain ground observatories, seemed to indicate that the universe is younger than many of its stars! That is, at least three independent measurements suggested that the cosmos is "only" eight to ten billion years old, whereas many of the globular clusters of stars in various galaxies are thought to be about 16 billion years old. On the other hand, a number of astronomers still insist that *their* measurements show the universe to be about 20 billion years old.

At any rate, it is obvious that they have not yet found their holy grail. Other important cosmological concepts — such as whether the universe is open, closed, or flat, whether most of it consists of invisible dark matter, whether the general theory of relativity has to be changed, and other such mysteries — are dependent in one degree or another on this search.

The cosmologists (with a number of notable exceptions) are

committed to the "big bang" theory of cosmos origin, the date of which is the age for which they are searching. But the "big bang" itself is highly speculative, and there are a growing number of astronomers who are questioning it. Especially if the many younger astronomers advocating the 8 to 12 billion year age of the universe should prevail, it would be in serious trouble. Such an age ". . . suggests the universe is younger than its oldest stars, a logical contradiction that would destroy the big bang theory."[18]

The author of this particular observation quotes a Canadian astronomer, Sidney van den Bergh, who is trying to be neutral on this issue, and who then quotes Mark Twain as follows:

> The researches of many commentators have already thrown much darkness on this subject, and it is probably that, if they continue, we shall soon know nothing at all about it.[19]

But continue they will, no doubt, for that is how they make their living. Practically all leading astronomers are evolutionists, and most are either atheists or pantheists. They seem determined to find some means — any means — of eliminating the true God, the God of the Bible, from any role in the creation of the universe.

When the "big bang" theory began to run into serious difficulties about 20 years ago, it was supposedly rescued by the "Inflation" theory. This esoteric theory postulated a period of very rapid cosmic "inflation" (moving far more rapidly than the speed of light!) in an infinitesimal moment of time before the "big bang" took over.

But the original inflationary theory has been modified in various ways by various cosmologists, for it has also encountered many problems. A. D. Linde, for example, proposed a scenario called "chaotic inflation." These ideas are all intensely mathematical and impossibly abstruse (at least for laymen such as myself) and obviously cannot be tested experimentally.

One of the strangest ideas recently has been developed by Linde, based on his premise of chaotic inflation. He first notes that there have been many inflationary theories.

> The inflationary theory itself changes as particle physics theory rapidly evolves. The list of new models includes extended inflation, natural inflation, hybrid inflation, and many others.[20]

Dr. Linde, originally trained in Moscow and now at Stanford, proceeds to develop one of the most remarkable scenarios ever proposed. Instead of the universe inflating only to grapefruit size, as the original inflation theory proposed, he has it inflating almost instantaneously to a size many orders of magnitude greater than that of our whole observable universe! This inflationary bubble does not precede the "big bang" but includes it. Furthermore, it unceasingly produces other inflationary domains, each with its own big bang. Linde calls the process "eternal inflation," producing a fractal-like pattern of universes without end. Our own universe is merely one such inflationary bubble with an infinite number of sibling universes.

> In it the universe appears to be both chaotic and homogeneous, expanding and stationary. Our cosmic home grows, fluctuates and eternally reproduces itself for all types of life that it can support.[21]

But there is still a problem. Where and how did the first inflationary bubble, with its first "big bang," arise?

> What arose first: the universe or the laws determining its evolution? Explaining this initial singularity — where and when it all began — still remains the most intractable problem of modern cosmology.[22]

After 20 pages of examining the possibilities, one writer concludes as follows:

> Thus we reach a general conclusion: there is no philosophy of big bang cosmology that makes it reasonable to reject the fundamental thesis of big bang cosmology: that the universe began to exist without a cause.[23]

In other words, the universe is "simply one of those things that happen from time to time."[24]

Cosmological theory seems to be a never-never land of ever-changing naturalistic speculations about the origin and meaning of the universe. They will never find their "holy grail" that way.

The answer to their search has been there all along, though it's not what they want. The very first words of God's revealed word — in fact, probably the first words ever written — say it plainly. "In the beginning God created the heavens and the earth" (Gen. 1:1). Then, lest anyone misunderstand, God later wrote it down in stone, with His own hand: "In six days the Lord made heaven and earth, the sea, and all that in them is" (Exod. 20:11). And that's the way it was!

No cosmologist has ever yet disproved these majestic words of fiat creation by the omnipotent Creator who simply spoke the universe into existence; "By the word of the Lord were the heavens made: and all the host of them by the breath of his mouth. . . . For he spake, and it was done" (Ps. 33:6–9).

No Room for God

Some years back, a special issue of *Scientific American* (October 1994) reminded me of the famous line from Coleridge's *Ancient Mariner*:

> *Water, water everywhere,*
> *and all the boards did shrink;*
> *Water, water everywhere,*
> *nor any drop to drink.*

The eight feature articles in that magazine cover the evolutionary gamut from the evolution of the universe to the evolution of intelligence. The most remarkable thing about this anthology, however, is that not one of the 12 eminent authors (all of whom are on the faculties of very prestigious universities), in all their explorations of the origin of every facet of the universe and life, deign to give even a *"nod to God"* as having anything whatever to do with the origin of anything!

Every article is replete with speculation about how this or that might have happened, but without a shred of *proof* about the origin of any of it. God should at least have been included as one of their speculations, but there was not a nod toward Him at all.

Such scientists, studying firsthand the beauties and complexities and interrelationships of God's creation, ought to be able to see abundant evidence of God in the creation. Ordinary people have no difficulty in doing so, and God's word tells us it is inexcusable not to.

> Ye fools, when will ye be wise? He that planted the ear, shall he not hear? He that formed the eye, shall he not see? . . . He that teacheth man knowledge, shall not he know? (Ps. 94:8–10).

> The invisible things of him from the creation of the
> world are clearly seen, being understood by the things that
> are made . . . so that they are without excuse (Rom. 1:20).

There are innumerable evidences of design everywhere one looks in the creation, but these men seem to see no evidence whatever of God's handiwork.

For example, the four authors of an essay on "The Evolution of the Universe," assert sanctimoniously that:

> In science we adopt the plodding route: we accept
> only what is tested by experiment or observation.[25]

They write as if they could actually *observe* or conduct an *experiment* on the evolution of the universe! They proceed then to invoke the standard "big bang" cosmology as the way they *know* the universe to have evolved. They do admit, however:

> We do not know why there was a big bang or what
> may have existed before.[26]

Dr. Robert R. Kirshner, chairman of Harvard's Department of Astronomy, writing on "The Earth's Elements," is satisfied that all the chemical elements that compose the "matter" of the cosmos originated in this primordial bang.

> Matter in the universe was born in violence. Hydro-
> gen and helium emerged from the intense heat of the big
> bang some 15 billion years ago.

The heavier elements are then explained as arising later, either in "the burning depths of stars" or in "supernova explosions." However, he also indicates a degree of uncertainty, acknowledging that ". . . the rug in most astronomy departments is lumpy from all the discrepancies that have been swept under it." He concludes his contribution with this statement of faith in "Matter":

> But understanding the history of matter and search-
> ing for its most interesting forms, such as galaxies, stars,
> planets and life, seem a suitable use for our intelligence.

As to our own earth, however, he seems quite sure that "complex atoms, formed in stellar cauldrons, have organized themselves into intelligent systems."[27]

In further reference to the earth, the two distinguished authors of the article on "The Evolution of the Earth" are quite certain that it originated by accretion of rock fragments bumping into each other. They also give a nod to the Gaia hypothesis (though not to God), suggesting that the earth and life may have cooperated with each other in furthering their own evolution.[28]

One of the top researchers on the naturalistic origin of life is Dr. Leslie Orgel of the Salk Institute, who writes on "The Origin of Life on the Earth." He reviews the many unsuccessful speculations of the past and then makes quite a number of his own. He does recognize, however, that "at first glance, one might have to conclude that life could never, in fact, have originated by chemical means."[29]

Not to worry. Orgel, Francis Crick and others have come to the rescue.

> We proposed that RNA might well have come first and established what is now called the RNA world. . . . The scenario could have occurred, we noted, if prebiotic RNA had two properties not evident today: a capacity to replicate without the help of proteins and an ability to catalyze every step of protein synthesis.[30]

This is quite an "if." These properties are indeed "not evident today." RNA cannot even replicate *itself*, let alone catalyze *any* step of protein synthesis for further evolution. Orgel is hopeful, but he still must admit at the end, that:

> The precise events giving rise to the RNA world remain unclear. As we have seen, investigators have proposed many hypotheses, but evidence in favor of each of them is fragmentary at best.[31]

Dr. Steven Weinberg, in the first article of the symposium, discussed "Life in the Universe," surveying the various theories of cosmic origins and the origin and nature of life. Although he did not know the answer to these problems, he is sure we don't need God.

> The experience of the last 150 years has shown that life is subject to the same laws of nature as is inanimate matter. Nor is there any evidence of a grand design in the origin or evolution of life.[32]

That icon of the evolutionary establishment, the late Dr. Carl Sagan, discussed one of his favorite subjects in "The Search for Extra-terrestrial Life."

> While no one yet has found living organisms beyond the earth, there are reasons to be encouraged.[33]

His encouragement centered on the hope that other solar systems like ours will someday be discovered, and the fact that organic molecules (carbon-containing compounds) have been found in space. He is evidently not easily discouraged!

Dr. Sagan's chief rival for icon-hood in the evolutionary temple is Harvard's Stephen Jay Gould, who has written an article entitled, "The Evolution of Life on the Earth." He stresses the almost complete randomness of evolutionary history.

> Humans arose, rather, as a fortuitous and contingent outcome of thousands of linked events, any one of which could have occurred differently and sent history on an alternate pathway that would not have led to consciousness.[34]

There is neither design nor progress evident in Gould's evolutionary scenario, let alone any evidence of God.

Finally, Dr. William Calvin discusses "The Evolution of Intelligence," but he has difficulty in even defining the word. He does see that:

> Language is the most defining feature of human intelligence; without syntax — the orderly arrangement of verbal ideas — we would be little more clever than a chimpanzee.[35]

He seems to think that this attribute was somehow acquired by natural selection among "ideas" competing for "workspace" in the pre-human brain.

To a creationist it is humorous to read the speculations of evolutionists grasping at straws, as it were, in their almost paranoid attempts to get away from their own Maker.

If they really wish to know how the universe originated, for example, God has told them. "By the word of the Lord were the heavens made; and all the host of them by the breath of his mouth" (Ps. 33:6). Would they like to know how the earth, with its lands and seas, came to be? "The sea is his, and he made it: and his hands formed the dry land" (Ps. 95:5).

And how about life in all its varieties? "God created great whales, and every living creature that moveth" (Gen. 1:21). If they ask why and how man appeared on earth, God answers that man is no accident, "for I have created him for my glory, I have formed him; yea, I have made him" (Isa. 43:7). And can we expect to find life in outer space? No, for "the heavens, are the Lord's but the earth hath he given to the children of men" (Ps. 115:16).

There is water — spiritual water — everywhere one looks, and He calls, through His word: "Ho, every one that thirsteth, come ye to the waters" (Isa. 55:1). In the last invitation of the Bible, He still calls: "Let him that is athirst come. And whosoever will, let him take the water of life freely" (Rev. 22:17). It is sad that there is so much pure water everywhere, but nary a drop will they drink.

Still More Spaced Out

Those scientists (astronomers, astrophysicists, and cosmologists) whose professional activities focus on outer space seem to live in a strange wonderland of relativistic mathematics and quantum theory, which non-initiates find hard to believe. In fact, the evolutionary socialist Jeremy Rifkin says:

> Cosmologies are made up of small snippets of physical reality that have been remodeled by society into vast cosmic deceptions.[36]

Cosmologists speak of ten dimensions instead of the familiar three-dimensional space in which "we live, and move, and have our being" (Acts 17:28). We also read about curved space, quantum fluctuations in the infinite vacuum, cosmic inflation, causeless beginnings, and other marvels from their mathematical manipulations.

What is the purpose of all this esoteric theorizing in the study of extraterrestrial space? None of it seems to contribute to anything of practical value at all. In an article eulogizing modern science and its wonderful contributions, Judson admitted that:

> Still, even today certain major sciences offer scant prospect of practical application. Astronomy and cosmology are of little earthly use.[37]

But if any common purpose can be discerned in space research, it seems to be that of explaining the universe without God. A recent survey[38] found that 92.5 percent of the leading physicists and astronomers (those in the National Academy of Science) reject the idea of a personal God altogether.

Still, there are a few theistic astronomers (e.g., Dr. Hugh Ross) who claim that most astronomers accept the big bang as the act of cosmic creation recorded in Genesis 1:1. Unfortunately, many leading evangelical Christians today, fearful of being thought anti-intellectual, are buying this notion.

> Since the mid-1960s, scientifically informed theists have been ecstatic because of big bang cosmology. Theists believe that the best scientific evidence that God exists is the evidence that the universe began to exist in an explosion about 15 billion years ago, an explosion called the Big Bang. Theists argue that . . . the cause of the universe is God. This theory hinges on the assumption that it is obviously true that whatever begins to exist has a cause.[39]

Science has, indeed, always assumed the validity of the cause-and-effect principle, that every effect must have an adequate cause. But now evolutionary philosophers are questioning this most basic of all scientific laws.

An eminent cosmologist at the Fermi Labs "explains":

> One of the consequences of the uncertainty principle is that a region of seemingly empty space is not really empty, but is a seething froth in which every sort of fundamental particle pops in and out of empty space before annihilating with its antiparticle and disappearing — these are the so-called quantum fluctuations. . . . In a very real sense, quantum fluctuations would be the origin of everything we see in the universe.[40]

To us outsiders, this seems like an unreal never-never land. But evolutionary astrophysicists believe it is "very real," and that it proves the universe came into existence all by itself.

> The claim that the beginning of our universe has a cause conflicts with current scientific theory. The scien-

tific theory is called the Wave Function of the universe. It has been developed in the past by Stephen Hawking, Andre Vilenkin, Alex Linde, and many others. Their theory is . . . that a universe with our characteristics will come into existence without a cause.[41]

Probably the most eminent of this group of astrophysicists is Stephen Hawking, whose 1988 book, *A Brief History of Time*, has sold over 2.5 million copies. He has claimed that science is on the verge of developing a "theory of everything" including the origin of the universe.

> The problem is that the ultimate theory envisioned by Hawking and others never materialized. Theorists seeking that theory have become lost in a fantasyland of higher-dimensional mathematics that has less and less to do with reality. The theory of everything has become a theory of nothing.[42]

But, if the idea of the universe emerging naturalistically as a quantum fluctuation of nothing into something seems bizarre, there is a new theory going around now that seems even more "spaced-out" than that!

> We suggest that the Universe emerged from something rather than nothing — and that something was itself. . . . Such a thing is possible because Einstein's general theory of relativity permits closed time-like curves — loops of time.[43]

This theory has been advanced by J. Richard Gott III and Li-Xin Li of Princeton University and even suggests that time travel may be possible.

> Ruling out the possibility of traveling back in time has turned out to be trickier than many physicists had supposed. Two researchers have now shown that quantum effects do not necessarily prevent the occurrence of loops in time, Li-Xin Li and J. Richard Gott III of Princeton University present their case in the April 6 *Physical Review Letters*. "Hence," the researchers say, "the laws of physics may allow the universe to be its own mother."[44]

Marcus Chown comments that this theory, if true, would mean:

> . . . it's possible that a branch of space-time could loop backwards to form the tree trunk. . . . Space would have been in a loop of time perpetually recreating itself.[45]

But the observational facts with which to test such notions are very limited. One group of eminent astronomers has disparaged the entire big bang theory, with all its strange offshoots: "Cosmology is unique in science in that it is a very large intellectual edifice based on very few facts."[46]

Although these astronomers reject the big bang theory, they still believe in cosmic evolution: they are not believers in biblical creation.

They should be, however, and so should all the rest. "The heavens declare the glory of God" (Ps. 19:1), not the complexities of an imaginary cosmic evolution. "By the word of the Lord were the heavens made . . . For he spake, and it was done" (Ps. 33:6–9). There is not one *fact* of physics or astronomy that refutes these plain statements of the Word of God. "Praise him, ye heavens of heavens . . . for he commanded, and they were created. He hath also stablished them for ever and ever" (Ps. 148:4–6).

It is sad that so many brilliant space scientists are seeking to comprehend the cosmos without God. If God was not there at the beginning, neither will He be at the end, so they must try also to extrapolate its future without God.

And such a future is dreadfully dark, for the stars must eventually burn out, according to these theories, and even matter itself will disappear.

> Therefore, nothing made of ordinary matter — including atoms — will last.[47]

> In the beginning there may have been light, but in the end, it seems there will be nothing but darkness.[48]

Not so, however, for those who have trusted the Lord Jesus Christ as their Creator and Redeemer. This created universe will continue forever. "And they that be wise shall shine as the brightness of the firmament; and they that turn many to righteousness as the stars for ever and ever" (Dan. 12:3).

The Long, Long Stardust Trail

As earlier noted more or less in passing, most of the big bang cosmologists, as well as some Christians, believe that our human bodies are essentially "stardust," composed of elements generated long ago in exploding stars which disbursed their dust into space. The trail began some 15 billion years ago in the primeval big bang, which first produced simple chemical elements, then eventually stars and galaxies and planets and people through eons of evolution.

This idea is not scientific. Scientists have never observed stars or planets evolve, so such ideas are essentially based on naturalistic speculation supported mostly by esoteric mathematics, so they are not scientific, by definition.

As far as the stars are concerned, Abraham Loeb (of the Harvard University Center for Astrophysics) has frankly acknowledged that scientists do not know how they formed:"The truth is that we don't understand star formation at a fundamental level."[49]

The most favored theory at present is that the big bang explosion generated the simple elements hydrogen and helium, which eventually coalesced into the first simple stars.

These stars, known as Type-3 Stars, did not include any complex elements. The latter had to be generated when some of this first group of stars exploded as supernovas. From the resulting stardust evolved more complex stars and eventually planets and people.

The problem is that, out of the billions upon billions of stars in the observable universe, there do not seem to be any Type-3 Stars at all.

> The first generation of stars likely formed when the universe was only a few million years old (though these Population III stars have not yet been identified).[50]

It would seem that we should see plenty of them if they ever existed, since all the other stars supposedly keep coming from them.

Be that as it may, we are more interested in our sun with its solar system. There have been various theories of the evolution of the planets and their satellites, as well as the comets and asteroids. Most of these theories have encountered insuperable obstacles, so that the current theory (of last resort, actually) is a set of catastrophic theories based on multiple impacts of various rock bodies.

The moon (to take a "close to home" example) is said to

have originated in a gigantic impact on earth.

> Many models have been proposed for the forma-
> tion of the Moon, but no one has succeeded in showing
> the formation satisfactorily. The popular "giant impact"
> model states that a Mars-sized protoplanet hit the proto-
> Earth and generated a circumterrestrial debris disk from
> which the Moon accreted.[51]

While this theory may have fewer problems than others, it appears extremely imaginative and quite incapable of proof. Furthermore, it does encounter one serious difficulty.

> However, no reasonable means to rid the Earth/
> Moon system of the excess angular momentum has yet
> been proposed.[52]

One scientist in this field seems about ready to give up hope
that the origin of the moon can ever be explained, not to mention
the other planets and satellites.

> All in all, developing a theory of lunar origins that
> could make sense of data obtained from the Apollo lunar
> landing programme proved very difficult. So much so,
> in fact, that when I took a class on our planetary system
> from Irvin Shapiro two decades ago, he joked that the
> best explanation was observational error — the moon
> did not exist.[53]

The comets orbiting the sun present another problem. These
bodies lose considerable mass at every pass around the sun. They
cannot survive many orbits, and thus cannot be very old. To get
around this problem, evolutionists assume there is a vast cloud of
hibernating comets out near the edge of the solar system, which
releases new comets every so often.

This imaginary cloud is called the "Oort Cloud," named after
the astronomer who proposed it. The problem is that there is no
observational evidence such a cloud exists at all.

> We have never actually "seen" the Oort Cloud. . . .
> We infer the existence and properties of the Oort Cloud
> . . . from . . . the steady trickle of long-period comets into
> the planetary system.[54]

The underlying reason for space research is to explain the origin of the stars and planets without God having been involved. The ultimate hope is to find evidence of extraterrestrial life somewhere, for that would prove, they say, that life could evolve anywhere — not just on earth.

One hope is to locate some type of non-random radio signals from the stars. Very elaborate radio telescopes have been built and monitored for years hoping to catch them. But this effort has been a waste of much money.

> Scientists are systematically scrutinizing a thousand nearby sun-like stars for the faint signal that would betray intelligent habitation. So far, they have found nothing — not a single extraterrestrial peep. . . . we are, to our knowledge, still alone in a vast cosmos.[55]

Nevertheless, NASA is still hoping to find some evidence of extraterrestrial life — if not human life on some far-off planet, then at least microbial life on a nearby planet.

The only candidate remaining among the planets in the solar system is Mars. Although Mars seems to be devoid of any life at all, they still are searching for evidence that it used to be there. Two years ago, NASA generated global publicity by announcing they had found such evidence — a Martian rock with fossilized bacteria that had somehow traveled to earth and landed in Antarctica.

This claim has been well debunked by now.

> Eighteen months after David S. McKay and his colleagues . . . raised eyebrows with their claim . . . the team has made few converts . . . its critics have published dozens of new observations they believe make that theory increasingly improbable.[56]

On the other hand, this sensational claim of Martian life has been immensely successful in one sense.

> Scientists now working on . . . the possibility of extraterrestrial life are funded at levels that two years ago would have been unimaginable. Had NASA's publicity machine not turned McKay's paper into a global media event, this largesse would never have been granted.[57]

What is NASA up to? Two years ago, the agency thought it had discovered life on Mars and set the world ablaze with talk of a universe populated by aliens. Now it has discovered water on the moon and the world is already planning holidays at lunar resorts. . . . But we should not be cynical. NASA needs periodic blazes of publicity to keep the U.S. Congress interested in funding space exploration.[58]

But no matter how much money is spent and how many tests are run on the Mars rock: "Most researchers agree that the case for life is shakier than ever."[59]

The most recent NASA project has been the widely publicized adventure of sending an ex-senator and ex-astronaut (now 77 years old) back on a space mission, ostensibly to research the effects of space travel on the aging process. The public relations boost for NASA has again been enormous.

There is a lot of extraterrestrial life, of course. The Bible calls them angels! These are specially created beings "sent forth to minister for them who shall be heirs of salvation" (Heb. 1:14).

But the astro-scientists will not find any angels with their telescopes or space probes. Neither will they find any other humans or humanoids out there. Physical life was specially created, and earth was created uniquely to support that life. The stars were created for other purposes, not yet revealed. "The heaven, even the heavens, are the Lord's: but the earth hath he given to the children of men" (Ps. 115:16).

Evolutionary scientists would be well advised to "hit the sawdust trail" that leads to Christ and forget about the imaginary stardust trail that they think led to life.

The Coming Big Bang

For over 40 years now, the big-bang theory has been the reigning paradigm of evolutionary cosmology. It assumes a naturalistic evolution of the space/time cosmos from nothing into an infinitesimal universe which rapidly inflated and then "exploded," expanding eventually into our present cosmos of stars and galaxies, beginning somewhere between 10-and-20-billion-years ago.

The idea was initially developed by the Belgian astronomer Georges Lemaitre in 1927, then popularized by Sir Arthur Edington and George Gamow. Lemaitre called it the "primeval atom," but Gamow, as well as Sir Fred Hoyle (who popularized the opposing "steady state theory") began calling it the "big bang." With the discovery in 1964 of the pervasive "cosmic background radiation" (supposedly left over from the great explosion), the majority of astronomers became committed to the big bang.

As a result, a number of evangelical scientists have recently become promoters of the notion that Genesis 1:1 is God's way of identifying the big bang. The great majority of professional astronomers, on the other hand, do not believe in supernatural creation at all, although some would accept the pantheistic concept that the cosmos is its own "intelligent" creator. With respect to the attempt to identify Genesis 1:1 with the big bang, the British astronomer Paul Davies says:

> When the Big Bang Theory became popular in the 1950s many people used it to support the belief that the universe was created by God at some specific moment in the past, and some still regard the big bang as "the creation." . . . However, this sort of armchair theology is wide of the mark. . . . It is therefore scientifically plausible to consider a universe with no need for an external creator in the traditional sense.[60]

Not only have these evangelicals thus been denied a seat on the big bang bandwagon by its professional occupants, but also the bandwagon itself is now developing many cracks and dents. Even though the big bang is still the cosmogony of choice for the majority of astronomers, there is a rapidly growing body of very competent dissenters. One of these is the astronomer David Darling.

> Don't let the cosmologists try to kid you on this one. They have not got a clue either. . . . "In the beginning," they will say, there was nothing — no time, space, matter, or energy. Then there was a quantum fluctuation from which — whoa! Stop right there. You see what I mean? First there is nothing, then there is something — and before you know it, they have pulled a hundred billion galaxies out of their quantum hats.[61]

Five eminent astronomers, in a significant article in a leading scientific journal, have raised many near-fatal objections to the big bang theory, with an understated conclusion as follows:

> The above discussion clearly indicates that the present evidence does not warrant an implicit belief in the standard hot Big Bang picture.

Then they go on to say:

> Cosmology is unique in science in that it is a very large intellectual edifice based on a very few facts.[62]

There are a number of alternative evolutionary cosmogonies that are now being offered in competition with the big bang. There is the plasma theory for example, and a modified steady state theory, as well as numerous variants of the big bang inflationary theory, and others. All have fallacies and, consequently, have been unable to displace the big bang in the allegiance of the evolutionary establishment as a whole.

There is one cosmogony, of course, which does correlate perfectly with all actual astronomic data, and it is the simplest of all.

> By the word of the Lord were the heavens made; and all the host of them by the breath of his mouth. . . . For he spake, and it was done (Ps. 33:6–9).

> Praise him . . . all ye stars of light. . . . for he commanded, and they were created (Ps. 148:3–5).

> And God made two great lights; the greater light to rule the day, and the lesser light to rule the night: He made the stars also. . . . And the evening and the morning were the fourth day (Gen. 1:16–19).

The heavens did have a beginning, but it was by divine fiat, not by a quantum fluctuation of nothingness through a big bang that then evolved over billions of years into a highly complex universe.

Now, although the cosmos *did not originate* with a big bang, many scientists are becoming concerned that it may well end with a big bang. Evolutionary cosmologists are now speculating not only about how the world began but also about how it might end!

This trend has been stimulated especially by the widespread recent acceptance of the notion that the extinction of the dinosaurs was caused by the catastrophic impact of a comet or an asteroid on the earth about 60 million years ago. We may be due for another gigantic impact any day now, some are saying, since the heavens are cluttered with such objects. Davies says:

> Estimates suggest that 10,000 objects half a kilometer or more in diameter move on Earth-intersecting orbits. . . . Many of these objects are capable of causing more damage than all the world's nuclear weapons put together. It is only a matter of time before one strikes.[63]

That would indeed be a big bang! It might well destroy all life on earth.

Davies suggests other possible earth-destroying cataclysms that might occur. Our galaxy might collide with another galaxy. A nearby supernova might immerse the planet in lethal radiations. We might even be pulled into a black hole!

There is also the possibility of a big crunch — the opposite of the big bang — when the universe quits expanding and begins falling back on itself by gravity. Since the light from approaching stars might take longer to get here than the imploding stars themselves, we might even get thoroughly "crunched" before we would know it was about to happen. Davies says:

> The "big crunch," as far as we understand it, is not just the end of matter. It is the end of everything . . . time itself ceases at the big crunch.[64]

Davies ends his book on an incredibly morbid note:

> If there is a purpose to the universe, and it achieves that purpose, then the universe must end, for its continuing existence would be gratuitous and pointless. Conversely, if the universe endures forever, it is hard to imagine that there is any ultimate purpose to the universe at all. So cosmic death may be the price that has to be paid for cosmic success. Perhaps the most that we can hope for is that the purpose of the universe becomes known to our descendants before the end of the last three minutes.[65]

A remarkable commentary on our times is the fact that the famous annual million-dollar Templeton Prize for contributions to the scientific understanding of religion was awarded in 1995 to this same Professor Davies!

In any event, we can assure him, on the authority of the Word of the Creator himself, that the universe does have a wonderful purpose and that it will endure forever!

> He hath also stablished (the heavens) for ever and ever: He hath made a decree which shall not pass (Ps. 148:6).

> And they that be wise shall shine as the brightness of the firmament; and they that turn many to righteousness as the stars for ever and ever (Dan. 12:3).

> And there shall be no more curse: but the throne of God and of the Lamb shall be in it; and his servants shall serve him . . . and they shall reign for ever and ever (Rev. 22:3–5).

However, the earth in its present form will indeed end with a big bang. God's Edenic Curse, pronounced on Adam and all his dominion (including the very elements) because of sin, must first be purged.

> The day of the Lord will come as a thief in the night; in the which the heavens shall pass away with a great noise, and the elements shall melt with fervent heat, the earth also and the works that are therein shall be burned up (2 Pet. 3:10).

This will not be the end of the world, of course, for:

> We according to his promise, look for new heavens and a new earth, wherein dwelleth righteousness (2 Pet. 3:13).

And that new (literally "renewed") heavens and earth will last forever. So will all those who have been cleansed of sin and given eternal life through saving faith in the Lord Jesus Christ.

Endnotes

1   Cheryl J. Beatty and Richard Tresch Fienberg, "The Big Bang Challenge," *Sky and Telescope*, vol. 87, March 1984, p. 20–22.

2 Harold Puthoff, "Everything for Nothing," *New Scientist*, vol. 127, July 28, 1990, p. 55.

3 Robert Oldershaw, "What's Wrong with the New Physics?" *New Scientist*, vol. 128, December 22/29, 1990, p. 59.

4 Ibid.

5 Geoffrey Burbridge, "Why Only One Big Bang?" *Scientific American*, February 1992, p. 120.

6 Cited in Corey S. Powell, "A Matter of Timing," *Scientific American*, October 1992, p. 30.

7 Jay Gallagher and Jean Keppel, "Seven Mysteries of Galaxies," *Astronomy*, volume 22, March 1994, p. 39, 41.

8 Paul Davies, "What Hath COBE Wrought?" *Sky and Telescope*, January 1993, p. 4.

9 Ibid.

10 Andrew Scott, "Update on Genesis," *New Scientist*, vol. 106, May 2, 1985, p. 30.

11 Richard Morris, *Time's Arrow: Scientific Attitudes Toward Time* (New York: Simon & Schuster, 1984), p. 212.

12 Isaac Asimov, *In the Beginning* (New York: Crown Publishers, 1981), p. 24.

13 Ibid.

14 Abraham Loeb, as cited by Marcus Chown, "Let There Be Light," *New Scientist*, vol. 157, February 7, 1998, p. 30.

15 Hugh Ross, *Creation and Time* (Colorado Springs, CO: Navpress, 1994), p. 131.

16 Ron Cowen, *Science News*, vol. 146, October 8, 1994, p. 232–234.

17 Ibid., p. 232.

18 Ken Croswell, "The Constant Hubble War," *New Scientist*, vol. 237, February 13, 1993, p. 22.

19 Ibid., p. 23.

20 Andrei Linde, "The Self-Reproducing Inflationary Universe," *Scientific American*, vol. 271, November 1994, p. 54.

21 Ibid., p. 55.

22 Ibid., p. 48.

23 Quentin Smith, "Did the Big Bang Have a Cause?" *British Journal of the Philosophy of Science*, vol. 45, 1994, p. 666.

24 Puthoff, "Everything from Nothing," p. 55.

25 J. E. Peebles, D. N. Schramm, E. L. Turner, and R. G. Kron, *Scientific American*, volume 271, October 1994, p. 53.

26 Ibid., p. 57.

27 Robert R. Kirshner, "The Earth's Elements," *Scientific American*, vol. 271, October 1994, p. 59, 65.

28 Claude H. Allegre and Stephen H. Schneider, "The Evolution of the Earth," *Scientific American*, vol. 271, October 1994, p. 67–68 70–71.

29 Leslie E. Orgel, "The Origin of Life on Earth," *Scientific American*, vol. 271, October 1994, p. 78.

30 Ibid.

31 Ibid., p. 83.

32 Steven Weinberg, "Life in the Universe," *Scientific American*, vol. 271, October 1994, p. 47.

33 Carl Sagan, "The Search for Extra-terrestrial Life," *Scientific American*, vol. 271, October 1994, p. 93.

34 Stephen Jay Gould, "The Evolution of Life on the Earth," *Scientific American*, vol. 271, October 1994, p. 86.

35 William H. Calvin, "The Evolution of Intelligence," *Scientific American*, vol. 271, October 1994, p. 102.

36 Jeremy Rifkin, "Reinventing Nature," *The Humanist*, volume 58, March/April 1998, p. 24.

37 Horace F. Judson, "Century of the Sciences," *Science 84*, November 1984, p. 42.

38 Edward J. Larson and Larry Witham, "Leading Scientists Still Reject God," *Nature*, vol. 394, July 23, 1998, p. 313.

39 Quentin Smith, "Big Bang Cosmology and Atheism," *Free Inquiry*, Spring 1998, p. 35.

40 Rocky Kolb, "Planting Primordial Seeds," *Astronomy*, vol. 26, February 1998, p. 42–43.

41 Smith, "Big Bang Cosmology and Atheism," p. 36.

42 John Horgan, "The Big Bang Theory of Science Books," *New York Times Book Review*, December 1997, p. 39.

43 J. Richard Gott III, as quoted by Marcus Chown, "In the Beginning," *New Scientist*, vol. 157, January 24, 1998, p. 14.

44 J. Peterson, "Evading Quantum Barrier to Time Travel," *Science News*, vol. 153, April 11, 1998, p. 231.

45 Marcus Chown, "In the Beginning," *New Scientist*, vol. 157, January 24, 1998, p. 14.

46 Halton Arp, G. Burbridge, Fred Hoyle, J. Narlikar, and N. Wickramasinghe, "The Extra-Galactic Universe: An Alternative View," *Nature*, vol. 346, August 30, 1990, p. 812.

47 Fred C. Adams and Gregory Laughlin, "The Future of the Universe," *Sky and Telescope*, vol. 96, August 1998, p. 37.

48 Robert Matthews, "To Infinity and Beyond," *New Scientist*, vol. 158, August 1, 1998, p. 30.

49 Cited by Marcus Chown in his article "Let There Be Light," *New Scientist*, vol. 157, February 7, 1998, p. 30.

50 Fred C. Adams and Gregory Laughlin, "The Future of the Universe," *Sky and Telescope*, vol. 46, Aug. 1998, p. 34.

51 Shigeru Ida, Robin Canup, and Glen Stewart, "Lunar Accretion from an Impact-Generated Disk," *Nature*, vol. 389, Sept. 25, 1997, p. 353.

52 Ibid., p. 357.

53 Jack J. Lissauer, "It's Not Easy to Make the Moon," *Nature*, vol. 389, Sept. 25, 1997, p. 327.

54 Paul R. Weissman, "The Oort Cloud," *Scientific American*, vol. 279, no. 6, September 1998, p. 84.

55 Seth Shostak, "When E.T. Calls Us," *Astronomy*, vol. 25, Sept. 1997, p. 37, 41.

56 Gibbs W. Wayt, "Extra-Terrestrial Life Endangered," *Scientific American*, vol. 278, April 1998, p. 19.

57 Charles Seife, "Money for Old Rock," *New Scientist*, vol. 159, Aug. 1, 1998, p. 20.

58 Alun Anderson, "Giant Steps," *New Scientist*, vol. 157, Mar. 14, 1998, p. 3.

59 Richard A. Kerr, "Requiem for Life on Mars?" *Science*, vol. 282, November 20, 1998, p. 1398.

60 Paul Davies, "What Hath COBE Wrought?" *Sky and Telescope*, January 1993, p. 4.

61 David Darling, "On Creating Something From Nothing," *New Scientist*, vol. 151, September 14, 1996, p. 49.

62 Halton C. Arp et al., "The Extra-Galactic Universe: An Alternative View," p. 810, 812.

63 Paul Davies, *The Last Three Minutes* (London: Orion Books, 1995), p. 3.

64 Ibid., p. 123.

65 Ibid., p. 162.

Chapter VII

Defending Biblical Geology

n chapter 3 of this book, we surveyed the biblical
evidences that would seem to compel Bible-believing
Christians (and even Jews and Muslims, for that
matter, since they profess also to accept the Genesis
record) to believe in a recent creation and worldwide
flood. The problem, of course, is that practically all professional
geologists insist on their teaching that the earth has gone through
about 4.6 billion years of geological ages and that there never was a
worldwide flood. Thus, we must now look at the actual geological
and other scientific data to see whether or not they can really be
explained in terms of the biblical geology implied by the revelation
of recent creation and worldwide flood.

If the Bible record is true (as we must surely believe it is), then
the so-called "geologic column" (that is the great thickness of
sedimentary rocks with their fossils) is not really a record of the
evolution of life over many ages, but of the sudden destruction of
life in one age with its residual effects in the continuing "after-shocks"
of the great flood. The column thus would actually represent the
buried remains of the wonderful world as God had created it back in
the beginning. God had pronounced it to be a "very good" world,
but the effects of sin had contaminated it for some 1,656 years (by
the Ussher chronology) between the creation of Adam and the
entrance of Noah and his family into the ark. Therefore we shall
look first at what we know about that first world (now the lost world)
in the days of Noah.

The World That Then Was

To discuss the antediluvian world meaningfully, we necessarily must think in terms of a recent creation. Otherwise, if there have really been almost five billion years of earth's history, about one or two billion years of life's history, and about one or two million years of human history, the study of the world before the flood would be more or less without meaning. One would then have to think in terms of a local flood, and the world before such a flood would be no different than the world after the flood.

The apostle Peter says that the whole world at that time perished by a great cataclysm of water. Our belief that the entire world was destroyed in the flood is based especially on 2 Peter 3:6, where it says the "kosmos," the whole world that then was, was "cataclysmed" (Greek, *kataklusmos*) with water and perished. The entire structure, the entire system that then was, perished. This is why we don't know too much now about how it happened or what the antediluvian world was like.

We might look first for clues in secular history. There was certainly a civilization before the flood and, presumably, the people had a written language. We read in Genesis 3 of the "Book" of the generations of Adam (Gen. 5:1), for example. Genesis 4 also tells us that they were able to develop musical instruments, metal-working instruments, etc., and this all implies some kind of means of written communications and records. The problem there is that the very purpose of the flood was to destroy mankind and all his works. Only Noah and what he took with him were preserved. Undoubtedly, Noah took some records with him in the ark. These almost certainly would have included the records written by the antediluvian patriarchs Adam, Noah, etc., perhaps on tablets of stone or clay. They then ultimately formed the basis of Genesis as written and edited by Moses.

We also have the mythologies of the early peoples. Many of these legends speak of a golden age long ago in history. These may be recollections, perhaps wishful thinking, of a world their forefathers on the ark once knew and handed down by word of mouth. There are stories about Atlantis and other vanished civilizations.

We do have a few books that have come down to us, which purport to describe the conditions before the flood — for example, the Book of Enoch. Actually there are at least two so-called "Books of Enoch." These, however, were mostly written a century before the time of Christ. We do know from the Book of Jude, however, that Enoch was a prophet, and he prophesied that the Lord would come someday to exercise judgment on all men (see Jude 14). This seems to be an actual remnant from an original book written by Enoch that now has been preserved in the Book of Jude. But we do not know how much of the rest is genuine. The same question applies to other such books (e.g., Book of Jubilees, Book of Jasher, etc.).

Mostly, therefore, we have to rely on the geological deposits to supplement the Genesis record of the pre-flood world. If the old world was indeed destroyed by a worldwide flood, then the rocks, fossils, and sediments must bear record to the great fact of the flood. However, the standard geology textbooks are all written around the framework of evolution and uniformitarianism.

From a geological viewpoint, if there was actually a universal flood, then all the pre-flood geological and geographical structures must have been changed very drastically. Therefore, we must take full cognizance of the flood in producing that record. For example, there are many great deposits of fossils, often in extensive "graveyards" of fossils. These seem to speak very clearly of some kind of a catastrophe. Fossils, especially fossils in large numbers, don't get preserved unless they are buried quickly. In order to be preserved in the sediments, be lithified, and be preserved for ages, they certainly would have to be buried quickly in an aqueous catastrophe.

We also see great faults, fractures, uplifts, and earth movements of a nature entirely incommensurate with anything happening today. We think also of the great region-wide lava flows of the Northwest, and of continental glaciers. Almost every geological phenomenon that we may study today indicates that forces in the past must have been operating on a far greater scale than we have now. More and more of even the orthodox geologists today are accepting at least local catastrophism. The old type of uniformitarianism is beginning to go out of vogue. The neo-catastrophists, however, are only speaking of many local catastrophes, rather than one global cataclysm.

As a matter of fact, some are indeed advocating worldwide catastrophes, but not the biblical flood. Books have been written promoting close fly-bys of planets, shifting poles, a slipping crust, astral visitors, cometary encounters, asteroid swarms, meteoritic impacts, axis flipping, and all sorts of things. Each one is advocated by different proponents of catastrophism as being the explanation of earth's geological history. All these claim a certain amount of evidence and may in some cases be partially valid. But all such proposed global catastrophes are altogether outside the domain of experimental science, and there can thus be no solid data here to build any understanding of the world before the flood. It seems to me that we are finally driven to the Word of God alone if we are to obtain any really reliable information concerning the pre-flood world. The fact that some men don't believe the Bible is not an argument against it. It is still the Word of God. Romans 3:3–4 says that the unbelief of some does not make the Word of God ineffectual. "Let God be true, and every man a liar." The surest position to take is to believe what the Bible says, exactly and fully.

The Water Canopy

On the second day of creation week, God separated the waters that were under the firmament from the waters that were above the firmament. These two reservoirs were separated by a firmament, or "expanse," which He called heaven. Later the birds would fly in the open firmament of that heaven. This is the space, the thinness, the open expanse in which the birds would fly — in other words, the open atmosphere.

This atmosphere separated the initial waters that covered the whole earth into two great reservoirs. It says that the waters were above the firmament, not in or scattered through it. This ties in very well with other statements made in the early chapters of Genesis.

The fact that the light from the sun, moon, and stars shone through indicates that the upper waters were in the form of water vapor, not ice or clouds. Water vapor, of course, is invisible and thus fully transparent. If this were true, certain inferences would follow.

The greenhouse effect in our present atmosphere, for example, would have been tremendously augmented. The present greenhouse effect of the atmosphere is provided by the water vapor, ozone, and carbon dioxide now in the atmosphere. There may also have been more carbon dioxide in the antediluvian atmosphere than in the present.

This strong greenhouse effect would have meant that the earth was everywhere in a warm and mild climate. The latitudinal differences in temperature would have been minimal. This would have meant also, since the wind is mainly the result of latitudinal differences in temperature, that there would have been only mild air movements. The great storms of the present world would have been altogether absent in the antediluvian world.

All of this would mean, too, that the present hydrologic cycle would not have been in effect. Although evaporation took place then in somewhat the same way as now, there could have been no large-scale transfer of evaporated water from the oceans to land by air movements, as at present. This would preclude continental precipitation. The condensation of water vapor also requires dust particles or other nuclei of condensation, and these would have been largely absent. Thus, snow, rain, or hail, such as at present, would have been absent before the flood. Genesis 2:5 says that God had not caused it to rain on the earth, and there is no indication that this situation was changed before the time of the flood. The watering of the earth was evidently accomplished primarily either by a sort of a ground fog, or mist, that rose up, "and watered the whole face of the ground" (Gen. 2:6), or by irrigation from subterranean waters or from the antediluvian rivers.

According to Genesis 2:10, there were four rivers that parted out of the one river coming from Eden. These waters must have been fed by some kind of artesian spring. It seems reasonable that there were also similar rivers in other parts of the world. Together with the daily "mist" and the intricate network of shallow "seas," they would have provided water for abundant plant life and animal life.

The antediluvian world was then completely changed by the flood. The Bible says there were torrents of rain that came down continuously all over the world for 40 days and 40 nights and, on a lesser scale, for 110 days after that. Literally, the "flood gates" of heaven were opened. This, today, would be impossible. There is only an inch and a half of water vapor in the present atmosphere. There must have been then, before the flood, far more water vapor in the atmosphere than we have today. This seems to have constituted the "waters that were above the firmament" before the flood.

One other effect of this water vapor canopy would be that, as a thermal blanket, it would reduce the amounts of ultra-violet rays, cosmic rays, and other harmful radiations reaching the earth's surface. Even the present-day water vapor does this to a sufficient extent to make life possible on the earth. This would have made the environment much more conducive to longevity. Men did die before the flood, of course, for the curse of sin was upon them. But it wasn't until after the flood that there began a very rapid reduction in human life spans.

If these waters from the canopy were precipitated and came down in this flood, then they would be now in our present oceans. This would mean that the land and the sea ratio would be different in the antediluvian world from that today. The oceans would be shallower, there would be more land area, the mountains smaller. The Genesis account says there were mountains but they were not as high as now. Most of the mountain ranges of the present world — the Himalayas, the Rockies, the Andes, and others, give indications of having been uplifted in geologically recent times, probably even in the so-called Pliocene or Pleistocene Epochs. In terms of flood geology, this implies mountain uplifts in the closing stages of the flood year or even later. The continental and oceanic structures before the flood would seem by this to have been significantly different then. There were also intricate systems of shallow seas, more or less in the areas of the present mountain ranges, which served as the geosynclinal troughs into which tremendous thicknesses of sediment were washed during the flood. The mountains today give evidence of tremendous thicknesses of stratified sediments of such a nature that they must have been formed in shallow water, and then somehow, later, the entire land mass was uplifted, with the still-soft geosynclinal sediments especially subject to great compressive forces and structural distortion in the uplift process.

As there were waters above the firmament, so there were also those below the firmament. Genesis 7:11 says the fountains of the great deep were broken up. The word "deep" is mentioned before in Genesis 1:2. This great deep was broken up at the time of the flood. Probably great subterranean pockets of compressed waters, associated with molten rock, or magma that were restrained before the flood, under the antediluvian crust then broke forth. Perhaps some of these waters had provided the source for the artesian rivers before the flood. Then, at the time of the flood, on one day, all these were broken up. After 150 days, Genesis 8:2 says that God stopped the fountains of the great deep. This means that for 150 days great masses of water and lava and magma came out of the earth onto the surface. This surely means that the present system of isostasy, with its balance between continental and oceanic crustal weights, would have been different before the flood. In geophysics today it is suggested that below a certain depth most of earth's materials are in a plastic state and the earth's crust is thus more or less floating on the mantle. It is thought that this implies a uniform distribution of weights around the entire earth's sphere. Where the earth's crust is thin, as in the ocean basins, there the density of the crust is heavy, as with basaltic rocks, but where continents and mountains have been uplifted, the earth's crust is less dense. Now, if for 150 days tremendous amounts of materials were coming out of the fountains of the deep, this would mean that the isostatic balances must certainly have been different before the flood than now. It would mean that there would be many changes in the earth's crust, and this would demand rifts, earthquakes, and other movements, to help achieve after the flood a new isostatic and hydrologic balance. We should not be surprised then to find there are evidences in the geological strata that there have been such great earth movements.

The resulting picture of the world before the flood is bound to be largely speculation, because there is no way of checking it out scientifically. There will always be problems, but we can at least try to imagine what the pre-flood world was like in the framework of the Bible and the data we have. One thing we should not do is to change or distort what the Word of God says. Geological data are subject to varying interpretations, but we cannot do this with the Bible. Geographically, there would surely have been a much greater land surface and smaller ocean basins. The land surface would be gentler and more rolling than now. The seas might have occupied the areas, roughly, of the present mountain ranges because of the geosynclines found there. The Bible does indicate that there were many "seas" (rather than one great ocean) occupying one "place," and therefore all interconnected (Gen. 1:9–10).

There is a general consensus among geologists today about continental drift and plate tectonics. But the dynamics involved in moving great continental blocks are very difficult and no adequate mechanism has yet been determined to reconcile these movements with the forces needed to accomplish them. In any case, it is probable that many of these remarkable features of the face of the earth today are best subject to explanation in terms of the huge tectonic forces and tremendous movements of the earth during and following the flood year.

The antediluvian meteorology and hydrology would have been

controlled by the greenhouse effect of the vapor canopy. Some think that with all this water in the upper atmosphere, in the water canopy, the atmospheric pressure at the earth's surface would have been intolerable, in terms of both pressure and temperature. However, there is much evidence that life thrives better under what is called hyperbaric pressures than under present pressure conditions. The heating problem is the subject of current research and indications are that this also could have resulted in feasible temperatures.

Biologically, with the greater extent of land areas and the more congenial environment, one would anticipate that there would be a much more virile, varied, and abundant life upon earth before the flood than afterwards. This is supported by the tremendous fossil deposits of plant and animal life we find, as well as the tremendous coal deposits. Coal, of course, is made up mostly of fossilized plant life. There is thus evidence that there was very lush vegetation and very abundant animal life before the flood. There were undoubtedly ecological niches for the various assemblages of life forms, with a variety of topographic and zoologic relationships at all latitudes and longitudes. Dinosaurs and other extinct forms existed simultaneously with present forms, including man, but probably in different areas.

It is significant that we find very few human fossils. The reason probably is that most men, representing the highest form of life, and the most mobile, would be able to reach the high hills before being caught by the flood waters. After finally being overtaken and drowned, they would float on the surface and would only rarely be trapped and then buried in the sediments. Actually, the problem of the scarcity of human fossils is more serious for the evolutionist than for the creationist. If the earth were really billions of years old, and if man has actually lived several million years on earth, we ought to be able to find multitudes of prehistoric human fossils rather than only a few widely scattered bone fragments. Especially should we find many fossils of primates evolving from animal life to modern man, but instead have found no such halfway creatures at all.

The thermal effect of the canopy blanket of the pre-flood world would mean that the latitudinal differences in climate we now have in the world would not exist. Today we have different forms of life in the Arctic than at the equator. There would still be ecological zones as the result of differences in elevation, but otherwise the same general forms of animals and plants would be distributed throughout the world. Thus, Noah did not have to send expeditions to Alaska or elsewhere to find representatives of exotic forms of life to put on the ark. All the main forms would have been close by. Of course, he did not have to hunt for them anyway, because God sent the animals to him, according to Genesis 6:20.

In spite of the ideal climatic conditions of the antediluvian world, man did die. He might have lived 900 years, but he did die. We find evidence in all the geological strata that the whole earth was under the bondage of corruption, decay, and death in the geological past as well as in the present. The strata abound with evidences that the whole earth was groaning and travailing in pain under the Curse of God. Romans 8:21–23 explains this by saying all of nature is under the bondage of corruption, the result of sin. Before the flood, man filled the earth with people, but also with violence. Every imagination of his heart was only evil continually (Gen. 6:5). The main lesson we receive from the world before the flood is not the physical one, although this is astounding. The main lesson is spiritual, and this is given by Jesus in Matthew 24:37–39: "But as the days of Noah were, so shall also the coming of the Son of man be. For as in the days that were before the flood they were eating and drinking, marrying and giving in marriage, until the day that Noah entered into the ark. And knew not until the flood came, and took them all away; so shall also the coming of the Son of man be." We must learn to see the awful judgment of God on man's sin when we study the pre-flood world, and this must drive us to the Lord Jesus Christ as man's only hope of salvation.

The Flood and Geology

The "geologic ages" are actually nothing but a philosophical construct, formally organized in what is known as the "geologic column." This column is a theoretical cross-section through the earth's crust, from the surface down to the crystalline rocks that compose the "basement." The sediments comprising the crust have obviously been transported from various source areas mostly by moving water, then deposited and usually hardened to become lithified sedimentary rocks (limestones, shales, sandstones, etc.). It is commonly assumed that the "oldest" sediments are at the bottom of the column, with the "youngest" on top. All of this is supposed to have taken hundreds of millions of years to accomplish — hence the geologic "ages."

Since the same lithologic types of rocks and types of structural features occur throughout the entire column, the only way the different "ages" of the rocks are identified is by the different types of once-living plants and animals found buried and fossilized therein. Thus, rocks that contain what are considered "ancient" forms of fossils are considered old, while rocks containing more "modern" forms are assumed to be young. This summary is over-simplified, but essentially does represent how rocks are "dated" and assigned to specific geologic "ages." The following statements from the standard geologic literature convey the significance of fossils in age dating:

> The geologists utilized knowledge of organic evolution, as preserved in the fossil record, to identify and correlate the lithic records of ancient time.[1]

> The only chronometric scale applicable in geologic history for the stratigraphic classification of rocks and for dating geologic events exactly is furnished by the fossils. Owing to the irreversibility of evolution, they offer an unambiguous time-scale for relative age determinations and for worldwide correlations of rocks.[2]

> Fossils have furnished, through their record of the evolution of life on this planet, an amazingly effective key to the relative positioning of strata in widely separated regions and from continent to continent.[3]

> The age of rocks may be determined by the fossils found in them.[4]

> Ever since William Smith at the beginning of the 19th century, fossils have been and still are the best and most accurate method of dating and correlating the rocks in which they occur.[5]

These statements are from older geological writings, but the concept and method of dating rocks by their fossil contents — assuming evolutionary progression — has not changed. To the objection that this method of dating was in use before Darwin popularized evolution, the answer is that evolutionism was being advocated long before Darwin. In fact, before very many fossils had ever been found and analyzed, it was assumed that they should be arranged chronologically to conform to the assumed "Great Chain of Being," a pantheistic concept originating in ancient Greece, and very prominently utilized by humanists during the Renaissance and later by pre-Darwinian evolutionists in particular. This concept assumed that there was an unbroken chain of entities in nature from the simplest to the most complex, and the early attempts to organize the fossil record in a chronologic sequence were, to a large extent, based on this ancient pagan idea.[6]

It has long been recognized that the geologic column is an arbitrary construct, existing nowhere in full in any *local* geologic column. Various concepts were used in the early 19th century to combine all the scattered local columns into one global *standard* column.

> By application of the principle of superposition, lithologic identification, unconformities, and reference to fossil successions, both the thick and the thin masses are correlated with other beds at other sites. Thus there is established in detail the stratigraphic succession for all the geologic ages.[7]

More recently, in a very comprehensive study of all the local columns on all the world's continents everywhere, creationist geologist John Woodmorappe demonstrated that the standard column was actually non-existent anywhere. He concluded that:

> . . . 42% of earth's land surface has 3 or less geologic periods present at all; 66% has 5 or less of the 10 present; and only 14% has 8 or more geologic periods represented at all.[8]

He also concluded that "slightly less than 1% has all 10 periods simultaneously in place" (p. 67). Even that 1 percent is too high because it represents only the land surfaces. If the ocean bottoms are factored in (so far as known, none of these have the complete column in place, usually only containing Tertiary and possibly Cretaceous sediments), the portion of the earth's surface containing the complete column in place is only 1/3 percent or less.

Not even this small percentage tells the whole story, since none of the ten geologic periods are *fully* represented anywhere. The average thickness of local geologic columns is only about one mile, whereas the standard column with all ten periods and their subdivisions represented in their fullness would be *at least* 100 miles in thickness![9]

The identification of the various geologic ages, as noted above, is based on their fossil contents, but fossil taxons normally persist through many of these ages. Thus, only certain index fossil assemblages are actually used to date the strata. Furthermore, fossils are not infrequently found out of their assumed places in the evolutionary sequences (an anomalous situation supposedly caused by reworking and secondary deposition) and whole formations are sometimes found out of the standard evolutionary order (a phenomenon supposedly attributed to the remarkable process of "overthrusting"). Even in those cases where the few ages in a local column are in the proper order, they often are not sequential, with much of the standard column missing. In addition, every geological period from Cambrian to Tertiary can often be found resting on the basement, just as every period can often be found right on the earth's surface. There seems to be nothing very standard about the standard geologic column!

The standard column does serve evolutionists well, of course, as their best argument for evolution. The fossil record, even though it contains *no true transitional fossils*, is still presented as a persuasive evolutionary argument by means of its organization into the geologic column.

> . . . fossils provide the only historical, documentary evidence that life has evolved from simpler to more and more complex forms.[10]

> Naturalists must remember that the process of evolution is revealed only through fossil forms.[11]

> . . . we must look to the fossil record for the ultimate documentation of large-scale change. In the absence of a fossil record, the credibility of evolutionists would be severely weakened. We might wonder whether the doctrine of evolution would qualify as anything more than an outrageous hypothesis.[12]

In view of the vital importance of the standard geologic column and its associated fossil record to the whole question of evolution, and in view of the ephemeral and variable nature of the local columns which supposedly can be fitted into it, as well as the utter non-existence of genuine scientific evidence for evolution at all, it is surely appropriate to ask whether there might be a better explanation for the fossil record than the geologic column and its assumed evolutionary ages.

Indeed there *is* a better explanation. The divinely inspired record of the Bible describes a global hydraulic cataclysm that devastated the antediluvian world, killing all of its land-dwelling animals and humans (except those in Noah's ark), covering all the mountains of the world at its crest and continuing for a whole year. If such a cataclysm (involving tectonic and volcanic activity on a massive scale, as well as torrential rains and violent winds, affecting the entire world) really occurred, then it would definitely and profoundly affect the geologic record. If any earlier geological deposits had ever been formed, they would almost certainly be overthrown, reworked and redeposited, as well as destroying all the pre-flood topography. After it was all over, including its after-effects, the resulting worldwide "geologic column" would be a record, not of the evolution of life over many long ages, but rather of the destruction of life in one short age, that of the flood period.

This, in fact, was exactly the belief of the founding fathers of the science of geology — men such as Steno, Woodward, Burnet, Whiston, and others, and endorsed by leading scientists in other fields such as Isaac Newton. This paradigm later shifted to evolutionary uniformitarianism, especially through the publications of Lyell and Darwin, with the way being eased by the compromising multiple-flood views of Cuvier, Buckland, Sedgwick, and others.

The current complaint of so-called "progressive creationists" that an emphasis on six-day creation and the global cataclysmic flood is somehow hindering their efforts to win scientists and other intellectuals to Christ is falsified by the fact that a whole century of advocating progressive creationism and other compromise theories resulted only in alienating practically the whole intellectual world. The modern revival of strict creationism, on the other hand, has resulted in great numbers of intelligent and well-educated people turning back to God and His Word.

There are, indeed, still many unresolved geological problems in the flood model of geology and recent creationism, but there are many more serious biblical problems with the uniformitarian old-earth model. For those of us who really believe the Bible to be God's inerrant Word, *that* premise ought to govern our interpretations of the geologic data. We should *not* allow the latter to determine how we interpret the Bible!

With the coming of the flood, the greatest regime of death and destruction the world has ever known came on Planet Earth.

Job said later that the terrible floodwaters had "overturned the earth" (Job 12:15). Jesus said that "the flood came and destroyed them all" (Luke 17:27), and Peter said that "the world that then was, being overflowed with water, perished" (2 Pet. 3:6).

There has never, in all human history, been another event remotely comparable to this cataclysmic worldwide flood. If the biblical record is true and understandable — *and all creationists ought to believe this* — the greatest quantity and extent of erosion and sedimentation in world history must have been caused by the flood, and therefore also the greatest amount of fossilization.

All this, of course, was still further augmented by great tectonic and volcanic activity, when "all the fountains of the great deep were broken up" (Gen. 7:11). Still more geologic activity occurred in the latter stages of the flood, after the first 150 days, when "God made a wind to pass over the earth, and the waters assuaged; The fountains also of the deep and the windows of heaven were stopped, and the rain from heaven was restrained; And the waters returned from off the earth continually" (Gen. 8:1–3). The waters continued to go down for another five months before those in the ark, resting on one of the Ararat mountains (probably present-day Mount Ararat, the highest peak in the very mountainous region in eastern Turkey, a volcanic mountain now 17,000 feet high), could even see the tops of other high mountains nearby (Gen. 8:5).

The "assuaging" of the waters, as they drained rapidly off into new ocean basins (with, no doubt, much additional erosion and deposition of sediment) was caused by great tectonic uplifts, as described in Psalm 104:6–9:

> Thou coverest [the earth] with the deep as with a garment: the waters stood above the mountains. At thy rebuke they fled; at the voice of thy thunder they hasted away. They go up by the mountains; they go down by the valleys unto the place which thou hast founded for them. Thou hast set a bound that they may not pass over; that they turn not again to cover the earth.

The phrase "go up by the mountains" can as well be translated "the mountains go up," and many versions so render it. The total picture is one of rapid orogenies and high velocity run-off as the mountains rose up.

The end result of such tremendous geologic upheavals (hydraulic, volcanic, tectonic, atmospheric) is that, as Peter says: "The world that then was, being overflowed [literally, 'cataclysmed'] with water, perished." There could never have been greater death and burial of plants and animals in flood and volcanic and wind sediments in all world history than during this uniquely devastating cataclysm. Surely, the great majority of fossils now entombed in the sedimentary rocks of the earth's crust must be attributed to the flood, at least as far as the Bible is concerned.

The Bible does mention other great catastrophes such as earthquakes and local floods. But these were all *local* and *brief* in duration — in no way comparable to the mountain-covering, year-long flood of Noah's day.

There is, of course, a very brief reference to a time when "the earth was divided" in the days of Peleg, who was presumably born 101 years after the flood, assuming no gaps in the genealogical chronologies of Genesis 10 (note especially Gen. 10:25 and 11:10–16). Some young-earth creationists suggest that this statement may refer to a splitting and separation of one great post-flood continent into the seven continents and many islands of earth's present geography, resulting in a worldwide visitation of volcanic eruptions and destructive tsunamis.

It seems very likely, however, that such a monumental event as this, producing the planet's new continental/oceanic configurations in a brief time, as well as another global devastation like the flood itself, would be given a much more prominent description in the Bible than a few words in one single verse! Not too much later, for example, God's Word devotes a whole chapter (Gen. 19) to the much smaller geological catastrophe of the destruction of Sodom and Gomorrah. The latter catastrophe is also mentioned several times in later books of the Bible, but nowhere else is there even a hint of the continents splitting and moving apart.

There have indeed been other later floods, earthquakes, landslides, and other geological catastrophes in earth history, and some of these no doubt left much death and even occasional fossils in their wake. These were all relatively local and brief, however, warranting only superficial mention, if any, in the Bible. As far as God's Word is concerned, the great flood of Genesis must have produced many times more fossils than all the others combined. Everything else is trivial in relation to the geological effects of the flood (these effects include the resulting glacial period and other residual catastrophism). The Pleistocene Ice Age, for example, was caused by the flood, as an after-effect. This has been shown very persuasively by meteorologist Michael Oard.[13]

The record of the flood does not specifically mention the death and fossilization of marine animals, but this phenomenon must have been very widespread, with the breaking-up of all the fountains of the great deep. The record *does* state, of course, that "all that was in the dry land died" (Gen. 7:22). Every terrestrial mammal, every reptile, every bird, every amphibian, died. Undoubtedly many of these were trapped in the great shifting sediments and eventually buried and fossilized.

This would not necessarily be the case with human beings, however. More than any other creatures, men and women would be able to escape burial in sediments — by running, swimming, climbing, floating on rafts, etc. — even though they would finally have drowned in the flood waters. Their bloated, floating bodies would seldom have been trapped in the underwater sedimentation. Fossilization normally requires rapid and permanent burial, in addition to death, and relatively few humans, in comparison to land animals, would be preserved as fossils. Any that *were* preserved would probably never be found, with any remains scattered throughout the enormous volume in the global sediments laid down during the flood.

Science and the Geologic Column

Remember that the geologic column is largely an artificial construct, not existing as a whole in any one location. *Local* geologic columns do exist, however, and it is these that preserve the remnants of geologic history.

In general, the few distinct geologic "ages" represented in any given local column actually reflect the habitat elevations and ecological communities that once existed at that location, or else at the location from which they had been transported — possibly *en masse*. That is, *other factors being equal*, they would be deposited in the same communities of organisms with which they had lived and roughly in the same relative elevations at which they had lived, even though transported considerable distances. Marine invertebrates would tend to be buried at low elevations, fishes at higher elevations, amphibians at the original interface between sea and land, reptiles a little higher, birds and mammals still higher. Marine sediments would be deep down in the column, land sediments at the top, other things being equal.

This is exactly the order usually found in each local column. Many exceptions to this generalization can be found, of course, due to hydrodynamic sorting, reworking and mixing of sediments, etc., but this is the usual order. Furthermore, the older ideas of the uniformitarians, who thought that every formation was laid down very slowly over long ages, are rapidly being abandoned by the modern school of geologists. More and more it is acknowledged that all geologic events now preserved in the geologic column must have occurred very rapidly. For those who still think in terms of slow processes, note the following typical statements from leading evolutionary geologists — geologists who still believe in evolution, but in a catastrophic (or *episodic*) context rather than one of uniformitarianism.

The British geologist, Derek Ager, has been in the vanguard of this neo-catastrophist movement. He said:

> . . . the evolution of continents and of the stratigraphical column in general, has been a very episodic affair, with short "happenings" interrupting long ages of nothing in particular.

> In other words, the history of any one part of the earth, like the life of a soldier, consists of long periods of boredom and short periods of terror.[14]

In Ager's last book, written shortly before his death, he noted:

> . . . we cannot escape the conclusion that sedimentation was at times very rapid indeed and that at other times there were long breaks in sedimentation, though it looks both uniform and continuous.[15]

Ager noted two interesting examples of catastrophism, among many others.

Probably the most convincing proof of the local rapidity of terrestrial sedimentation is provided by the presence in measures of trees still in position of life.[16]

One of the most remarkable geological sights I have ever seen was at Mikulov in Czechoslovakia, where an excavation in Danubian loess shows the remains of literally dozens of mammoths.[17]

These mammoth fossils deposits, of course, are only one example of multitudes of fossil graveyards all over the world. In fact, as we have noted, the geological "ages" are identified by their fossil contents, and the very existence of fossils — particularly of any size — requires catastrophic burial.

In a review of Ager's last book, a geologist at the Paleontological Research Institution near Cornell University in Ithaca, New York, has made the following cogent observations.

Indeed geology appears at last to have outgrown Lyell. . . . The last 30 years have witnessed an increasing acceptance of rapid, rare, episodic, and "Catastrophic" events.

The volume is the summation of a lifetime of global geological work by one of the most influential stratigrapher-paleontologists of his generation, a highly eclectic compilation of the author's geological observations from around the world in support of the general view that the geological record is dominated not by slow, gradual change, but by episodic rare events causing local disasters, . . . this volume may mark the arrival of catastrophism at the status quo.[18]

Previously, Robert Dott, prominent American geologist, had made the same point in his presidential address to the Society of Economic Paleontologists and Mineralogists.

. . . the sedimentary record is largely a record of episodic events rather than being uniformly continuous. My message is that episodicity is the rule, not the exception.[19]

A leading European geologist rejects uniformitarianism in favor of what he calls "actualistic catastrophism."

In my presidential address to the International Association of Sedimentologists, I pointed out the fallacy of the Lyellian dogma and coined the term actualistic catastrophism.[20]

Catastrophism is enjoying a renaissance in geology. . . . Many of us are accepting that unusual catastrophic events have occurred repeatedly during the course of Earth's history.[21]

A prominent younger paleontologist calls uniformitarianism an albatross.

Our science is too encumbered with uniformitarian concepts. . . . Detailed paleo-environmental data tell us that the past is the key to the present, not vice versa.[22]

Another influential American geologist lists and describes many fallacies of uniformitarianism, and makes the following observation.

The idea that the rates or intensities of geological processes have been constant is so obviously contrary to the evidence that one can only wonder at its persistence.[23]

Similar quotations and examples could be multiplied at great length. Although many geologists continue to harbor a sort of emotional attachment to uniformitarianism in the old Lyellian sense, the facts of geology are against them, and this realization is leading to a plethora of literature on mass extinctions, asteroid impacts, climatological revolutions, and other catastrophic "rare events." Nevertheless, they all with one voice continue to reject the global flood of Noah's day, and continue to believe in long ages and evolution. They are almost neurotically afraid of being associated with the Bible and biblical creationists. Derek Ager was particularly insistent on this distancing posture.

This is not the old-fashioned catastrophism of Noah's flood and huge conflagrations. I do not think the bible-oriented fundamentalists are worth honoring with an answer to their nonsense [that is an easy way of ignoring the overwhelming evidence in favor of our "nonsense"— *writer*]. No scientist could be content with one very ancient reference of doubtful authorship [Ager's easy way of ignoring the overwhelming evidence for the divine inspiration of the Bible—*writer*].[24]

Dr. Ager once wrote to the writer, complaining about my quoting him, and wanting me to know that he did not believe in creationism or in *biblical* catastrophism. I had never implied that he did, of course, but his evidence for catastrophism was worth noting.

As Ager (and all the others quoted above) imply, the catastrophes they are postulating are intermittent, local or regional — sometimes even global — catastrophes, but they are all assumed to be separated from each other by millions of years when nothing much was happening geologically. They each may have caused mass extinctions, which they assume provided opportunities for the evolutionary "punctuations" so urgently needed by modern evolutionary biologists, in the absence of true transitional forms in their billions of fossils.

These geological "gaps" have left little or no legible record, except the necessity to provide time for evolution.

> Thus it appears that indeed the geological record is exceedingly incomplete. . . . If erosion and other ravages of time are the cause of the missing record, one should expect the incompleteness to increase with age. This, however, is not the case, and the explanation cannot be so simple.
>
> The geological record may thus be a record of rare events separated on any time scale by numerous and long gaps.[25]
>
> I maintain that a far more accurate picture of the stratigraphical record is of one long gap with only very occasional sedimentation.[26]

In other words, what we *see* in the "geologic column" is catastrophism. What we *do not see* is the long ages when nothing was happening in between the catastrophes.

Except, that is, when macroevolution must have been happening, and happening so rapidly that no intermediate forms could be fossilized to provide any evidence that it was happening. So the story goes.

At one time in the honored past, science was supposed to be

based on sound factual data, on observation and experimentation, not on the metaphysical speculations which evolutionists would pass off as science today. Many uniformitarians have finally been willing to admit that Lyell was wrong, because all geologic observations bear witness of catastrophe, not uniformity with the present. But they still cling to the notion of *unobserved* millions of years in between their catastrophes.

The reason why they must do this is that they would otherwise have to give up their evolutionism as well as their uniformitarianism. Other than this, there is no truly objective reason why all these individual catastrophes could not be merged into one gigantic global cataclysm, exactly as described in the Bible!

As a matter of fact, this is exactly what the evidence indicates. That is, there are no physical, chemical, or structural differences between the different "ages." As mentioned before, there are limestones, shales, sandstones, basalts, faults, folds, thrusts, marine formations, etc., in rocks of every assigned "age." There are the same metals and minerals in rocks of every age.

The only differences are in the fossils and, as we have seen, the "ages" are based on special index fossils. Every phylum of animal life is represented in every "age," as well as most classes and orders. Many — probably most — taxons extend through many ages, so not even fossils are useful in age dating, in most cases. The index fossil assemblages that are used, as we have noted, are essentially arranged in accordance with evolutionary presuppositions. Yet the resulting fossil record is, as we have also noted, taken as the best evidence for evolution.

All of this adds up to the fact that there is no real evidence for the geologic ages except evolution, and no real evidence for evolution except the geologic ages. In any other field of science, such a system would be called flagrant circular reasoning. There is, therefore, no real evidence that the entire geologic column (to the extent that it actually exists) could not have been formed in a single worldwide complex of catastrophes extending over a relatively short duration of time, finally comprising a unique hydraulic/volcanic/tectonic cataclysm. This, of course, is also what the Bible teaches.

No Time Break in the Column

There is one other very important point to note in this connection. The geologic column, as it has been constructed, is supposed to have worldwide validity, with each early age (i.e., lower in the column) grading into the next age above it. Even though the complete column exists nowhere, it is argued that one can locate adjacent regions where the uppermost layers in a formation truncated by erosion in any given local column will grade upward into the lowermost layer in an adjacent overlapping column, and so on. In this way, as noted before, "there is established in detail the stratigraphic succession for all the geologic ages."[27] Although there may be a local "unconformity" at the erosion surface (whereas a "conformity" would indicate uninterrupted deposition), such an unconformity would only extend a limited distance before grading into a conformity.

At one time, in the early 19th century especially, it was believed that each of the major periods was separated from those above and below it by worldwide "unconformities," assumed to be erosion surfaces representing unknown durations of time. Thus, the Cambrian Period was separated everywhere from the Ordovician Period above it by a worldwide break in the stratigraphy, marking a time period of unknown length. There are, of course, many local unconformities, which may well represent time gaps, or even boundaries between "ages," in various *local* columns.

It is now known, however, that there are no worldwide unconformities, and therefore no worldwide time gaps, in the standard geologic column. Deposition of sediments continued at some point or points in the world throughout the entire period of deposition of the geologic column on the crystalline basement rocks, at least until reaching the still unlithified sediments near the surface.

This is an important point, so needs documentation. Note a few such confirmations.

> The employment of unconformities as time-stratigraphic boundaries should be abandoned. . . . Because of the failure of unconformities as time indices, time-stratigraphic boundaries of Paleozoic and later age must be defined by time — hence by faunas.[28]

Here it is once again! Geologic ages are marked by their fossils, and nothing else — not by unconformities, not by type of rock, not by superposition or anything else — only by fossils on the basis of their assumed stage of evolution, or location in the Great Chain of Being.

It is widely acknowledged that chronostratigraphic units [that is, geologic systems representing a given age] . . . do not coincide everywhere with the diachronous boundaries of lithostratigraphic and biostratigraphic units [that is, specific geologic formations].[29]

Many unconformity-bounded units have been erroneously regarded as lithostratigraphic units, even though they are characterized not by lithologic unity but by the fact of being bounded by unconformities. . . . Similarly, many unconformity-bounded units have been erroneously considered to be chronostratigraphic units in spite of the fact that unconformity surfaces are apt to be diachronous [that is, crossing supposed time boundaries] and hence cannot constitute true chronostratigraphic boundaries.[30]

Finally, Dr. Amos Salvador, Chairman of the International Subcommission on Stratigraphic Classification, has said:

Bounding unconformities were the basis for establishing many of the earliest stratigraphic units, recognized in western Europe. Many of the systems of the presently accepted Standard Global Chronostratigraphic Scale were originally unconformity-bounded units. This procedure has not been restricted, however, to the earliest days of stratigraphic work or to western Europe; it has been used, and continues to be used, in all parts of the world. Unconformity-bounded units became very popular at the time tectonic episodes were considered essentially synchronous worldwide, but did lose favor among geologists when synchroneity was found not to hold true.[31]

It is evident that, if unconformity surfaces are not isochronous surfaces and do not extend worldwide, there is no worldwide time gap in the geologic column. For example, somewhere the middle Ordovician grades conformably into the upper Ordovician and somewhere the upper Ordovician grades into the lower Silurian, and so on. The deposition of the entire column — whether or not it is believed to represent the geologic ages — proceeded from bottom to top (Proterozoic through Tertiary) with no worldwide interruption in its deposition.

That being true (and it is), and if also every deposit has been formed very rapidly (as the neo-catastrophists now recognize), then it follows as day follows night that *the entire column was formed rapidly*! If all formations represent local catastrophes, as acknowledged now by Ager and most other active geologists, then they must all be interconnected and essentially continuous, forming the tremendous record of a global hydraulic/volcanic/tectonic cataclysm — nothing less than the great flood of the Bible!

The Martian Flood

An interesting commentary on the reluctance of secular scientists to accept the historicity of the global Genesis flood is their eager acquiescence in the attempt by NASA geologists to promote a global Martian flood. This is all a part of the desperate attempt to find evidence of life in other worlds, as discussed in chapter 6.

In their unrelenting attempt to find evidence for extraterrestrial life, governments have spent many billions of dollars on space probes of various kinds and giant radio telescopes vainly searching the cosmos for intelligible signals from other worlds. On the popular level, reports of UFO sightings and alien landings have proliferated enormously in recent decades. The entertainment media have feasted on mega-profits from this mania (*Star Wars, E.T., Contact, Independence Day, Star Trek*, etc.) for many years, with no end in sight.

Why? What is the meaning of this fascination with the heavens and the possibility of life out there? It still seems completely impossible that "earthlings" could ever travel to other planets where there are intelligent beings — or that such beings could ever travel to earth. Even if such creatures exist — for which there is not the slightest evidence as yet — they are just too far away.

The atheist Isaac Asimov wrote many best-selling novels about these other worlds, but as a scientist he knew they were beyond reach.

> Asimov also disposes of another popular myth — that one day we will journey to the stars — Only if we use antimatter as a fuel can we make a return trip to the nearest star, and that form of energy is likely to remain forever beyond our grasp. In any case, the effort would never justify the visit; our intrepid voyagers, or their descendants, would not arrive back before A.D. 50,000. Because we can never visit another star, so we can never be visited by

aliens from another Solar System. Asimov, you're a spoil-sport![32]

Yet both scientists and laymen persist in believing that the vast universe must be teeming with intelligent beings. Says the astronomer Jastrow:

> Why would the Earth alone — an undistinguished body among trillions of similar ones — be chosen by nature or the deity as the only planet on whose soil the seeds of life have taken root?[33]

No one has seen even *one* of these trillions of planets, of course — only a number of questionable "perturbations" on several stars. Nevertheless, evolutionary statistical speculation suggests they just *might* be there.

> If one chooses to avoid speculation and stick solely with observations, one can ask the same question that Nobel physicist Enrico Fermi put forth in 1950: If the Galaxy is teeming with intelligent life, where are they? The sobering reality is that there is no observational evidence whatsoever for the existence of other intelligent beings anywhere in the universe.[34]

Be that as it may, the space search is now focusing on finding life of any kind — intelligent or not — in the solar system. The moon probes turned out negatively and so did those of the Viking landers on Mars. The other planets seem too inhospitable for life even to be seriously considered, although hopes have recently been expressed for some of their satellites. The problem is that for any form of life to be even possible, an abundance of liquid water is essential.

The earth has been called "the water planet," with more than two-thirds of its surface covered by water, but there is no liquid water at all on the moon or on Mars, as far as anyone can tell.

But since it is so important to evolutionists to find *some* evidence of extraterrestrial life, they are currently pinning their hopes on Mars. The announcement by David McKay and other NASA scientists in 1996 that fossil bacteria had been found in a meteorite from Mars has created a sensation that is being exploited to the full. But consider the following:

Even the premise that the meteorite came from Mars is disputable. . . . Several reasons for caution on the micro-fossils came from William Schoff at the NASA press conference: they are a hundred times smaller than any such fossils found on Earth, there is no measurement of the composition of the cells to show whether they are organic or not, and there is no sign of any cavities within the cells in which fluids necessary for life could reside.[35]

The whole scenario is fascinating. Four billion years or more ago, there was — they say — enough water on Mars to permit minute organisms, much smaller than any ever seen on earth, to evolve, then to die, become fossilized in a magma rock, which was somehow blasted out into space about 16 million years ago and then, amazingly, settled down on earth about 13,000 years ago, to be discovered in Antarctic ice by meteorite hunters 12 years ago, finally to be recognized by NASA scientists just when they needed additional funding for more space ventures.

Trying to be politically correct, yet realistic, a recent summary of the evidence concludes as follows:

> Even if some Martian organic matter is present, it may be impossible to disentangle its properties from the apparent overprint of terrestrial contamination.[36]

But what about the water that was so necessary to get all this started? There is apparently no liquid water on Mars now. This important deficiency can be overcome, however, by assuming that enough water used to be there to scour out great channels and form vast flood plains. Certain surface features on photographs taken by the Viking craft that orbited Mars in 1976 have been interpreted as formed by water in tremendous quantities in what would have amounted essentially to global flooding of the planet.

The Pathfinder "rover" received even more enthusiastic media coverage than the Martian meteorite. It landed on a site assumed to be a vast flood plain, and proceeded to sample various rocks on the plain.

> But team scientists were already doing impressionistic science on images from the site, finding evidence that it was swept by one of the largest floods — or mud slides — in solar system history.[37]

Matthew Golombeck of Pasadena's Jet Propulsion Laboratory, which organized the Pathfinder mission, and other NASA geologists now believe in a mammoth Martian flood long, long ago, and the flood water presumably would have made life possible there.

> Golombek and his colleagues believe that the first images confirm their suspicion that billions of years ago a great flood of a billion cubic meters per second swept the region for weeks, carrying a variety of rocks from distant highlands.[38]

A newspaper account called it "a flood of biblical proportions." Which raises a question. Why are evolutionists so anxious to believe in a global flood on Mars, where there's no water at all, and no evidence but a few questionable land forms, while they flatly reject a global flood on earth, where there is a great amount of water and an abundance of evidence?

When creationists talk about the Genesis flood, skeptics frequently ask: "If the flood was global, where did all the water come from, and where did it go?" The Bible does provide an answer, of course: the water is in the ocean and changes in the atmosphere and geosphere both caused and removed the floodwaters.

But how about on Mars? Where did *that* water come from, and where did it go? They don't know.

> Determining what could have unleashed the water, which was presumably stored beneath a dry surface, is one of the enduring mysteries of Mars.[39]

The question would probably not even be raised if it were not for the urgent need to find extraterrestrial life somewhere. Similar "flood channels" and "flood plains" have been noted on Venus, but life would be impossible on Venus for other reasons, so its "flood" features have been attributed to rivers of lava.

But if it can just be shown that there was once life on Mars — any form of life — that would supposedly prove that life is a natural phenomenon that occurs whenever the conditions are right.

> Confirmation of the Mars report will demonstrate that the universe is teeming with life.[40]

That would mean that life is a product of evolution and we

don't need God to explain it. Or at least, that is the reasoning that many employ. Of course, theistic evolutionists might still argue that God could have allowed life to evolve on many planets if He so chose.

But it is not a question of what God *could* do. What He *says* is that our planet earth is where He created life, earth is where He himself became man and died for our sins, and earth is where He will reign forever over His whole creation.

> The heaven, even the heavens, are the Lord's; but
> the earth hath he given to the children of men (Ps. 115:16).

God has other purposes for the stars, and other planets, if they exist, and we shall have eternity to learn about them.

> And they that be wise shall shine as the brightness
> of the firmament; and they that turn many to righteous-
> ness as the stars for ever and ever (Dan. 12:3).

The Question of Radiometric Dating

I shall conclude this chapter with a necessarily brief and inadequate discussion of radiometric dating. The geological evidence as just discussed ought to be sufficient to show that the earth is quite young, since all of its fossil-bearing rocks are best explained in terms of the Genesis flood and its after-effects. However, there are thought to be certain non-geological evidences that the earth is old, and this subject needs also to be treated.

The dating of rocks by the radioactive decay of certain minerals is undoubtedly the main argument today for the dogma of an old earth.

But the Bible clearly teaches a recent creation of both the heavens and the earth, so Christians have often tried to reinterpret this doctrine to accommodate the long ages required by radioactive dating. For those Christians who believe that Genesis (like the other historical books of the Bible) should be understood as literal history, it has therefore been necessary to show the fallacies in the so-called "scientific proofs" of an old earth.

Before the discovery of radioactivity, this usually meant arguing against the evidences from crustal cooling, sedimentation rates, or salt influx in the oceans. The development of radiometric dating during the early decades of the 20th century, however, soon displaced all these arguments, since the latter method seemed to allow much more time for evolution. As this dating method began to be developed, a Committee on the Measurement of Geologic Time was formed by the National Research Council with Professor Alfred C. Lane, geology professor at Tufts University, as chairman. The Committee first met in December 1923 and then began publishing in "Annual Reports," reviewing and discussing all the papers on radiometric dating during each successive year, continuing until 1955 or so. When I first heard of these (about 1946), I purchased all the back issues and subscribed to all future issues, trying to note all studies and comments potentially useful to creationists. They are now in our ICR Library.

During the century after Lyell and Darwin and up until about 1950, the reaction of practically all Christian leaders was to accept uniformitarianism and the radiometric ages, accommodating them by either the gap theory or the day-age theory.

There were a few exceptions. Perhaps the first was Dudley Joseph Whitney, an agricultural scientist who had graduated from Berkeley and then edited various agricultural journals. Whitney's article, "The Age of the Earth: Comments on Some Geologic Methods Used in its Interpretation," appeared in the *Bulletin of Deluge Geology* in December 1941, and was apparently the first modern defense of a recent creation. In this paper, Whitney developed the evidences for a young earth based on: (1) influx of sodium and other chemicals into the ocean; (2) depletion of the land by leaching; (3) sedimentation rates; (4) build-up of helium in the atmosphere; (5) disintegration of comets; (6) influx of meteorites and their nickel-iron contents on the earth; and (7) efflux of water from earth's interior by volcanism. Most of these evidences are still relevant.

Whitney then added a brief critique of the assumptions in radioactive dating. He commented on the many discordances in results, the problem of separating "common lead" from radiogenic lead, the possibility that some of the supposed radiogenic elements could have been added either before or after deposition, the possibility of changes in disintegration rates, the possibility of selective leaching, and the many conflicts with previously assumed geologic ages. These criticisms also are still valid.

Whitney published many other papers, as well as two small books, all advocating recent creation and flood geology. He was even able to get at least one paper included in the Reports of the Committee on Geologic Time (he was on good terms with Professor Lane) and in the *Pan-American Geologist*.

There were a few others in the old Creation-Deluge Society who believed in recent creation, but the next important article — so far as I know — was one by geologist Clifford Burdick entitled, "The Radioactive Time Theory and Recent Trends in Methods of Reckoning Geologic Time." The paper had been written earlier, but was finally published in 1946, in volume I of *The Forum*, a short-lived journal established by the "old-earthers" who had taken over the Creation-Deluge Society. It covered much the same ground as Whitney had done, but in more detail and with better documentation.

My first book, *That You Might Believe* (published in 1946), had briefly questioned the reliability of radioactive dating, but also had allowed for the gap theory. But then I read Burdick's paper and was convinced that such a compromise was unnecessary scientifically. In the meantime, I had made a verse-by-verse study of the whole Bible on this subject and found that the Bible could not legitimately allow for an old earth (see my 1993 book, *Biblical Creationism*, which demonstrates this fact by analyzing every relevant biblical passage).

In 1953, I presented a paper at the annual convention of the American Scientific Affiliation (where I first met John Whitcomb) entitled "Biblical Evidence for a Recent Creation and Worldwide Flood." The response to this paper finally disabused me of the idealistic notion that the leading members of the A.S.A. could be swayed by biblical evidences. They and others like them will accept literal creationism only when they are convinced that secular scientists believe it.

However, this conference and my later correspondence with John Whitcomb did lead finally to the book, *The Genesis Flood*, and this in turn to the Creation Research Society and the modern revival of literal biblical creationism. My portion of *The Genesis Flood* included a 48-page discussion of radiometric dating and its fallacies (as I saw them, at least) with suggested resolutions.

The Creation Research Society was formed in 1963 and its quarterly publications have included a few papers critiquing radiometric dating, but these have been relatively few, considering the critical importance of the subject. The most extensive was a paper by John Woodmorappe, "Radiometric Chronology Reappraised," published in the *CRS Quarterly* in September 1979 and recently reissued by

ICR in an anthology of Woodmorrappe articles entitled *Studies in Flood Geology.*

Woodmorappe's paper, as well as later more precise research studies by Drs. Steve Austin and Andrew Snelling (both on the ICR geology faculty)[41] have shown numerous gross inconsistencies in many published radiometrically determined ages (e.g., an age of hundreds of thousands of years or more for the 1980 lava flows from Mount St. Helens). However, the reason why calculations from radioisotopes should give such vast "apparent ages" at all is still unsettled.

An ICR-formed committee of well-qualified geoscientists is (at this writing) working diligently in search of an answer to this question. There seem to be three main assumptions in such calculations, any one or all of which could be the problem.

First, the mineral being measured is not a closed system, so that the "parent" may be leached out or the "daughter" filtered in, thus making the apparent age too great.

Secondly, the decay rate may have been greater in the past — say, during the creation period or the flood period. This also would make the apparent age too large.

Perhaps most likely of all, the "daughter" may already have been placed in the mineral along with the "parent" in the original magma, which then eventually came to the surface as igneous rock, and thus was not formed by the decay process at all.

All these possibilities, along with others, are being studied in depth by the committee. In any case, with so many potential errors in the assumptions, even if the measurements are accurate, there is no good reason to rely on radiological age values at all.

The biblical revelation, of course, must be our constraining guide in seeking a firm answer. Whether or not we creationists can ever come to a firm consensus on the significance of the radiometric data, we must never forget that the evidence for the inspiration, integrity, and clarity of God's Word is far greater than the illusory and self-serving arguments offered by evolutionists and compromising creationists for an ancient earth. We need to remind ourselves over and over that there is no hint whatever — anywhere in the Bible — that the earth is significantly older than the few thousand years of recorded history.

There are numerous biblical statements, on the other hand, that clearly require a young earth. For example, there is no evidence in context that the word "day" in the first chapter of Genesis means anything but a literal day. The word (Hebrew, *yom*) is specifically defined by God as the daylight period in the diurnal succession of day and night the very first time it is used (Gen. 1:5). God himself unequivocally confirmed in the fourth commandment (Exod. 31:18) that He had made everything in heaven and earth in six days — days that were the same kind of days as man's days.

Furthermore, the Lord Jesus Christ clearly affirmed in Mark 10:6 that "from the beginning of the creation God made them male and female"—not 4.6 billion years *after* the beginning of the creation! The very concept of billions of years of a groaning, travailing creation (Rom. 8:22) with animals suffering and dying during the long geologic ages before God could get around to creating men and women in His own image, is an insult to a loving, omniscient, omnipotent God. Death is, under such a concept, not "the wages of sin" as the Bible says (Rom. 6:23), but the method of "creation," as evolutionists say.

Therefore, there *must* be a true and satisfying answer to this troublesome radiometry problem. The earth *is* young, and the data *must* confirm this, if they are rightly understood.

God has provided the basic direction for our research on this vital issue in 2 Peter 3:3–6. This passage clearly informs us that the unique processes during two brief periods of history — creation and the flood — make the uniformitarian assumptions in the use of radio-decay rates for dating earth history quite invalid.

Endnotes

1 O.D. von Engeln. and K.E. Caster, *Geology* (New York: McGraw-Hill, 1952), p. 423.

2 O.H. Schindewolf, comments on some stratigraphic terms. *American Journal of Science*, 255:394, 1957. Schindewolf was one of Europe's leading paleontologists.

3 H.D. Hedberg, "The Stratigraphic Panorama," *Bulletin of the Geological Society of America,* 72:499, 1961. Hedberg was president of the Geological Society of America, and the quote was taken from his presidential address.

4 S.P. Welles, "Paleontology," *World Book Encyclopedia*, 15:5, 1978. Welles was Research Associate in the Museum of Paleontology at the University of California at Berkeley.

5 D. Ager, "Fossil Frustrations," *New Scientist*, 100:415, 1983. Ager was a past president of the British Geological Association.

6 Henry M. Morris, *The Long War Against God* (Grand Rapids, MI: Baker Book House, 1989), p. 183–195.

7 von Engeln and Caster, *Geology*, p. 417.

8 John Woodmorappe, "The Essential Non-existence of the Evolutionary-Uniformitarian Geologic Column," *Creation Research Society Quarterly*, 18:47–71, 1981. Also in J. Woodmorappe, *Studies in Flood Geology* (Santee, CA: Institute for Creation Research, 1993).

9 von Engeln and Caster, *Geology*, p. 417.

10 C.O. Dunbar, *Historical Geology* (New York: Wiley, 1960), p.47. In its various editions, this textbook was one of the most widely used of this century.

11 P. Grassé, *Evolution of Living Organisms* (New York: Academic Press, 1977), p. 4. Grassé taught evolution at the Sorbonne for 30 years.

12 S.M. Stanley, *Macroevolution: Pattern and Process* (New York: W. H. Freeman, 1979), p. 2. Stanley is one of the leading paleontologists active today, especially in the field of "macroevolution."

13 M. Oard, *An Ice Age Caused by the Genesis Flood* (Santee, CA: Institute for Creation Research, 1990).

14 D. Ager, *The Nature of the Stratigraphic Record*, 3rd edition (New York: Wiley, 1993), p. 132, 141.

15 D. Ager, *The New Catastrophism* (New York: Cambridge University Press, 1993), p. 49.

16 Ibid., p. 47.

17 Ibid., p. 51.

18 W.D. Allmon, "Post-gradualism," *Science*, 262:122–123, 1993.

19 R.H. Dott, "Episodic View Now Replacing Catastrophism," *Geotimes*, 10:16, 1982.

20 K.J. Hsu, "Actualistic Catastrophism and Global Change," *Paleongeography. Paleoclimatology, Paleoecology* (Global and planetary change section), 89:309–313, 1990.

21 K.J. Hsu and J. A. McKenzie, "Rare Events in Geology Discussed at Meeting," *Geotimes*, 31:11–12, 1986.

22 E. Kauffman, "The Uniformitarian Albatross," *Palaios*, 2(6):531, 1987.

23 J.H. Shea, "Twelve Fallacies of Uniformitarianism," *Geology*, 10:455–460, 1982.

24 Ager, *The New Catastrophism*, p. xix.

25 T.H. Van Andel, "Consider the Incompleteness of the Geological Record," *Nature*, 294:397–398, 1981.

26 Ager, *The Nature of the Stratigraphic Record*, p. 52.

27 von Engeln and Caster, *Geology*, p. 417.

28 H.E. Wheeler and E. M. Beasley, "Critique of the Time-Stratigraphic Concept," *Bulletin, Geological Society of America*, 59:75–86, 1948.

29 S.G. Lucas, discussion of "A critique of Chronostratigraphy," *American Journal of Science*, 285:764–767, 1985.

30 K.H. Chang, "Rethinking Stratigraphy," *Geotimes*, 26:23–24, 1981.

31 A. Salvador, "Unconformity-bounded Stratigraphic Units," *Bulletin, Geological Society of America*, 98:232–237, 1987.

32 John Emsley, in a review of *The Relativity of Wrong*, by Isaac Asimov (New York: Oxford University Press, 1988) in *New Scientist*, vol. 122, April 8, 1989, p. 60.

33 Robert Jastrow, "What Are the Chances for Life?" *Sky and Telescope*, June 1997, p. 62.

34 Robert Naeye, "O.K. Where Are They?" *Astronomy*, vol. 24, July 1996, p. 42.

35 Monica Grady, Ian Wright, and Colin Pillinger, "Opening a Martian Can of Worms," *Nature*, vol. 382, August 14, 1996, p. 575.

36 Harry V. McSween, Jr. "Evidence for Life in a Martian Meteorite?" *Geotimes,* vol. 7, July 1997 , p. 5.

37 Richard A. Kerr, "Pathfinder Strikes a Rocky Bonanza," *Science*, vol. 277, July 11, 1997, p. 173.

38 Ibid.

39 Ibid.

40 Jastrow, "What Are the Chances for Life?" p. 63.

41 S.A. Austin, *Catastrophes in Earth History* (Santee, CA: Institute for Creation Research, 1984). Also, see the associated Catastroref software (1994).

Chapter VIII

Defending Against Compromise

he four previous chapters have especially emphasized the defense of our faith — especially its creationist foundations — against its overt enemies, the evolutionary atheists, pantheists, and humanists. We have focused in particular on the fields of biology, astronomy, cosmology, and geology, for these are the sciences in which evolutionism is most pervasive, and in which the biblical revelation of creation and ancient history is most widely rejected.

In this chapter, however, we need to examine the all too common tendency of Christians to compromise on these vital issues, trying somehow to accommodate the evolutionary ages of the geologists and astronomers in their theology. No doubt most of these Christian accommodationists sincerely believe they should do this in order to win over the hard-core evolutionary scientists to a Christian world view. They argue that a literal acceptance of the Genesis records is difficult or impossible scientifically and therefore turns educated young people away from Christianity.

We have already shown in chapter 3 that the traditional attempts to accommodate these ages in Genesis — via the day/age theory, gap theory, local flood theory, etc. — will not work biblically. Nevertheless, Christian compromise on this foundational issue is still so widespread, among evangelicals as well as main-line denominations, that further examination of current trends of this sort is needed here.

Bible-believing Christians really need to defend traditional biblical Christianity today not only against its overt enemies but also against the compromises advocated by its friends. The criterion must always be to interpret scientific data in terms of the inerrant Word of God — not to use current "science" to determine our biblical interpretations.

The Mythical Genesis

Back to Genesis, the epic first book of the Bible that takes readers from stories of the creation of the world through the first centuries of human history.[1]

These are among the opening lines of a 1996 feature story on the current revival of interest in the Book of Genesis. This revival is said to be spawning an imminent deluge of books and media events praising the religious and moral worth of Genesis while flatly denying its record of real history. The author, Sandi Dolbee, goes on to exclaim (and don't miss the Noahic metaphor!): "Now, over the next 40 days and 40 nights, more or less, Genesis will be awash in a flood of new attention. At least nine books, by one count, will rain down on bookstores. Interview czar Bill Moyers will add to the deluge with a ten-episode public television series on the subject."[2]

However, the combination of Bill Moyers (the liberal once-Southern Baptist bureaucrat, commentator, and media personality ever since the presidency of Lyndon B. Johnson) and public television (with its anti-creationist bias as particularly imposed on its tax-paying audience with the one-sided *Nova* program which had confused the creation-evolution question several years before) was enough to quickly dispel any euphoria we might experience over this sudden interest of government in religion.

The author of the article cited many writers and editors as they attempt to evaluate the renewed interest in this ancient Book of Genesis, which — they all agree — is nothing but myth and legend. Rabbi Harold Kushner offered the interesting idea that it is connected with "a sense of an end of days, a sense of cycles closing," because of the imminence of the year 2000. Phyllis Tickle, an editor of *Publishers Weekly*, attributed it to "overwhelming religious nostalgia." Bill

Moyers called Genesis "the mother of all books" — speaking more profound truth than he may have intended.

It is natural for us to be glad for this upsurge of interest in the foundational book of God's inspired Word. Moyers, by the way, said he got the idea for the Genesis series from a Genesis seminar he attended about five years before. I do not know who sponsored this seminar, of course, or what its perspective may have been, but at least it caused him to think about origins and meanings. Whether readers believe its records or not, the narratives in Genesis are magnificent literature, if nothing else, and it does speak solemnly and beautifully of the existence, character, and purposes of God.

It is sad, however, that these writers and religionists refuse to take the Genesis record as it stands. Rabbi Kushner, for example, said that the story of Adam and Eve should be understood as "the biblical metaphor of evolution. How the first human beings rose above the animal level and entered the world of knowledge of good and evil."[3] One of the book writers, Karen Armstrong, former Roman Catholic nun, interprets the story of Jacob wrestling all night with God as symbols "of the human struggle to relate to God."[4]

And so on. Moyers said a key purpose of his 10-part television series on Genesis would be to get people to engage "in a dialogue that will help us work ourselves through to a new cultural identity."[5] At least that's what the article says he said!

We can at least be thankful if this spate of books and television programs causes people to go back and read the actual Book of Genesis itself. Genesis can speak for itself, if it is read with an open heart and mind. Serious readers will find they don't need Rabbi Kushner and other theological liberals to tell them what they think it means. The fact is that God himself wrote it, using His chosen patriarchs to record it, and it means exactly what it says. All the other Bible writers, as well as Christ himself, accepted it as true, literal history.

While Moyers and his liberal friends are, in effect, "damning it with faint praise," as the old saying goes, others continue to attack Genesis — especially its accounts of creation and the flood — head-on.

The American Civil Liberties Union, in one of its latest high-pressure, fund-raising, and membership-soliciting letters from Executive Director Ira Glasser, cites with great pride its part in the Scopes trial and in the 1987 Supreme Court rejection of the Louisiana creation law. Glasser boasts that: "Our success in the Scopes trial played a major part in ending forced religious teaching in public schools." He said that the ACLU's victory in the Louisiana case ended "a seven-year struggle by the ACLU to prevent the imposition, by law, of religious beliefs in the public schools."[6]

A similar high-pressure, fund-appeal, and membership solicitation letter by Barry Lynn, executive director of Americans United for Separation of Church and State, warned that "the Religious Right" is determined to "require that biblical accounts of how the world began be taught in public school science classes."[8]

One wonders why the ACLU and AUSCS and other such groups did not oppose the proposed airing of the 10-part series on "Genesis: A Living Conversation" on public television, since they are so zealously opposed to any mixing of government and religion.

However, they don't seem to be opposed to the state's endorsement of religion as such, but only to the *true religion*! Especially as founded upon Genesis!

The government has itself indirectly been promoting the rejection of Genesis as the true account of origins by its ongoing funding of projects to support evolution. The most expensive of these, of course, is the space program, which for decades has been trying urgently to find evidence of extra-terrestrial life. Such evidence, of course, is needed if the Genesis record that God created life on earth in six days is to be rejected. If life evolved on earth (so the reasoning goes) it must also have evolved in other worlds. So probes are sent to the moon and the planets, and radio telescopes monitored for space messages, all at great cost to taxpayers, in the vain hope of finding some hint somewhere of extra-terrestrial life.

The unbroken chain of failures, however, together with the sky-rocketing national debt, had tempted Congress to curtail the funding of such ventures. As noted in chapter 5, however, that situation suddenly changed with the supposedly fortuitous revelation that a small, supposed meteoritic rock, found 12 years before in Antarctica, had supposedly been formed 4.5 billion years ago in Mars, then supposedly fractured about a billion years later, allowing minerals to form that supposedly contained some structures that might have been primitive bacteria, then supposedly blasted into space by a cometary impact or something about 16 million years ago, finally settling down on earth supposedly 13,000 years ago. The minute structures supposedly might have been primeval Martian bacteria, although there were known to be inorganic processes that could have produced similar structures.

But with such supposedly overwhelming and profoundly convincing evidence that life once existed on Mars (it doesn't now, of course), immediately evolutionists just *know* that life must have evolved at many places through the universe.

And, most importantly, our government's exobiology research programs, which they hope will disprove Genesis, are no longer in danger of being defunded!

It is rare enough for a scientific discovery with no practical applications to draw an enthusiastic response from politicians, but it is almost unheard of for House Speaker Newt Gingrich (R-GA) and U.S. Vice President Albert Gore to agree on the need for more government spending. The startling claim that a meteorite, consisting of a chunk of Mars rock, bears evidence of ancient life has provoked just such a reaction, however. Both political leaders told NASA Administrator Daniel Goldin separately in recent days that they are willing to find more money to beef up the agency's Mars exploration effort. If that happens, the first hints of extra-terrestrial life could jump-start the struggling U.S. space science program.[9]

And President Bill Clinton himself has said: "I am determined that the American space program will put its full intellectual power and technological prowess behind the search for further evidence of life on Mars."[10]

It does seem very important indeed to our political, scientific, and theological establishments to prove once and for all that the Genesis record of creation is only a myth.

I can't help but think of the ironic verse in Psalm 2:4 in this situation. "He that sitteth in the heavens shall laugh: the Lord shall have them in derision."

Old-Earth Creationism

Many evangelical leaders today, unfortunately, have capitulated to the evolutionary time-scale of modern unbelieving geologists and astronomers. They feel that they must somehow reinterpret the Genesis record of creation to allow for billions of prehistoric years, which the evolutionists must have in order to make cosmic evolution and biological evolution seem feasible. This compromise is necessary, they say, in order to win scientists and other intellectuals to the Lord.

Perhaps the most influential of these evangelical scientific speakers and writers is Hugh Ross, with his "Reasons to Believe" organizations, but there are many others. Many large evangelical churches, as well as most evangelical seminaries and liberal arts colleges, today favor one of the various accommodationist theories. So do the leaders of many para-church organizations, such as the American Scientific Affiliation, along with a host of others. Some claim neutrality on the issue, but this is a cop-out that ignores the clear statements of God's Word.

In addition, there are the many liberal denominations, seminaries, and other professedly Christian organizations that no longer hold even to the verbal inspiration of the Bible, practically all of which now teach theistic evolution. The term "evangelical" is used above to denote only those individuals and organizations that still hold to the full inspiration and authority of the Bible, as well as the deity of Jesus Christ and salvation through faith in the substitutionary death and bodily resurrection of Christ. Yet even many of these seem willing to distort the Bible's teaching on creation and the flood, simply to accommodate the supposed geologic and cosmic ages required by evolution.

We strongly believe that it is a serious mistake when Bible-believing Christians compromise with the great ages demanded by the evolutionists. Various interpretive devices have been suggested by Bible expositors as they try to convert the six-day creation record of Genesis into billions of years. Some will frankly advocate "theistic evolution," but others will call it "process creation," "progressive creation," "multiple creation," or some other term, implying that they still believe in some sort of "creation." Some do criticize and reject Darwinian evolution, but then will still allow some other form of evolution — "creative evolution," "pantheistic evolution," "punctuational evolution," or something. Some still resort to the unscientific "gap theory" which seeks to insert the "ages" between the first two verses of Genesis. Every such group must turn to either the "local flood theory" or the "tranquil flood theory" if they are going to hold to the geologic ages, since a global cataclysm such as the Bible describes would have destroyed all evidence for the geologic ages.

Then they go on to patronizingly deplore the supposed anti-intellectualism of what they call "young-earth creationism" (this is *their* term; we prefer "biblical creationism" or "literal creationism"). They think this position is an embarrassment (one has even called it a "scandal") to evangelicalism.

However, those who believe in a recent literal creation of all things do not consider themselves anti-scientific or anti-intellectual! Many are fully credentialed scientists, quite as familiar with the scientific and biblical evidences as anyone else. Indeed there are *now thousands of scientists* who believe in recent six-day creation. There are also organizations of scientists who are young-earth creationists in at least 15 different countries, as well as in many states in this country.

The difference is this: we believe the Bible must take priority over scientific theories, while they believe scientific theories must determine our biblical interpretations.

It all seems to hinge on one overriding question. Do we really believe the Bible to be God's inerrant Word or not? If the Bible is *really* the Word of our Creator God, then — by definition — it *must* be inerrant and authoritative on every subject with which it deals. This assumption leads clearly to the conviction that the creation took place in six literal days several thousand years ago. We believe this simply because God said so and said it quite plainly! And then we find also that this revealed fact would fit all the facts of science much better than the long-age evolutionary scenario does.

It is no good to say, as one evangelical leader said recently: "Well, I believe that God could create in six days or six billion years — it makes no difference."

Yes it does, because it has to do with God's truthfulness! It is not a matter of what God *could* do. The question is what God *says* that He *did*! And what He said in writing was this, recorded with His own finger on a table of stone: "In six days the Lord made heaven and earth, the sea, and all that in them is, and rested the seventh day" (Exod. 20:11; see also Exod. 31:15–18).

For a discussion of every passage in the Bible dealing with creation or the flood, see the writer's book, *Biblical Creationism*. There

218 ~ Defending the Faith

is *not a hint* anywhere in the Bible of evolution or long ages of earth or cosmic history.

Others have said: "But God *could* have created by a long evolutionary process if He wanted to."

No, He couldn't! God can do everything *except* contradict himself and His own nature. Evolution is the most wasteful and most cruel process that one could ever devise by which to "create" men and women. Christians should not accuse God of being responsible for the evolutionary process.

Nor does it help any to say that God interspersed various acts of special creation at different times throughout the long geological ages. This is what is usually meant by the term "progressive creation." Modern evolutionary biologists and paleontologists are increasingly turning to a similar concept today — only they just call it "punctuated equilibrium." They explain the many gaps in the fossil record, not by sporadic creation events, but as sudden evolutionary developments triggered by mass extinctions that punctuate long periods of "stasis," or equilibrium.

Their atheistic theory is, it would seem, actually more reasonable than that of the progressive creationists. The latter have to attribute all these massive waves of extinction to God. There were also the multiplied billions of animals that suffered and died during the long periods of stasis. This problem applies even to the populations of supposed pre-Adamic human-like beings (*Homo erectus*, Neandertal, etc.) that presumably became extinct before Adam and Eve were created.

To literal creationists, on the other hand, it seems unthinkable that the God of the Bible — the God who is omniscient and omnipotent, merciful and loving — would do anything like that. Surely He could devise and implement a better plan than this. It is true, of course, that in this present age "the whole creation groaneth and travaileth in pain together until now" (Rom. 8:22), but God did not *create* it as a groaning, dying world. At the end of the creation week, "God saw everything that he had made, and, behold, it was very good" (Gen. 1:31).

The problem is sin. "By one man sin entered into the world, and death by sin, and so death passed upon all men, for that all have sinned" (Rom. 5:12). It will not do, of course, to argue that death affected only Adam and his human descendants, for "death reigned

— even over them that had not sinned" (Rom. 5:14). God's curse was on Adam's whole dominion, even the very elements. "Cursed is the ground for thy sake," God told Adam (Gen. 3:17).

Nor will it do to say that the curse applied only to "spiritual" death, on the premise that Adam would eventually have died physically anyway. If *that* were the case, the bitterly cruel *physical* suffering and death of Christ on the cross for our sins becomes a travesty.

Unbelievers seem to have a better understanding of this obvious truth than old-earth creationists do. By accepting the geological ages, such creationists are accepting billions of years of suffering and death in God's creation even before sin entered the world — not only man's sin, but even Satan's sin. Thus, God would be directly responsible for creating a world which is *not* good!

Therefore, the wonderful saving gospel of Christ is essentially subverted and destroyed if we accept the vast ages of the evolutionary cosmologists and geologists, with their eons-long spectacle of suffering and death as recorded in the global fossil graveyard. Sound theology must say no to any such concession! Fossils speak of death, and death results only from sin and judgment. "Sin . . . bringeth forth death" (James 1:15). Death is only a temporary intruder into God's very good creation, of course, and in the new earth which is to come, "there shall be no more death" (Rev. 21:4).

"But science has proved the earth is old," they still insist, "and we dare not alienate the academic community by insisting on a literal Genesis."

No, "science" has *not* proved the earth is old! The oldest written records we have, apart from the Bible, are in Egypt and Sumeria, and these only go back a few thousand years. The great fossil "record," instead of displaying vast ages of evolution, really shows the remains of a worldwide hydraulic cataclysm. Nowhere in the fossil record are there any genuine evolutionary transitional forms between kinds, and certainly no one has ever observed true evolution taking place in all recorded history. Furthermore, many geologists now recognize that *all* formations were laid down very rapidly. Uniformitarian speculation applied to a few radiometric decay systems may suggest great ages, but other more reasonable assumptions applied to scores of other global processes indicate much younger ages. (See *The Defender's Study Bible*, Appendix 5, p. 1505–1510, for a listing of such processes, with references.)

Also see the book, *The Young Earth*, by Dr. John Morris, for an excellent exposition of several such key processes, along with a critique of radiometric dating.

In any case, the only way we can know anything about the date of creation (and remember that the word "science" means knowledge!) is for God — who was there — to tell us when He did it. And, of course, He has told us, in His inspired Word. The question is, do we really believe what He says?

Evolution and the Pope

According to the Vatican Information Service, in a news release on October 23, 1996, Pope John Paul II declared that evolution is "more than just a theory." This seems to mean, despite the tenuous wording, that he now considers evolution a scientific fact. His written message to his science advisers, the Pontifical Academy of Sciences, speaks of "a series of discoveries made in different spheres of knowledge" which have convinced him to make this bold statement supporting evolution and suggesting that his millions of followers do the same. Some people said he had been misquoted, but official Catholic sources later confirmed that this understanding of his affirmation was correct. That is really what he said and meant.

One cannot help suspecting that the recent spate of events and media articles "puffing" evolution is being orchestrated somewhere to combat the modern resurgence of creationism around the world. The facts are so trivial but the propaganda has been so high and mighty. There was that widespread furor, for example, about the lone Colorado student who had the temerity to ask his local school to tone down its dogmatic teaching of the naturalistic origin of life.

And what about the sudden media announcement that a small rock found in Antarctica "proved" that life has evolved all over the universe? There is also the widespread publicity about Bill Moyer's series of public telecasts rethinking Genesis. And a new series of anti-creationist articles in such establishment journals as *Time, Harper's, Life, Scientific American, Newsweek,* and others.

Then came the pope with his "surprise" announcement that it is acceptable for Catholics to believe and teach evolutionism. He did include the small proviso that they should still allow God to create each human soul. Atheism thus remains inappropriate for Catholics, and that's a relief to know!

As a matter of fact, this public papal evolutionism is hardly a surprise to anyone who has followed the pronouncements of the last four popes, or who is familiar with the teachings of the various Catholic colleges and seminaries in this country. Even the last true conservative pope, Pius XII, in his famous 1950 encyclical, *Humani Generis*, while not promoting evolutionism and still seeming to lean toward special creation, did make a point of allowing Catholics to study and accept evolution as a scientific theory of origins, again with the limitation that God created the soul, and that all men are descendants of Adam, along with the doctrine of original sin as inherited from Adam.

The freedom to study and teach evolution with this constraint seemed very quickly to result in the widespread acceptance of theistic evolutionism in Catholic institutions and churches everywhere. As far as the present pope, John Paul II, is concerned, he has been an evolutionist in this sense probably since his youth. Despite this sudden supposed surprising pontificating, it is nothing new to his personal beliefs.

Pope John Paul II was Karol Wojtyla, cardinal of Krakow when he was named pope in 1978. He had earlier been an actor and was apparently quite comfortable as a government-approved ecclesiastic in Communist Poland. When he was elected pope, his election was enthusiastically endorsed by Poland's Communist Party and by world communism in general, in spite of his popular reputation as an anti-Communist. Since his election, he has seemingly been promoting a syncretistic agenda, not only with Protestants but also with Hindus, Lamaists, and others. In any event, he is not a recent convert to evolutionism, as the media have implied.

Perhaps the most influential evolutionist among Catholic theologians was the Jesuit priest, Teilhard de Chardin, now considered in effect to be almost the "patron saint" of the New Age movement with his strong pantheistic evolutionism. Teilhard was involved in the controversial discoveries of both Piltdown Man and Peking Man, and vigorously promoted total evolutionism all his life, greatly influencing such leading secular evolutionists as Theodosius Dobzhansky, George Gaylord Simpson, and Sir Julian Huxley. His books were banned at one time by the Catholic church but have apparently become respectable, and even very influential among Catholics during the reigns of the recent more liberal popes.

There have been many other leading evolutionary scientists in the domain of Catholicism, and this description would certainly apply to the scientists of the Pontifical Academy. On the other hand, we need to recognize that there are many strong creationists, not only among lay Catholics, but also among Catholic scientists as well. We could mention Dr. Guy Berthault of France, for example, whose studies on sedimentation have been profoundly significant in refuting geological uniformitarianism. Two Italian creationists, Dr. Roberto Fondi (paleontologist) and Dr. Giuseppe Sermonti (geneticist) have published important scientific books and papers refuting evolution. There are many others.

In this country, Dr. Wolfgang Smith, born in Austria but educated in this country (at Cornell, Purdue, and Columbia, in physics and mathematics) and having served since 1968 as Professor of Mathematics at Oregon State, after previous faculty positions at M.I.T. and U.C.L.A., has written a devastating critique of de Chardin's teachings and evolutionism in general. In this book, he says that the doctrine of macroevolution "*is totally bereft of scientific sanction.*" He then adds that "there exists to this day not a shred of bona fide scientific evidence in support of the thesis that macroevolutionary transformations have ever occurred."[10]

It is too bad that Pope John Paul II (who is not a scientist) did not consult such real Catholic scientists as Wolfgang Smith before glibly stating, as he did, that "new knowledge leads us to recognize in the theory of evolution more than a hypothesis." Just what new knowledge would that be, Pope John Paul II? Possibly the Mars rock? Or the fantasy of a walking whale?

One wonders whether he might be thinking of Teilhard's famous definition of evolution when he says it is more than a hypothesis. Here is what Teilhard said:

> Is evolution a theory, a system, or a hypothesis? It is much more: it is a general condition to which all theories, all systems, all hypotheses must bow. . . . Evolution is a light illuminating all facts, a curve that all lines of thought must follow.[11]

Evolution was, to all intents and purposes, Teilhard's "god," and his goal was globalism, a unified world government, culture, and religion, with all religions merged into one.

There are more and more signs that such globalism is also the aim of Pope John Paul II and other modern liberal Catholics. If so, this publicized commitment to evolutionism would contribute substantially to such a goal. All world religions — including most of mainline Protestantism, as well as Hinduism, Buddhism, and the rest — except for biblical Christianity, Orthodox Judaism, and Fundamentalist Islam, have embraced some form of evolutionism (either theistic, deistic, or pantheistic) and rejected or allegorized the true record of origins in Genesis. The pope has participated in important meetings with leaders of communism, Zen Buddhism, Hinduism, Taoism, Lamaism, and others, as well as the World Council of Churches, the Trilateral Commission, the B'nai B'rith of liberal Judaism, and a wide assortment of still others. He has traveled to India, Australia, the United States, and all over the world in his bulletproof "popemobile," speaking to immense crowds everywhere.

All cults and movements associated with the "new world order" of the so-called New Age movement have two things in common — evolutionism as their base and globalism as their goal. It is disturbing now to see even many large evangelical movements (e.g., Promise Keepers, charismatic ecumenism) inadvertently drifting into the same orbit while eulogizing this evolutionist pope.

The pope insists, of course, that Catholic evolutionists must still believe that God started the universe with its big bang and still creates each human soul. The scientific establishment, however, will never be content ultimately with anything less than total evolutionism.

The man who is believed by many to be the world's greatest living scientist, Stephen W. Hawking, has an insightful comment regarding his own audience with the pope, in his best-selling book, *A Brief History of Time*. He had been a speaker at a high-level papal scientific conference on cosmology, after which he describes his encounter thus:

> At the end of the conference the participants were granted an audience with the pope. He told us it was all right to study the evolution of the universe after the Big Bang, but we should not inquire into the Big Bang itself because that was the moment of creation and therefore the work of God. I was glad then that he did not know the subject of the talk I had just given at the conference—the possibility that space-time was finite but had no boundary, which means that it had no beginning, no moment of creation.[12]

That being the case, according to his cosmological mathematics, he concludes: "What place, then, for a Creator?" Hawking's book refers frequently to God, but he ends up concluding in his heart: "There is no god." And such must inevitably be the ultimate logical conclusion of any consistent evolutionism.

Among the most poignant verses in the Bible, with its reality coming more and more into focus these days, are the words of the Lord Jesus in Luke 18:8: "When the Son of man cometh, will He find faith on the earth?"

Neocreationism

Creationism is being fitted for new clothes today by a number of very articulate writers and speakers, and it is hoped by many that this will help it gain acceptance in the elite company of academics who have heretofore opposed it. They usually call it the "intelligent design" movement. One leader of the opposition to any form of creationism, Dr. Eugenie C. Scott, executive director of the National Center for Science Education, calls this development *neocreationism*.

> Phrases like "intelligent design theory," "abrupt appearance theory," "evidence against evolution," and the like, have sprung up, although the content of many of the arguments is familiar. This view can be called "neocreationism."[13]

Scott notes that the arguments for neocreationism are the same arguments that have been used by traditional creationists for many years. The new clothing is not so much what has been added, but what has been taken off.

> Neocreationists are by no means identical to their predecessors, however. . . . Neither biblical creationists nor theistic evolutionists. . . . Most of them are "progressive creationists."[14]

This new creationism is really not very new, except perhaps for the terminology. Progressive creationists, as well as traditional creationists, have been documenting intelligent design (that is, the magnificently organized complexity of every living creature) and "abrupt appearance" (that is, the complete absence of any true transitional forms in the fossil record) for well over 150 years.

But note what is missing. The neocreationists are not "biblical creationists," Scott says. They may believe that the Bible is the word of God, but they assume its testimony is irrelevant to their arguments. As Nancy Pearsey says:

> Design theory is also redefining the public school debate. At issue are not the details of evolution versus the details of Genesis; it's the stark, fundamental claim that life is the product of impersonal forces over against the claim that it is the creation of an intelligent agent.[15]

Now, this approach is not really new, either. During the past quarter century, ICR scientists have participated in well over 300 creation/evolution debates with university professors on college and university campuses, and each debate was intentionally framed to deal *only* with the scientific evidences, never with "the details of Genesis." Other creation lectures have been given on hundreds of campuses and scientific meetings with the same format, dealing only with science.

In fact, ICR has also been involved in the publishing of a number of books[16] that present the case for creation strictly from a scientific perspective with no reference to religion. These debates and books have been successful in winning many individual scientists and others to belief in creation and frequently as a tool in winning them eventually to saving faith in Christ.

But what it will *not* do is displace evolutionism as the reigning paradigm in the intellectual community. One form or another of evolutionism, either atheistic or pantheistic, has been the reigning paradigm in every age since the beginning of human history (with one exception), and the prophetic Scriptures indicate that it will still be so when the Lord Jesus Christ returns at the end of this age to set up His own eternal kingdom.[17] That one exception consists of those small communities in many different nations and times who have believed in a personal Creator God who created all things, and who has revealed His purposes in creation and redemption through His written word, the Holy Scriptures.

In more modern times, William Paley popularized the design argument with his great book *Natural Theology*, first published in 1802, profoundly influencing the English speaking world of his day — even including Charles Darwin! The book began with a detailed description of the "irreducible complexity" of a functioning watch, noting that even the most rabid skeptic would acknowledge that the watch — or at least its prototype — must have been designed and made by a skilled watchmaker. Just so, he argued persuasively, the much more complex universe required a universe-maker. These themes of intelligent design are compellingly developed at great length in Paley's 402-page book.

Darwin, however, wanted to find a way to escape Paley's conclusion, not for scientific reasons, but because he refused to accept a God who would condemn unbelievers like his father to hell.[18] Many modern Darwinians now follow him in maintaining that what appear to be evidences of design can also be explained by natural selection.

Richard Dawkins, Professor of Zoology at Oxford University, is the most articulate present-day advocate of neo-Darwinism, which maintains that evolution proceeds gradually through the preservation of small beneficial mutations by natural selection. Dawkins, a doctrinaire atheist, has published an influential book called *The Blind Watchmaker*. Dawkins comes down hard on "fundamentalist creationists" but even harder on modern anti-Darwinists who try to insert God somehow into the supposed Darwinian "science" of origins.

> I suppose it is gratifying to have the Pope as an ally in the struggle against fundamentalist creationism. It is certainly amusing to see the rug pulled out from under the feet of Catholic creationists such as Michael Behe. Even so, given a choice between honest to goodness fundamentalism on the one hand, and the obscurantist, disingenuous doublethink of the Roman Catholic Church on the other, I know which I prefer.[19]

Dawkins is gloating over the fact that the pope is an evolutionist,[20] but he is also impatient with the pope's insistence that the human soul has been "created." *Everything*, according to Dawkins and the modern neo-Darwinians, is attributable solely to the action of time and chance on matter, so that what *appears* to be evidence of design is really evidence of the creative power of random mutation and natural selection. Although Dawkins calls Behe a creationist, Behe himself claims to be an anti-Darwinian evolutionist.

More and more evolutionary biologists these days, in fact, are rejecting neo-Darwinism, acknowledging that the gaps in the fossil record (which have repeatedly been emphasized by creationists ever since Darwin's day, especially by the scientists representing the creation revival of the past four decades) make gradual evolution very hard to defend. Very few of these (if any) are becoming creationists, however — not even neo-creationists. The evidence of "abrupt appearance" is interpreted by them as "punctuations" in the "equilibrium" of the natural world. The increasing complexity of organisms in so-called evolutionary history is not interpreted as coming from intelligent design but as order emerging from chaos, probably by the mechanism of so-called "dissipative structures."[21]

Other evolutionists recognize that there is, indeed, evidence of intelligent design in the world, but they take it as evidence of Gaia (the Greek earth goddess, or Mother Nature) or of some "cosmic consciousness." This New Age movement is essentially a return to ancient evolutionary pantheism, a complex of religions now growing with amazing rapidity all over the world. Thus, Darwinians interpret the evidence of design in nature as natural selection, punctuationists interpret it as order through the chaos of dissipative structures, and New Age evolutionists interpret it as the intelligence of Mother Earth.

Getting people to believe in "intelligent design" is, therefore, neither new nor sufficient. People of almost every religion (except atheism) already believe in it. The only ones who do not, the atheists, have rejected it in full awareness of all the innumerable evidences of design in the world. These cannot be won by intellectual argument, no matter how compelling. As Isaac Asimov said:

> Emotionally, I am an atheist. I don't have the evidence to prove that God doesn't exist, but I so strongly suspect he doesn't that I don't want to waste my time.[22]

King David, by divine inspiration, had a comment on the attitude of such atheists: "The fool hath said in his heart, There is no God" (Ps. 14:1; also Ps. 53:1). Similarly, in Romans 1:21–22, the apostle Paul, discussing such people, said: "When they knew God, they glorified him not as God, neither were thankful; but became vain in their imaginations, and their foolish heart was darkened. Professing themselves to be wise, they became fools."

This is strong language, and "design theorists" might recoil from using it, especially concerning their own academic colleagues, but it

was God who said it! And intellectual fools are not won by intellectual arguments; if they are changed at all, it will be through some
traumatic experience brought about by the Holy Spirit in answer to
prayer.

Such Scriptures are speaking of those who are atheists "in their
hearts." Like Asimov (and Dawkins et al.), they are "emotional" atheists who have tried to ignore or subvert the real evidence with the
pseudo-science of evolutionary speculation. There are, on the other
hand, many "reluctant atheists" — those who have been so influenced by the doctrinaire atheists among their teachers and other intellectuals, that they feel they *cannot* believe in the God of the Bible
even though, in their hearts, they would like to believe.

People like this *can* be reached by sound evidence and reasoning. In our debates, for example, we know from many personal testimonies that a good number of students and young professionals in
the audiences who had felt they had no choice but atheistic evolutionism, have indeed been won to solid creationism and soon to saving faith in Christ, at least in part by the scientific evidence. We hope
this will be the experience of those who are now stressing "intelligent design," just as has often been true in the past.

But it will *not* be so if they stop with just the evidence for design and leave the Designer — the God of the Bible — out of it. Even
though we intentionally limit our debates (and some of our books) to
the *scientific* evidence, everyone in the audience and among our readers is well aware that we are really undergirding *biblical* creationism
(including recent creation and the global flood), because that is our
clearly stated position.

But modern "intelligent design theorists" intentionally
emphasize that, while they oppose materialism and Darwinian
evolutionism, they are *not* arguing for biblical creationism. At a
conference on what was called "Mere Creation," held at Biola
University in November 1996, the main speaker, Phillip E. Johnson,
said in his concluding remarks:

> For the present, I recommend that we also put the
> biblical issues to one side. The last thing we should want
> to do, or seem to want to do, is to threaten the freedom of
> scientific inquiry. Bringing the Bible anywhere near this
> issue . . . closes minds instead of opening them.[23]

In a widely reprinted article, a *New York Times* writer said:

> These new creationists avoid one pitfall of their predecessors by not positing, at least publicly, the identity of the creator. "My decision is simply to put it off," Mr. Johnson said, "and I recommend that to others."[24]

Now that may be all right as a temporary agreed-on constraint for a particular discussion — as in one of our scientific debates. But that cannot be the goal, and we need to be honest about this if we really believe the Bible to be the word of God. The innumerable evidences of intelligent design in nature really do not point to theistic evolution or dissipative structures or Gaia, but if we stop our program without arriving at the true God of the Bible as the Creator of all things, then many converts to "design" will gravitate to one of these other beliefs and never come to know Jesus Christ as their Savior.

As faith without works is dead, so is design without the Designer!

The Fruits of Creation Evangelism

One of the most frequent objections by compromising Christians to biblical literalism, especially what they call "young-earth creationism," is that our teaching of six-day creation and a worldwide flood will cause young people to reject the gospel. They have been taught evolutionism and billions of years all through their schooling, and so assume they must believe it. Therefore, the progressive creationists and other compromisers insist we must reinterpret the Bible to accommodate these beliefs of the secular scientists, or else we will turn people away.

Nothing could be further from the truth. These compromise theories do not win skeptics to Christ and the Bible. Rather, they lead professing Christians to become skeptics. Intelligent people can read and they can easily deduce that a book which has it all wrong concerning events which can be checked out empirically cannot be very reliable when it tells about salvation and heaven and other concepts which have to be accepted entirely on faith. As Jesus told Nicodemus: "If I have told you earthly things, and ye believe not, how shall ye believe, if I tell you of heavenly things?" (John 3:12).

The fact is that a straightforward, no-compromise presentation of the literal truth of God's Word concerning creation, the flood, and related events has borne more spiritual fruit in the past 40 years or so (the years of the modern revival of literal creationism) than the 200 years of Christian compromise with Lyell, Darwin, and their followers. This fact is illustrated by the many unsolicited testimonies we have received from people reached in this way.

At each Thanksgiving season especially, it has been good for me to think back over the countless blessings from God on the ICR ministries in our earlier days. From extremely small and unimpressive beginnings in 1970, it does seem that God may have called ICR "to the kingdom for such a time as this" (Esther 4:14).

Before we moved into our present building in 1985, ICR had experienced 15 years of slow but steady growth while located on the campus of Christian Heritage College, and many people were being reached for the Lord and His Word. Recently, in culling through my old files, I have run across numerous letters of testimony to this effect from that earlier period, and I'd like to share excerpts from some of them with you.

Listen, for example, to this heart-felt expression from a Christian lady: "You caused me to love the Bible more. You taught me to love God *more*. Your writings made my heart respond and leap to the Savior in new ways, and at times I couldn't read because of the tears in my eyes."

In an early letter from a New Mexico pharmacist was the following testimony: "I have listened to the tapes that were recorded here when you and Dr. Gish were at the University of New Mexico. The information you gave has been very instrumental in my own conversion, as evolution was a real problem in my coming to the Lord Jesus."

Here's one from a pastor in British Columbia: "I want to thank the Lord for the tremendous ministry you have had and are having. I had been a confirmed atheist and evolutionist, but the truth sets people free. It was because of one of Dr. Morris' books that I accepted the Lord Jesus Christ as my personal Lord and Savior."

A Christian man in England wrote the following back in 1977: "To the teaching of Dr. Henry Morris and his associates I owe an intellectual conviction in the Christian faith for which I can never hope to express adequately my gratitude."

Closer to home was the following letter from Illinois: "Just a note to let you know that a fellow who attended a creation lecture given by you and Dr. Gish in Oshkosh, Wisconsin, had his thinking regarding evolution shaken. He left the lecture with the conviction that Genesis is probably true and if Genesis is true, Revelation and the coming judgment are also. He acquired some Christian literature, read it, and accepted the Lord. He is now involved in full-time Christian service.

From a student in the Medical College of Georgia came the following testimony: "I praise the Lord for the work that you and the other scientists at the Institute have done, and I appreciate your testimony to the living creation. Some lectures and books by Dr. Morris had a big influence on me to reexamine Christianity and subsequently made a decision to receive Christ as my Lord and Savior."

A man whom the Lord has since used in a ministry of creation evangelism first wrote to me some 20 years ago. He said: "This letter is nearly 20 years late. . . . In many ways, *The Genesis Flood* was a turning point in my life. As a geologist . . . I was full of the textbook teaching. . . . the absolute evolutionary emphasis taught in college and in graduate school. This had taken its toll. . . . at that point I was introduced to *The Genesis Flood*. At last! Something that made sense! After that beginning, I read everything I could find on creationism and the ever-changing thoughts of the adherents of the evolutionary hoax. . . . For the past several years I have been lecturing in creation and the various aspects of the creation/evolution debate to anyone who would listen. . . . Thanks again for *The Genesis Flood* and all the books that followed; all have been used by God to profoundly affect many lives."

A young man who was a student at V.P.I. (Virginia Tech) while I was there on the faculty (although we never met) wrote to me about his own personal experience. "While a student at V.P.I. majoring in Biology, I became very despondent with the conflict I was having with evolution and the Bible. . . . As I looked around for some good books to read, in a religious bookstore I came across your little book, *The Bible and Modern Science*. . . . Dr. Morris, when I got through reading it, I knew my whole life was going to be different. . . . I was about to shipwreck, but your little book sent me away under full sail. . . . At the present time I am teaching a general biology course at [a Christian college]. I plan on entering seminary next fall."

Then I found a letter, written in 1980, from a pastor in whose church I had been privileged to speak two months earlier. "After the evening service you spoke with a young man about creationism and the accuracy of the Bible. Your messages and that short conversation proved to be the turning point in his spiritual pilgrimage. . . . He had been heavily involved in the anti-war movement in the early seventies. After that he became a policeman. . . . Your sermons and that conversation sparked a deep interest inside him. It made him believe that Christianity had a credible base. Sometime over the Christmas holidays, alone with his thoughts, Dennis gave his heart to Jesus Christ."

This same pastor had written earlier about his own personal testimony. "I remember the first time I saw a book by Henry Morris . . . I wasn't a Christian then. The book was called *The Twilight of Evolution*. Dr. Morris argued that with all the evidence evaluated, the case for evolution falls to the ground. Such an idea astounded me. . . . His book opened my eyes and changed my life. . . .That book made me seriously consider the truthfulness of the Bible. I began to study the subject on my own, and eventually came to faith in Christ."

We hear occasionally from a faithful Christian lady in New Zealand. In her first letter to me, about ten years ago, she gave this testimony. "I was an evolutionist before I was saved, and this was a tremendous barrier to believing the Bible. After I was saved, I was taught the day-age theory and spent many hours trying to manipulate God's Word to make it fit into science falsely so called! Then I read *The Remarkable Birth of Planet Earth* and discarded the geological ages forever, and everything fell into place. Thank you — thank you from the bottom of my heart. May the Lord continue to use you mightily to help others as you have helped me."

My old files are bulging with dozens and dozens of thrilling letters like these, and I praise God for every one of them. I've been trying to cull them out, for space seems at a premium these days, but I'm finding it almost impossible to discard any of them.

And these are only my *personal* files — which, of course, is why they seem to refer mostly to my own books and messages. Please excuse this imbalance. I am sure that other creationist writers and speakers receive many such letters referring to *their* books and other ministries, too.

Furthermore, most people who have been touched by an ICR lecture or book or radio message never write at all, but they are being reached nevertheless. Everywhere any of our men have held meetings, they have received many verbal testimonies similar to those cited in this little review. All of this helps to assure us that the Lord is indeed using creation evangelism in a vital way in these last days, even though only a few of those so affected (percentage-wise, that is) will ever have opportunity to tell us so before we all meet in heaven.

It is certainly true that creation seminars, creation-oriented books, and other means of spreading the message of scientific, biblical creationism are effective tools for evangelism and discipleship. We need not be surprised at this, for the Bible itself makes it plain that creation evangelism is a scriptural method for reaching both Christians and non-Christians who have been influenced by the evolutionary humanism that dominates our schools and news media.

Here is another testimony, one received by Dr. John Morris at a seminar in Mason City, Iowa.

> For most of my life I was completely lost. Though raised in a home some might term "Christian," I was never presented the true gospel of Jesus Christ with any degree of enthusiasm. I therefore eventually dismissed any church affiliation as an archaic predilection rooted more in Western tradition than propositional truth. I claimed agnosticism but was a practical atheist, and when I did acknowledge God it was to curse His name and dare Him to retaliate, "knowing" that such response was impossible since there was no God.
>
> I found myself in this precarious position in relation to God for one primary reason. I was a scientifically oriented, self-proclaimed intellectual for most of my life. One thing I had to my credit was enough intellectual integrity to realize that, if prevailing scientific opinion regarding origins was true, then the Bible was a dubious and ignoble work of fancy. By no means could it be considered a divine oracle by which to determine the course of one's destiny. Because I believed its foundation to be a whimsical illusion, I rejected the entire structure of the Christian faith.
>
> The course of my life took an entirely unexpected turn a few years ago. As the result of the concerted efforts of a very dear friend, I was coerced into attending my first

"Back to Genesis" seminar in Castro Valley, California. I cannot describe the thoughts and feelings that rushed throughout my entire soul as truths that seem now obvious to me were unfolded. All I can say is that at one point I began to wonder if anyone noticed the tears rolling down my cheeks. It was not the dry data that stirred me to such a display, but their implications. My rejection of God had been predicated on the fallacy of Genesis 1:1. If it were possible that the creation account were true, then God was real and I was in trouble! Strangely enough, however, my most intense emotion at that moment was not the fear of imminent divine retaliation, but a deep sense of agony at having for so long spat in the face of the loving God who created me. A few weeks later, I dedicated my life to the Lord. Although I didn't realize it at the time, God had not only called me to salvation, but also to the ministry of His gospel. At the time of this writing I am a licensed Baptist minister and am currently in the process of gaining a seminary degree.

I have spent the bulk of my life on the path to hell. If it were not for the ministry of the Institute for Creation Research, I might never have departed from that path. I thank the Lord Jesus Christ for ordaining this vital ministry to His service.

Another heart-felt testimony was received recently in a letter from a lady in New England.

I want to extend my heartfelt thanks to you for your book, *The Genesis Record*, that was sent to my husband by ICR. I cannot express the joy and tenderness of his heart that I have witnessed in the intense reading of your book. It has made him a strong dedicated man, a man that I can see Christ in. It (the book) was sent at a time that I experienced a deep loss and as a result, a hurt so deep that I became both physically and emotionally drained and in despair, losing my faith in a God that is alive and that even cares about me. Nick has been slowly and tenderly sharing your book with me. Thank you so very much, Dr. Morris. There is most certainly a special place in my heart for you.

Here is a fine letter from a Chinese student studying in Iowa.

I have just finished reading your book, *Science and the Bible.* I just bought the book this morning and read through it in the evening. I could not put it down except for dinner and I am blessed by your book very much. Praise the Lord!! I am a man that loved science very much and find the Bible is contradictory (or at least that was what I thought) to sciences or facts. The Lord is right!! I shall know the truth and the truth will set me free. I was overfilling when I was reading chapter two to the end of the book. No wonder many Christian scientists said they were being lied to and now I know exactly why.

The reason I wrote this letter is to tell you the above mentioned and to tell you that I am really blessed!! Please can you also send me a list of your publications and other similar books to me. I give thanks to you in the name of Christ.

The following is a testimony from a medical doctor in Arkansas who is now a strong and articulate creationist and soul-winning Christian.

Through my many years of scientific and medical training I had agreed with the idea that evolution was fact. Since I had a personal relationship with the Creator, I believed that God was behind it all. Thus I was a theistic evolutionist. Scientific creation was a farce!

Dr. Henry Morris, a scientist, had been invited to speak at our church on the scientific evidence of creation. At that time I was embarrassed by the promotion of his talk in our community.

On the night before Dr. Morris was to speak, a friend asked if I would please take Dr. Morris out for breakfast. I spent that evening preparing many questions designed to humble this man who believed in creation as science. He politely answered questions on the age of the earth, carbon 14 dating, fossils, biochemistry, physics, genetics, geology, biology, history, anatomy, etc. His answers showed irrefutable, clear evidence of a designer. I quickly shifted to the "weaknesses" of the Bible: a seven-day creation, the flood, Cain's wife, languages, races, Jonah and the whale, etc. His answers were clear, simple, and easily understood. For the first time in my scientific life I was hearing understandable truths and seeing facts that answered my most difficult questions. I did not need faith to believe the obvious.

A wife and mother in Minnesota writes that she and her husband had both graduated from a denominational college but that all of their textbooks and classes had been heavily weighted toward evolution. One day they happened to hear our ICR radio program. She goes on to say:

> . . . he had heard someone from ICR on the radio and was very excited about what he had heard. I bought him *The Genesis Record* and he read it from cover to cover. . . .

Their childhood faith was restored, and all her family soon joined a Bible-believing church where they are happy in the Lord and studying God's Word.

A man in England writes about the way in which God brought him to saving faith in Christ.

> I went to church up to the end of my teens and I then stopped. I considered myself a Christian, but accepted evolution as proved, and tried to fit in what the Bible had to say with it, obviously with no success. . . . I started to think about evolution and wonder how it worked. It made no sense to me. While I was doing this, I was looking at the books about the Bible in our central library. One of the books that caught my attention was *The Genesis Flood*. What you had to say made more sense to me than evolution ever did. I decided to look into it, and what I found absolutely appalled me. I decided to fight it at every opportunity I could get. It was this and a couple of other Christian books that the Lord used to lead me to himself, and I accepted Him as my Lord and Savior in 1983.

From a college student in Arkansas:

> While I was at my parent's home during spring break, I came across a book I had read during junior high entitled *Evolution and the Modern Christian*, by Henry

Morris. I am rereading it now and again I am struck (as I was in the eighth grade) by how well it refutes the doctrine of evolution. . . . This book transformed me from a skeptical doubter into a defender of the faith armed with scientific knowledge to refute the false and unscientific concept of evolution.

From a student at the University of Papua, New Guinea:

I am a second year biology student at the above mentioned university. . . . I never realized the supreme importance of the question of origins until I came to university. The devil is attacking the Book of Genesis and Christians on university campuses are silent! It seems much easier to go and win souls than to get tangled up in a controversial issue — while our very foundations are being destroyed.

I thank God for the tremendous work you guys are doing. I first got to hear about ICR through my Baptist chaplain. He does seminars on creation versus evolution, backed up by slides and films that he's bought from your Institute. He has also bought a lot of books and tapes and we keep them in a little book centre that we've started. . . . My chaplain is leaving at the end of this year and we want to continue learning from you through *Acts & Facts*.

We hear many such testimonies at our meetings and I would like to put them all in this book, if I could. In any case, although we never give altar calls or use other such methods that are common in evangelistic meetings, we are confident that the creation-oriented message is effective in evangelism, both in winning people to saving faith in Christ and in strengthening the faith and testimony of those who are already Christians but who have doubts that are hindering their own effectiveness in the Christian life.

Of course, we do get some negative "testimonies" from skeptical intellectuals, but far more thrilling testimonies of God's blessings on personal lives through the uplifting message of creation, redemption, and divine purpose which is now going out all over the world.

From a missionary in Venezuela comes the following: "Please be encouraged that the ministry of ICR has been and continues to be an inspiration and blessing to everyone serving on our field."

Here is a heart-warming word from a reader in Connecticut: "Lonely, depressed, and a drug abuser living in Hollywood, it dawned on me that I had forgotten about God . . . my brother gave me your book, *Science and the Bible*, to read. . . . In my heart I decided for Christ and put my trust in Him alone for salvation, about two weeks after I began reading your book. . . . Since then, everything is new. My interests have turned now to apologetics and true science. . . . Let God be praised continually, for it is He that 'giveth the increase' always."

Finally, note the testimony (perhaps of special interest to me) from a university professor in Indiana. "Like you, I have a Ph.D. in civil engineering with a specialty in hydraulic engineering. More importantly, I am a Christian who never really understood creation. . . . As I read your book, the Holy Spirit gently instructed me and helped me develop a better understanding of God's Word. . . . I can only 'Praise the Lord' for the renewed hunger that I now have for reading and studying the Bible."

Such testimonies could easily be multiplied a hundred-fold. True biblical creationism is effective in evangelism and Christian growth simply because it takes God at His Word, and seeks to present the truth graciously, but without compromise.

The Creationist Faith of Our Founding Fathers

Many of the foundations of our American heritage are being undermined in today's hedonistic society, and this sad fact is surely related to the prior undermining of biblical creationism in our schools and colleges. It is therefore relevant to the theme of this book to note that most of the founding fathers of our nation believed in special creation as taught in the Bible. Thus, defending our Christian creationist faith is a vital component of the true defense of our country and its system of constitutional government "under God."

A favorite patriotic song of yesteryear, "My Country, 'Tis of Thee," is not sung much anymore, especially in our public schools. I assume this is because the last verse is a prayer, directed to "Our fathers' God . . . Author of liberty . . . Great God our King." As we all know, our Supreme Court decided several years ago that it is unconstitutional to pray in school.

In fact, it is now considered unconstitutional to acknowledge God in any way at all in school, especially as our "Author" and

"King"—that is, as our Creator and Lord. Yet, when our nation was first established on that memorable fourth day of July in 1776, the signing of the Declaration was preceded by prayer, at the urging of old Ben Franklin, to the Author of liberty. It was no accident that the Declaration of Independence acknowledged God as Creator (that is, as "Nature's God") in its very first sentence. Then, in its second sentence, the Declaration affirmed that "all men are *created* equal, . . . endowed by their *Creator* with certain unalienable rights." In its last sentence, it expressed "firm reliance on the protection of *Divine Providence*." Our nation's first and founding document thus expressed faith in God as both Creator and sustainer of men, and there is bound to be a correlation between our nation's strong foundation and God's blessing on it for these some 225 years since that first fourth of July.

Franklin may not have been an orthodox Bible-believing Christian, but he did believe in God and creation. He wrote, for example, as follows:

> Here is my creed. I believe in one God, the Creator of the universe. That he governs it by His Providence. That He ought to be worshiped.[25]

The same could be said of Thomas Jefferson, reputedly a deist, but nevertheless a believer in God and special creation. Some of his testimonies are actually inscribed on the walls of the Jefferson Memorial, in Washington, DC. For example:

> Almighty God hath created the mind free. All attempts to influence it by temporal punishments or burthens . . . are a departure from the plan of the Holy Author of our religion. . . .
> God who gave us life gave us liberty. Can the liberties of a nation be secure when we have removed a conviction that these liberties are the gift of God?

A modern evolutionary historian has noted Jefferson's keen insight in reference to the growing pre-Darwinian propaganda for uniformitarianism and evolution, as follows:

> When Jefferson, in his old age, was confronted with the newly developing science of geology, he rejected the evolutionary concept of the creation of the earth on the grounds that no all-wise and all-powerful Creator would

have gone about the job in such a slow and inefficient way.[26]

It was Jefferson, of course, who had the major responsibility for the wording in the Declaration of Independence.

James Madison, who is often considered the chief architect of the Constitution as well as the Bill of Rights, was a profound Bible student studying for the ministry during his college days at Princeton (then known as the College of New Jersey). Although he eventually became a lawyer and statesman, his Christian convictions never wavered. It was especially his influence that eventually established religious freedom in our country. He later wrote that "belief in a God All Powerful, wise and good, is . . . essential to the moral order of the world and to the happiness of man."[27]

Madison's theology had been largely shaped by the teachings of President John Witherspoon of the College of New Jersey (also a signer of the Declaration) whose strong biblical Calvinist faith included the doctrine of the natural depravity of man. This truth in turn was behind Madison's unique insistence on a government of checks-and-balances in which the innate sinfulness of men attaining power could be prevented thereby from usurping total power. This doctrine, of course, rests squarely on the biblical record of the creation and fall of man.

His manuscripts also include elaborate notes on the four Gospels and Acts in particular, specifically acknowledging the deity and bodily resurrection of Christ, and praising the example of the Berean Christians in studying the Scriptures.[28]

John Hancock, who was the first to sign the Declaration, had been president of the Provincial Congress of Massachusetts a year before when he issued a proclamation calling for "A Day of Public Humiliation, Fasting, and Prayer," referring to "that God who rules in the Armies of Heaven and without whose Blessing the best human Counsels are but Foolishness — and all created Power Vanity."[29] That same year, the Continental Congress had also passed a stirring resolution expressing "humble confidence in the mercies of the Supreme and impartial God and ruler of the universe."[30]

George Washington (often called "the father of our country") was also a strong Bible-believing Christian and literal creationist. Among other things, he once commented as follows: "A reasoning being would lose his reason, in attempting to account for the great phenomena of nature, had he not a Supreme Being to refer to: and well has it been said, that if there had been no God, mankind would have been obligated to imagine one."[31]

Washington also said:

> It is impossible to account for the creation of the universe, without the agency of a Supreme Being. . . . It is impossible to govern the universe without the aid of a Supreme Being. It is impossible to reason without arriving at a Supreme Being.[32]

Consider also the testimony of John Jay, the first Chief Justice of the United States Supreme Court. In an address to the American Bible Society (of which he was then president) he said: "The Bible will also inform them that our gracious Creator has provided for us a Redeemer, in whom all the nations of the earth shall be blessed: that this Redeemer has made atonement for the sins of the whole world, and . . . has opened a way for our redemption and salvation."[31]

In fact, all the signers of the Declaration and the delegates to the Constitutional Convention, as well as the delegates to the various sessions of the Continental Congress — at least so far as known — were men who believed in God and the special creation of the world and mankind. Nearly all were members of Christian churches and believed the Bible to be the inspired Word of God.

This had been true of their forebears as well:

> In colonial times, the Bible was the primary tool in the educational process. In fact, according to Columbia University Professor Dr. Lawrence A. Cremin, the Bible was "the single most primary source for the intellectual history of Colonial America." From their knowledge of the Bible, a highly literate, creative people emerged. Their wise system of education was later replaced by a man-centered system that has caused a steady decline in literacy and creativity.[34]

An interesting admission from Fred Edwords, executive director of the American Humanist Association and a strong opponent of modern creationism, has noted the following regarding the nation's founders:

> . . . all mentioned God — and not merely the

clockwork God of deism, but a god actively involved in history. Their "public religion" . . . harked back to the Old Testament with its view of America as "the promised land." This was prevalent in many writings of the time.[35]

In many ways the history of the founding and further history of our country in modern times does seem to parallel that of God's chosen nation of Israel in ancient times. One fascinating example of this is found in a very early Independence Day address by Dr. Elias Boudinot, president of the Continental Congress in 1783.

> No sooner had the great Creator of the heavens and the earth finished His almighty work, and pronounced all very good, but He set apart . . . one day in seven for the commemoration of His inimitable power in producing all things out of nothing. . . . The deliverance of the children of Israel from a state of bondage to an unreasonable tyrant was perpetuated by the Paschal lamb, and enjoining it on their posterity as an annual festival forever. . . . The resurrection of the Savior of mankind is commemorated by keeping the first day of the week. . . . Let us then, my friends and fellow citizens, unite all our endeavors this day to remember, with reverential gratitude to our Supreme Benefactor, all the wonderful things He has done for us, in our miraculous deliverance from a second Egypt — another house of bondage.[36]

Sad to say, ancient Israel gradually forgot their Sabbaths and their Passovers, and even forgot God and served the gods of nature, so that God finally judged them and sent them into captivity.

Similarly our own nation was greatly blessed of God in its miraculous formation and early history. On that first great Liberty Day, when the Liberty Bell first rang out, the founders sent forth a testimony to all colonies taken from God's Word: "Proclaim liberty throughout all the land unto all the inhabitants thereof" (Lev. 25:10). Yet now, we also are rapidly forgetting the true God, His creation, His Word, and His great salvation. Will the time come when America, like Israel, will fall under the chastening hand of our offended Creator and be enslaved by the coming humanistic pagan world government?

Actually, multitudes of our people, including many of our national leaders, have already abandoned their God-given Christian American heritage of liberty through our Creator and Savior, and have thereby become slaves themselves — some to drugs, some to alcohol, some to crime, immorality, greed, pleasure, or various other exacting slavemasters. In a word, they have become slaves to sin, even in this once-sweet land of liberty. As Jesus said, "Whosoever committeth sin is the servant of sin" (John 8:34).

The agents of the enemy entrap many into such slavery by their deceptive promises of freedom from God and His Word, but "while they promise them liberty, they themselves are the servants of corruption: for of whom a man is overcome, of the same is he brought in bondage" (2 Pet. 2:19).

True liberty, for both time and eternity is secured only by faith in the saving work of Christ, and "if the Son therefore shall make you free, ye shall be free indeed" (John 8:36). America in general — and individual American men and women individually — need urgently to come back to the true God and Savior before it is too late.

Endnotes
1 Sandi Dolbee, "Back to the Beginning: A Flood of Attention on the Epic Book of Genesis," *San Diego Union Tribune*, August 30, 1996 (as well as other papers).
2 Ibid.
3 Ibid.
4 Ibid.
5 Ibid.
6 Ira Glasser, undated 1996 solicitation letter, ACLU, New York, NY.
7 Barry Lynn, solicitation letter, American United for Separation of Church and State, Washington, DC, 1996.
8 Andrew Lawler, "Finding Puts Mars Exploration on Front Burner," *Science*, vol. 273, August 16, 1996, p. 865.
9 Ibid.
10 Wolfgang Smith, *Teilhardism and the New Religion* (Rockford, IL: Tan Books, 1988), p. 5–6, emphasis his.
11 Teilhard de Chardin, *The Phenomenon of Man* (New York: Harper and Row, 1965), p. 219.
12 Stephen W. Hawking, *A Brief History of Time* (New York: Bantam Books, 1988), p. 116, 140.
13 Eugenie C. Scott, "Creationists and the Pope's Statement," *Quarterly Review of Biology*, vol. 72, December 1997, p. 403.
14 Ibid.

15 Nancy Pearsey, "Debunking Darwin," *World*, vol. 11, March 1, 1997, p. 14.

16 One of the most recent of these is *Science and Creation*, Volume II in *The Modern Creation Trilogy*, by Henry M. Morris and John D. Morris (Green Forest, AR: Master Books, 1996).

17 For documented evidence of the age-long, worldwide dominance of evolutionism, see *The Long War Against God*, by Henry M. Morris (Grand Rapids, MI: Baker Book House, 1989).

18 Charles Darwin, *Autobiography*, edited by Nora Barlow (New York: Norton, 1969), p. 87.

19 Richard Dawkins, "Obscurantism to the Rescue," *Quarterly Review of Biology*, vol. 72, December 1997, p. 399.

20 Ever since the publication of Pope John Paul II's October 1996 message on evolution, there has been controversy over what he actually said. The actual official English translation of his speech appeared in the October 30 edition of *L'Osservatore Romano*, and it does indeed affirm that he said that "the theory of evolution is more than a hypothesis" (*Catholic News Service*, November 19, 1996). He also spoke of "several theories of evolution," but by this he was referring mainly to the "materialist, reductionist, and spiritualist interpretations."

21 See my article, "Can Order Come Out of Chaos?" "Back to Genesis" No. 102, ICR *Acts & Facts*, June 1997.

22 Paul Kurtz, "An Interview with Isaac Asimov on Science and the Bible," *Free Inquiry*, vol. 2, Spring 1982, p. 9.

23 Phillip E. Johnson, "Separating Materialist Philosophy from Science," *The Real Issue*, vol. 15, November/December 1996. The "Mere Creation" conference involved over a hundred participants, almost all of whom were either theistic evolutionists or progressive creationists. According to Eugenie Scott, "most of them have appointments at secular institutions" ("Creationists and the Pope's Statement," *Quarterly Review of Biology*, vol. 72, December 1997, p. 403).

24 Laurie Goodstein, "New Light for Creationism," *New York Times*, December 21, 1997.

25 *The Writings of Ben Franklin* (New York: Macmillan Co., vol. 10, 1905–1907), p. 84.

26 Gilman M. Ostrander, *The Evolutionary Outlook, 1875–1900* (Clio, MI: Marston Press, 1971), p. 1.

27 *Princeton University Library Chronicle*, Spring 1961, p. 125, cited by Eldsmoe, p. 110.

28 See volume I in *Biography of James Madison*, p. 3, 34, as cited in *A Cloud of Witnesses*, by Stephen A. Northrop (Portland, OR: American Heritage Ministries, 1987) p. 307.

29 William J. Federer, *America's God and Country* (Coppell, TX: Fame Publishing Co., 1996), p. 275.

30 Ibid., p. 140.

31 John F. Schroeder, editor, *Maxims of Washington* (Mt. Vernon, VA, Mount Vernon Ladies Association, 1942), p. 209.

32 Ibid., p. 275.

33 Stephen A. Northrop, editor, *A Cloud of Witnesses* (Portland, OR: American Heritage Ministries, 1987), p. 251.

34 Mary-Elaine Swanson, "Teaching Children the Bible" *Mayflower Institute Journal*, vol. 1, July/August 1983, p. 5.

35 Frederick Edwords, "The Religious Character of American Patriotism," *The Humanist*, vol. 47, Nov/Dec 1987, p. 20.

36 Address in New Jersey on July 4, 1783, cited in *Foundation for Christian Self-Government*, July 1982, p. 3.

Index of Subjects

Index of Names

Index of Scriptures